Psychology Today

HERE TO HELP

breaking the bonds of

FOOD
ADDICTION

Psychology Today
HERE TO HELP

breaking the bonds of
FOOD
ADDICTION

Susan McQuillan, M.S., R.D.

ALPHA

A member of Penguin Group (USA) Inc.

ALPHA BOOKS

Published by the Penguin Group

Penguin Group (USA) Inc., 375 Hudson Street, New York, New York 10014, U.S.A.

Penguin Group (Canada), 10 Alcorn Avenue, Toronto, Ontario, Canada M4V 3B2 (a division of Pearson Penguin Canada Inc.)

Penguin Books Ltd, 80 Strand, London WC2R 0RL, England

Penguin Ireland, 25 St Stephen's Green, Dublin 2, Ireland (a division of Penguin Books Ltd)

Penguin Group (Australia), 250 Camberwell Road, Camberwell, Victoria 3124, Australia (a division of Pearson Australia Group Pty Ltd)

Penguin Books India Pvt Ltd, 11 Community Centre, Panchsheel Park, New Delhi—110 017, India

Penguin Group (NZ), Cnr Airborne and Rosedale Roads, Albany, Auckland 1310, New Zealand (a division of Pearson New Zealand Ltd)

Penguin Books (South Africa) (Pty) Ltd, 24 Sturdee Avenue, Rosebank, Johannesburg 2196, South Africa

Penguin Books Ltd, Registered Offices: 80 Strand, London WC2R 0RL, England

Publisher: Marie Butler-Knight
Product Manager: Phil Kitchel
Senior Managing Editor: Jennifer Chisholm
Acquisitions Editors: Mikal E. Belicove and Paul Dinas
Development Editor: Christy Wagner
Production Editor: Janette Lynn
Technical Editors: The Editors of *Psychology Today* magazine

Copy Editor: Kelly D. Henthorne
Cover Designer: Ann Marie Deets
Book Designer: Trina Wurst
Creative Director: Robin Lasek
Indexer: Julie Bess
Layout: Angela Calvert
Proofreading: Donna Martin

*This book is dedicated to my daughter, Molly,
who waited so patiently for me all these months—
everything is for you, always.*

Contents

Foreword

Who doesn't love to eat?

Food is one of life's greatest joys. It brings friends and families together, and it's one of the best and simplest pleasures we have. But sadly, many of us have lost sight of this basic celebration of life. The satisfaction of a good meal has been buried by compulsions, fears, anxieties, and guilt.

It's a paradox: The more we obsess over diets and weight loss, the fatter and unhealthier we get. It all seems strange, until you realize the basic fact that our emotions affect how—and what—we eat. We eat because we're lonely, frustrated, or sad. We also eat when we're happy—to celebrate a birthday, a promotion, a milestone. Many of us simply eat on autopilot in front of the TV, while others run from any mention of food.

The warning signs are all around us. That's why it is so important for us to understand that we may be the victims of food addiction— that unhealthy, unhappy psychological relationship so many of us have toward what we consume. We call it a food "addiction" because that's just what it is: the compulsion to eat (or not to eat) as a way of coping with life's emotional pressures.

Nutritionist Susan McQuillan has filled *Breaking the Bonds of Food Addiction* with the latest information to help you regain a better perspective on eating and what it means to you. This book teaches you how to recognize the feelings that drive you to eat compulsively or starve yourself on diets that don't work. It advises you how to figure out when and why you eat—your "triggers"—as well as teaches you what constitutes good food, enabling you to eat more mindfully and with renewed satisfaction.

Maybe you'd like to get closer to your "ideal body weight" by losing or gaining a few pounds. Maybe you'd like to get the most out of your food, both from the standpoint of nutrition or just plain enjoyment. Or maybe you'd like to change a bad eating habit or two. Whatever your goals, this book gives you the insights and tools to achieve them—making the entire experience of eating happier, healthier, and more fulfilling.

Kaja Perina
Editor in chief
Psychology Today

Introduction

To help you figure out whether or not this book is for you, I'll begin by telling you what this book is *not* about. This is *not* a book about eating disorders, although eating disorders are included because they are, without a doubt, food addictions. Although this book could help you lose weight, it is *not* a diet book. The last thing a food addict needs is another weight loss scheme.

This is a book for anyone and everyone whose psychological relationship with food is out of control. It is a guide for anyone who is trying to regain a sane attitude toward food and stabilize his or her eating habits. This book will help you ...

- Understand what it means to have a food addiction.
- Replace an anxious, guilty attitude toward food with a healthier, more positive approach.
- Put the brakes on starve-and-binge behavior.
- Improve your lifestyle and have a happier relationship with food.
- Appreciate what it means to have a healthy body.
- Seek further help if you need it.

Millions of people in the United States are obsessed with food and eating and are unhappy about their bodies. They are food addicts. If you're reading this introduction, you might be one of them. You might already have firsthand knowledge about what it means to be a food addict. You might be wondering, *Why me?* This book will provide a number of possible explanations, in addition to practical solutions.

Food addiction goes by many names: emotional eating, compulsive overeating, binge eating, eating disorders, eating disturbances, and disordered eating. You might not realize it, but chronic dieting is a form of food addiction. Avoiding or restricting food is a food addiction. A food addict is anyone who is overly preoccupied with food and body size. A food addict is anyone whose relationship with food is getting in the way of his or her physical or emotional well-being. Anyone, male or female, young or old, can develop a food addiction at any time.

Ongoing research points to the possibility that some people have an addictive personality type that might or might not have a biological basis. This theory supports the use of the word *addiction* to describe not only excessive alcohol or drug use, but also compulsive behavior related to eating, sexual activity, gambling, exercise, and even playing computer games. More and more researchers believe that because these activities, when done in excess, share similar characteristics (craving for more, tolerance for increased amounts, and withdrawal symptoms when the activity stops), they can all be classified as addictive behavior.

To understand your food addiction, you don't need to know everything there is to know about how your mind and body work. The more you understand about your brain chemistry, body chemistry, genetic blueprint, environmental influences, and emotional appetites that affect your relationship with food, however, the better you'll understand what you can and cannot change. That's why the first three chapters of this book are devoted to explaining the social, psychological, and biological factors that come together to create a food addiction.

Many people suffer from feelings of shame, guilt, low self-esteem, and isolation associated with their food addictions. For some, it's a lifelong struggle of trying to separate their emotions from their eating habits. For others, there is ultimately a peaceful resolution. For everyone, there is hope. There is always something you can do to take back control over an addiction that has been running your life.

The goal of this book is to help you get to the root of your addiction, understand it as best you can, feel better about your body, and develop a healthier relationship with food. What's most important is that you learn to recognize the internal and external triggers that drive your eating behavior. Once you recognize your triggers, your next step will be to mentally separate them from your eating habits and learn to deal with the two separately and more effectively.

Once you confront the behavioral, environmental, emotional, and food triggers that control your eating habits, you'll be able to listen better to what your body tells you about when you are hungry, how much you should eat, and when it's time to stop eating.

You will no longer feel guilty about what you eat, worry about good foods and bad foods, or have unrealistic ideas about your body shape and size. You'll spend a lot less time thinking about food, and that's how it should be.

What You'll Find Inside *Breaking the Bonds of Food Addiction* is organized into four parts:

In **Part 1**, "**Understanding Food Addiction**," you'll find the latest research from top experts who help explain what's going on in your brain and body when you suffer from a food addiction, and why certain types of thinking and behavior are unique to food addicts.

In **Part 2**, "**The Nature of Eating**," you'll consider how your personal eating habits and family background might be feeding your food addiction. You'll look at the many ways advertising, marketing, and other forms of media can and probably do affect the way you eat. You'll also find a primer on good nutrition and tips for changing your food routine in ways that will guide you back to healthier, happier eating.

In **Part 3**, "**Breaking the Bonds**," you'll start setting goals and taking real steps toward freeing yourself from your food addiction. You'll learn to identify four different types of eating triggers and what you can do to stop yourself from falling into an emotional eating trap. You'll also become aware of just how much help is out there for anyone who suffers from a food addiction.

In **Part 4**, "**A Personal Plan for Healthy Living**," you'll learn how to get your mind and body in fighting shape so you can work from a position of power and self-confidence to overcome your food addiction. You'll see that setbacks are normal, and you'll learn how to handle them in ways that won't hinder your progress or prevent you from reaching your long-term goals.

How to Use This Book To get the most out of this book, it's a good idea to read it from beginning to end. But this is what my seven-year-old daughter would call an "Anywhere All About" book. The "anywhere" part means you don't have to start at the beginning and read straight through to the end to get something from it. Because of its format, you can pick it up and start reading anywhere in the book or flip back and forth between chapters. You'll still learn something. The "all about" part means this is a reference book that contains most everything known about the subject of food addiction. I dare say you'll find that to be true. A reference book is a keeper; one that you'll turn to again and again for information and advice.

Extras

Bonus boxes filled with stories, advice, and guidance show up on just about every page of this book. Be sure to read them all, because they include some of the most important information you'll need to know about breaking the bonds of food addiction. Here's what to look for:

In most chapters, I anticipated what questions you might have and wrote them into these Q&A boxes. You'll be happy to know that I've also provided the answers.

GET PSYCHED

There are more experts in this book than there are chapters, and they all have something important to say. These Get Psyched boxes hold the experts' valuable advice and words of wisdom.

PsychSpeak

When the experts include neuroscientists, medical doctors, genetic researchers, psychologists, and other academic types, there's bound to be language that others don't understand. PsychSpeak boxes highlight and define some words you might find confusing. You can also check the glossary at the back of this book for unfamiliar terms.

WEB TALK: These Web Talk sidebars provide links to relevant websites. Given the ever-changing nature of the Internet, there's always a chance that a link won't take you where you thought you were going. The links provided here are to well-established government, educational, and professionally run organizations, so chances are they'll still be there when you get there.

you're not alone

I n every chapter, you'll find boxes called You're Not Alone that tell true stories from men and women who have struggled with one type of food addiction or another. They've shared very personal information in the hope that you'll be inspired by their progress and their ultimate solutions.

Acknowledgments My professional thanks go to Lybi Ma for recommending me to write this book; to Kat McGowan and Mikal Belicove for getting me off to a great start; to Christy Wagner for superb editing and providing words of praise and encouragement when they were most needed; and to Janette Lynn and Kelly Henthorne for attending to details and supplying valuable feedback.

My personal thanks go to my mother, Irene, for a lifetime of support and good advice; David Ricketts and Wendye Pardue, for 20 years of unfailing friendship; Juliette Knight, Esther and Jaimie Meyers, Diane Crawford, Eileen Gleason, Andrea Sperling, Dui Seid, and Sally Xuereb for a generous supply of food, friendship, understanding, and child care.

Very special thanks to the many people who helped write this book by contributing personal stories and professional advice: you are the best. I am deeply moved by the willingness of so many wonderful people to share their stories of personal struggle and triumph over food addiction so others might be inspired. I'm also proud to have written a book about food addiction with the help and support of some of the top experts in the country, including the following:

Tracy Tylka, Ph.D., assistant professor of psychology at Ohio State University, whose continuum of eating behaviors appears in Chapter 1.

Bart Hoebel, neuroscientist at Princeton University, whose research focuses on binge eating and addiction. Dr. Hoebel's work is described in Chapter 1.

Ron Ruden, M.D., New York City internist and author of *The Craving Brain*. Dr. Ruden's explanation of the role of serotonin in food cravings is presented in Chapter 1.

Gene-Jack Wang, M.D., scientist at the Brookhaven National Laboratory, whose research on biochemical addiction is described in Chapter 1.

Mark Gold, M.D., chief of addiction medicine at the University of Florida's College of Medicine. In Chapter 3, Dr. Gold describes how the brain might work against a food addict who struggles with overeating.

Alan R. Hirsch, M.D., neurological director of the Smell and Taste Treatment and Research Foundation and author of *Scentsational Weight Loss*. Dr. Hirsch's explanations of how we taste and smell, and how our senses help determine our food preferences, are found in Chapters 3 and 5.

Kelly Brownell, Ph.D., director of the Yale Center for Eating and Weight Disorders and noted author of *Food Fight: The Inside Story of the Food Industry, America's Obesity Crisis, and What We Can Do About It,* for his insights on the food industry in Chapter 6.

Warren Berland, Ph.D., New York psychologist and author of *Out of the Box,* whose approach to fearless eating appears in Chapter 8.

James Prochaska, Ph.D., professor of clinical and health psychology at the University of Rhode Island. Dr. Prochaska is internationally recognized for his behavior model of change, which he applies to food addiction in Chapter 9.

Anne Fletcher, R.D., dietitian and author of the *Thin for Life* books and *Sober for Good,* whose views on behavioral change appear in Chapter 9.

Sarah Leibowitz, Ph.D., professor of behavioral neurobiology at The Rockefeller University in New York. Dr. Leibowitz's research on brain chemistry and cravings is described in Chapter 11.

Part 1

Understanding Food Addiction

Both the brain and the body are involved in food addiction. In these first few chapters, you'll learn all about the physical, emotional, and behavioral issues that can undermine your relationship with food.

What Is Food Addiction?

I f you are preoccupied with food, eating, or your body size to the extent that it interferes with your health, happiness, relationships, or normal day-to-day activities, chances are you have a food addiction. That doesn't mean you have an eating disorder, although eating disorders certainly are food addictions. You might, however, be acting out disordered eating behaviors such as bingeing, purging, eating secretly, compulsive eating, or compulsive dieting that are similar to the behavior of someone with a diagnosable eating disorder (and that could possibly lead to an eating disorder). These behaviors are all symptoms of food addictions.

Many theories exist about the nature of food addiction, and just as many unanswered questions. Some people say it's all in your head. Others say it's a starving soul. Still others say specific foods like carbs are to blame. Your genes and brain chemistry play a role, and so do your emotions, but what about the theory that food addiction is a form of substance abuse? Can you really become addicted to sugar the same way a drug addict becomes addicted to cocaine? In recent years, research in the area of eating behavior has shed new light on the mystery of why so many people develop an unhealthy relationship with food.

Pieces of the Puzzle

A food addict can be an overweight woman who tries diet after diet. She can be a thin woman who never eats enough food and is hungry all the time because she's afraid of getting fat. A food addict can be a man who eats double helpings of dinner after snacking on junk food all day long to help deal with the stress of his job. He can be a lonely guy with nothing to do on a Friday night except watch television and demolish several bags of potato chips. A food addict might graze all day and into the night to help alleviate the boredom of an unchallenging job or an unsatisfying social life. A food addict can be a mother who turns to junk food and overeats because she feels guilty about yelling at her kids or because she's angry with her ex-husband. A food addict can be a compulsive overeater who binges and then purges by vomiting or using laxatives on a regular basis. She also can be what some researchers call "the hidden anorectic," a teenager who starves herself but not to the degree that she can be diagnosed with a clinical disorder. Food addicts are often dissatisfied with their bodies, sometimes to the degree that they monitor themselves constantly to see what effect the food they eat is having on their bodies.

After years of on-and-off dieting, gaining weight and losing weight, indulging in food or avoiding food, your mind and body are understandably out of balance. You've developed a love-hate relationship with something you cannot live without. It will take more than balancing your eating habits to improve your relationship with food. You will also have to balance your inner self—that is, your emotional, mental, and spiritual self. To do that, you might have to take a break from worrying about how you look and how much you weigh.

Diets and weight loss programs often encourage you to change your eating habits immediately, but even though a change in diet might be warranted, it might not be your most important first step. If your food addiction takes the form of chronic dieting or emotional overeating, the place to begin developing a healthier

4

relationship with food is in your mind. Before you try to change long-standing eating habits, it might be more helpful to find ways to relax, uncover the physical and emotional stressors that are driving your unhealthy eating habits, and figure out what type of lifestyle changes you're willing to make.

Emotional Rescue To a psychologist, a food addict can be anyone who is preoccupied with food, eating, and body image or who relies on food to soothe the effects of underlying emotions. Often, food provides the fun, entertainment, comfort, or love that's missing in a food addict's life. At other times, food helps a food addict deal with stress or cover up fear, sadness, or other painful emotions that are too difficult to confront. Some food addicts eat too much; others don't eat enough. Inevitably, most food addicts suffer great anguish over their relationship with food.

Dr. Tracy Tylka, an assistant professor of psychology at Ohio State University, says most people who have an unhealthy relationship with food are acting out emotional issues. Whether they're happy or sad, food addicts often use the same unhealthy weight control techniques—dieting, bingeing, avoiding food— as someone with a bona fide eating disorder such as anorexia, bulimia, or binge eating disorder (see Chapter 4); they're just doing it less often. Food addicts might not have a diagnosable eating disorder, but they do show signs of an unhealthy relationship with food.

A food addict's eating behavior, whether it's overeating, emotional eating, or obsessive dieting, occurs on a *continuum,* which ranges from healthy eating habits to diagnosable eating disorders. According to Dr. Tylka, every other type of eating falls somewhere in between these two extremes. It's unclear exactly where on the continuum different types of food addictions fall, because a great deal of research has not

PsychSpeak

An eating behavior **continuum** is a rating scale that can be used to show a range of behaviors, from healthy eating to clinical eating disorders and everything in between.

been done on what's known as subclinical eating behavior. However, the farther to the right the unhealthy eating behavior falls along the continuum, the more critical the problem.

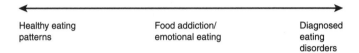

| Healthy eating patterns | Food addiction/ emotional eating | Diagnosed eating disorders |

Emotional eating and other forms of food addiction fall somewhere between the two extremes of healthy eating and clinical eating disorders on the same eating behavior continuum.

Brain Chemistry When you suffer from a food addiction, it might be hard to tell if it's your brain or your body that's out of whack. The fact is, your brain and body are in cahoots when it comes to what and how you eat. Your brain and body are always sending signals back and forth to communicate information about how hungry you are, how much you're eating, and whether you're craving salty potato chips, sweet pastries, or a juicy T-bone steak.

Normally, the brain and body also transmit signals of satisfaction and fullness. Some important research on food addiction and brain chemistry focuses on abnormalities in this communication system that might explain, at least in part, why some people can't stop eating.

Researchers at the U.S. Department of Energy's Brookhaven National Laboratory in Upton, New York, discovered that people who chronically overeat have a biochemical relationship with food similar to the relationship drug addicts have with controlled substances such as cocaine and heroin. Like drug addicts, food addicts have higher levels of a neurochemical called dopamine circulating in their brains than nonaddicts. Dopamine is involved in the regulation of appetites and drives. It motivates us to eat and thereby helps produce feelings of pleasure and satisfaction. These researchers believe food addicts might be like drug addicts, who have fewer dopamine receptors in their brains than people who don't overuse drugs. Tests showed that heavier people had fewer receptors. When there aren't enough dopamine receptors, the chemical is swirling around in the brain with no place to land. When the brain can't soak up dopamine through its receptors, the chemical messages it carries get lost, along with the pleasurable feelings that normally would arise. The food addict responds by overeating in an attempt to feel the normal pleasure that comes from eating a good meal.

These researchers speculate that people with fewer dopamine receptors possibly are predisposed to *compulsive* eating and other addictive behavior. Or it could be that chronic overeaters alter their brain chemistry over time and the result is abnormal dopamine activity and the resulting compulsive behavior. Unfortunately, the currently available drugs that can alter dopamine levels are not the solution because they're highly addictive. Researchers in this area say, however, that it might be possible to develop a drug that will correct the imbalance between dopamine and dopamine receptors, helping compulsive eaters control their obsessive relationship with food.

> **PsychSpeak**
>
> A **compulsion** is a behavior that provides relief from anxiety. Many food addicts are compulsive overeaters.

Dr. Ron Ruden, an internist in New York City and author of *The Craving Brain*, says, however, that dopamine is not the final answer when it comes to food addiction. Although dopamine motivates us to seek out and eat food, he says, another brain chemical called serotonin actually sets the stage for addiction. Normally, the two chemicals interact, with dopamine rising in anticipation of eating and motivating you to action while serotonin levels are rising to act as a calming, satiety agent as you're eating. In this manner, serotonin restricts the actions of dopamine, but in a food addict who overeats for emotional comfort, the brain perceives what Dr. Ruden calls "inescapable stress," and this stress causes serotonin levels to drop. When there's not enough serotonin, dopamine flows freely and eating becomes unstoppable. The food addict has to keep eating to get his serotonin levels to rise again. This rise in serotonin controls the dopamine levels, and the obsession with food begins to subside— at least for the moment. For the emotional overeater, this is a never-ending cycle.

In this respect, food addicts are just like any other addict. The brain perceives the compulsive behavior—whether it be overeating, gambling, or overindulging in alcohol, drugs, or sex—as necessary for survival. According to Dr. Ruden, this is why the key to addictive behavior lies in the landscape of the brain, or more specifically, in the relationship between dopamine and serotonin in the brain, rather than in the drugs, foods, or habits that the addict turns to. Even for food addicts, it's not really about the food, he says. Eating food releases dopamine in everyone, but only people with a vulnerable neurological landscape will turn to addictive eating behavior.

How can self-destructive, obsessive behavior such as binge eating be necessary for survival?

In early man, the neurological system that regulates brain chemistry was set up to deal with the stress of basic survival, explains internist Dr. Ron Ruden. The primary stressors in those days came from fulfilling three primal needs: food, sex, and safe shelter. But this system was not set up to deal with the many stressors that are part of everyone's life today. It was not designed to cope with an angry boss, a dysfunctional family situation, an unhappy marriage, or complicated emotions. Obsessive thoughts and compulsive behavior is a response to these types of situations that allows the brain to adapt to modern stressors by balancing the brain chemicals originally designed to alleviate less complicated forms of stress.

The brain is also the center of the sensory response to food— how it tastes, smells, and feels. Some researchers speculate that obese people might be more sensitive to the pleasurable properties of food and that this might help explain why food has such powerful appeal and significance for some people. Using brain-scanning techniques, these researchers found that, as a group, obese people had higher metabolic activity than nonobese people in those areas of the brain that receive sensory input from the mouth, lips, and tongue. This indicates enhanced sensitivity to some of the more pleasurable aspects of food.

Some of the most interesting research to come from the Department of Energy's Brookhaven National Laboratory in Upton, New York, suggests that the mere sight or smell of food causes a significant rise in brain dopamine, increasing our desire to eat. Scientists think this might be a clue to why people give in to cravings and eat junk food.

> **GET PSYCHED**
>
> "Advertisers, marketing executives, and supermarket managers know that people respond to their senses. They use this information to their advantage when they create enticing food images and displays that stimulate customers to buy and eat their products. It's difficult for anyone who is struggling with weight issues to avoid this trap."
> —Gene-Jack Wang, M.D., scientist, Brookhaven National Laboratory

Genetic Links In the scientific community, it is well accepted that body shape and body weight are largely a function of genes, much like height, eye color, and a propensity for certain diseases. Genetic researchers acknowledge that lifestyle factors such as poor eating habits and lack of physical activity, along with psychological issues such as unresolved emotional problems, social pressures, and stress, all contribute to weight problems, but none of these factors are as powerful as individual genetics, they say. Genes also affect your propensity to gain weight by helping to establish your individual metabolic rate, which is the number of calories you burn in a given period of time.

Your genes are a blueprint for the many hormones and brain chemicals that work together to regulate your appetite and your metabolism. Some research even suggests that we inherit a weight range from which we deviate only about 10 percent. If you have a family history of obesity, you might be predisposed to gain weight easily and have trouble losing it. That doesn't mean you're destined to be overweight, but it does mean you might have to struggle harder with weight control than someone who is not genetically predisposed to obesity.

Back when human beings lived in caves and food was not as easy to come by, a genetic propensity for being overweight actually came in handy. Carrying some extra body fat was a way to prevent starvation. These days, however, in every country where weight control is a problem, high-calorie, high-fat foods are readily available. Add to that an increasing lack of physical activity and the unprecedented stressors of modern life, and the genes that once helped save early man from starvation are now contributing to an obesity epidemic.

In the mid-1990s, obesity researchers at Rockefeller University in New York announced they had discovered a gene in the fat cells of mice that controlled overeating. They called it the *OB geneROM,* short for *obese geneROM.* All genes have jobs to do, and one of the OB gene's jobs is to produce a hormonelike protein called leptin (for more about leptin and other obesity-related hormones, see Chapter 3). In the original studies, it was found that leptin sends a signal to the brain that tells the mouse its fat cells are full so it will stop eating. If the OB gene is defective, it produces little or no leptin, so the signal to stop eating never gets sent. Later research revealed that a lack of leptin also encourages fat production within fat cells—a process that has nothing to do with the brain. Either way, the end result is one mighty big mouse.

When a mouse with a defect in this gene is injected with leptin supplements, it stops eating and loses weight. When an obese human with a defective gene is injected with leptin, he loses weight, too. This discovery was pivotal because it was the first to show that human obesity can have a genetic basis. But excitement over leptin research subsided when scientists found that a faulty leptin gene is extremely rare and if someone isn't overweight because of a damaged leptin gene, leptin injections won't help that person. It is now known that many genes play varying roles in regulating body weight and scientists worldwide are investigating newly discovered genes that are involved both in increased risk of and protection against obesity.

Other genetic research focuses on the link between the neurological system and unhealthy human behavior. Kenneth Blum, a professor of pharmacology at the University of Texas Health Science Center in San Antonio, has been working in the field of addictive behavior and genetics for more than three decades. His research suggests that all addictive, impulsive, and compulsive behaviors, including food bingeing, might have a common genetic basis. Blum theorizes that those of us who fall prey to these behaviors might have a "reward deficiency syndrome," which he believes might begin with defective genes that cause a chemical imbalance and interfere with the dopamine pathways of the brain that normally help induce a feeling of well-being, or the "reward." This imbalance could lead to one or more behavioral disorders such as food bingeing, alcohol abuse, or drug addiction.

Pharmaceutical companies are very interested in genetic research on weight control and eating behavior. For now, there is little more than speculation. Down the road, however, we probably can expect to see tests for damaged genes, drugs that fix damaged genes, and drugs that will make normal genes work even harder to control our eating habits.

Substance Abuse The term *food addiction* evolved because the behavior of a food addict mimics that of an alcoholic, a drug addict, or a gambler. A food addict uses, abuses, and obsesses over food the way a drug addict uses heroin or an alcoholic abuses liquor. Many people believe that certain foods, usually anything made with white sugar or white flour, are addictive substances. They say these foods are controlling their lives, and as a result, their lives are out of control.

GET PSYCHED

"There's no solid scientific evidence that sugar addiction or any food addiction exists in people, but we've been able to prove that animals can become overly dependent on sweet foods and show signs of addictive behavior." –*Bart Hoebel, neuroscientist, Princeton University*

One theory behind this idea is that carbohydrates such as pasta, bread, crackers, starchy vegetables, cookies, and cakes prompt the body to release natural, calming opiates called endorphins. Endorphins are neurochemicals that produce something of a mental "high" by elevating mood and producing a feeling of satisfaction and well-being.

People who suffer from severe food addiction, however, say eating addictive foods triggers cravings for more. These cravings set off a cycle of uncontrollable bingeing. Not eating these foods also causes cravings, they say, along with withdrawal symptoms similar to those suffered by alcoholics when they don't have a drink. Even when she knows there will be a price to pay, both physically and psychologically, a food addict can't stop eating these foods any more than an alcoholic can turn down another drink.

Abstinence appears to be the best solution for people who believe they are addicted to specific foods. But even though a food addict must avoid the foods that are controlling his life, most experts say food addiction isn't really about the food itself. Unlike substances such as alcohol or nicotine, sugar, flour, and other foods that are "abused" don't create true addiction. The root of the problem, most experts say, can be found in a combination of genetics, brain chemistry, and underlying psychological issues unique to people who suffer from severe food addictions. If you binge on sweets when you're under stress or dealing with any overwhelming emotion and addiction runs in your family, bingeing might lead to addictive behavior and cause long-term changes in your brain chemistry.

Compulsive Eating

Food addicts often eat compulsively—not because they're hungry, but to help them cope with problems, deal with stress, or suppress emotions. Some compulsive overeaters go on eating binges, consuming huge quantities of food in a relatively short period of time, and afterward feel disgusted and depressed by their own behavior. Others continually graze, eating all the time and feeling equally depressed about it. Most compulsive overeaters are over-weight, and many are obese.

Compulsive overeaters often admit to having low self-esteem. They don't feel good about themselves, so they don't believe they can handle personal conflicts, stress, loneliness, or other emotional situations—in fact, they might not have the skills necessary to handle these situations. For this type of food addict, eating becomes a way of coping with and numbing their feelings of inadequacy. Food addicts often set unrealistic expectations for themselves, and when they can't live up to their own expecta-tions, they feel distressed and eat. Compulsive overeaters need help setting realistic expectations for themselves and finding a balance in their thinking and their behavior.

On a Binge

An eating binge is best described as an unrestrained episode of overeating. Some binges are so out of control that food addicts often say they don't even remember what they ate. A binge eater consumes abnormally large amounts of food at one sitting, past the point of being full to a point where he feels physically ill. In addition to physical discomfort, a binge eater usually feels quite distressed after a binge. Guilt and shame lead binge eaters to hide their problem from family and friends. They usually binge when they're alone.

Binge eaters are emotional overeaters. When researchers at Johnson State College in Vermont compared women who binge with women who don't binge, they found higher levels of depres-sion, anxiety, and lower self-esteem among the bingers. This was true regardless of whether the women were overweight or ideal weight. Nonbingeing women, whether they were ideal weight or obese, showed less emotional distress than women who binged.

Animal research at Princeton University suggests that bingeing on sweets could lead to a form of food addiction by inducing a dependency on the animal's natural brain opiates. In one experiment, lab rats were deprived of food for twelve hours, then fed regular food plus sugar syrup for the next twelve hours to mimic the pattern of deprivation followed by bingeing that is practiced by many food addicts. After a few weeks on this cycle, the rats consumed less regular food and an increasing amount of sugar syrup and developed more of a certain type of brain receptor for opiates and dopamine in a part of their brain that motivates eating behavior. These brain and behavior changes are characteristic of physical addiction. When the rats were given a drug that blocks the opiate receptors, they showed common signs of withdrawal such as teeth chattering and changes in brain chemistry. They had become dependent on the chemicals in their own brains, released in response to a sugary diet.

PsychSpeak

Opioids are natural brain chemicals associated with feelings of pleasure and well-being. They are similar to chemical opiates such as morphine, codeine, and heroin.

Rats that were fed a steady diet of their regular food plus sugar syrup without deprivation and bingeing showed no signs of withdrawal.

Approximately one third of the overweight adults surveyed reported episodes of binge eating. Even young children are known to have problems with bingeing. The difference between someone who binges on occasion and someone with a diagnosable binge eating disorder is largely a matter of degree. If you binge at least a couple times a week for at least six months straight and suffer extreme emotional distress as a result, you might have binge eating disorder (see Chapter 4).

Guilt and Obsession

Certain traits distinguish the food addict, chief among them obsessive thinking and compulsive behavior with regard to food, eating, and body image. Add to that the guilt she feels about her own eating behavior, and you can see how food addicts can become trapped by their addiction.

Food Fixation A food addict spends most of her time thinking about food, anticipating eating, planning her next meal or snack, and, more often than not, worrying about what effect the food she eats has on her weight.

For all the time and effort spent on food and eating, however, a food addict's obsessive thoughts and behavior have very little to do with *food* and have everything to do with *control*. Food addicts often try to control their eating to compensate for the lack of control they feel in other areas of their lives.

Finding Fault Guilt is a way of finding fault with yourself or with something you've done. Because of their need to feel in control, food addicts often feel guilty about one or more of the following:

- Eating too much
- Eating certain types of food
- Bingeing
- Vomiting
- Not losing enough weight
- Eating at night
- Regaining weight
- Wanting to give up

Guilt suggests you've done something wrong. It makes you feel bad about yourself, and it can make you want to hide what you've done. For instance, a compulsive overeater might eat healthful amounts of food in front of other people and then secretly overeat at home or anywhere she can hide it from people she knows because she's ashamed of her eating behavior. A compulsive eater might feel guilty just for existing as an overweight person. Guilt and shame work against a food addict who is trying to improve her relationship with food. It's impossible to move ahead in positive directions when you feel bad about yourself and blame yourself for something that isn't your fault.

15

Not for Women Only

Just as alcoholism was once considered a "man's disease," food addiction is often mistakenly thought of as a woman's problem. But in fact, of the approximately 130 million overweight adults in this country, 65 million, or half of them, are men. And of the one third of American adults who are classified as obese, 27 million of them are men. It is estimated that 10 percent of the people with bulimia and anorexia are men. Experts believe the number would be higher if compulsive eaters were included in that figure and more men sought treatment and were counted. It's clear that men can develop unhealthy relationships with food. The question is, why don't we hear more about them?

While growing up, boys often are discouraged by parents and peers from showing feelings or displaying signs of weakness. They are more often encouraged to be physically and emotionally strong, "manly," and to handle problems themselves. Yet boys have just as difficult a time going through adolescence and other stages of life as girls. Boys and men can have the same problems with low self-esteem, a history of abuse, and depression that often underlie food addictions in women—but it might be much harder for men to deal with these issues openly.

How do men's and women's views on their bodies differ?

Studies have shown that women are more concerned overall about weight and shape than are men. However, Dr. Brooke Whisenhunt, a psychologist at Southwest Missouri State University, says that men's concerns about their bodies are increasing. Men do care about their weight. Dr. Whisenhunt points out that most women worry about being overweight, but men have concerns about being overweight *and* underweight. Another difference when it comes to attitudes about weight is that men tend to focus more on their upper bodies—their chest, arms, and abs—while women focus more on their lower bodies—especially the waist, hips, and thighs.

Historically, men haven't been under the same pressure as women to be thin or "shapely," so body obsession hasn't been as strong a phenomenon in men. Times have changed, however, and body-building celebrities, male models in men's magazines, superstar athletes, and even a new gym-body GI Joe doll have helped change boys' and men's thinking about their health, fitness, and appearance. Many men now feel the same pressure as women to live up to an often unrealistic "ideal" body image. Unlike women, however, when men think about their bodies, they tend to be more concerned with their size and shape than with their weight. These days, many men at the gym are as motivated by vanity as they are by health concerns.

More and more, men are the subjects of research that explores their relationships with food. Some of the research is specific to men, such as the work of Italian scientists who recently discovered a "beer belly" gene that predisposes some men to gain weight around the abdomen. Most of the available research, however, focuses on gender differences in attitudes and behavior when it comes to eating styles, weight control, and body image. It is clear that men and women have different opinions on everything from what constitutes a binge to how they perceive their own bodies, but it is also clear that men and women are responding in many similar ways to the emotional issues and societal pressures that underlie food addictions.

you're not alone

One Guy's Story

"I'm a guy, and guys aren't supposed to think about how much they weigh, right? Well, I've been thinking about it for about ten years now, and I'm finally getting to the point where I'm starting to feel comfortable with my own look and feel.

"As I got older, I got lazy and became cynical about my own ability to positively impact my health. I gained weight. Diets didn't work out, exercise felt too much like work, and I quickly became disillusioned and complacent. In short, I gave up on myself.

"I started walking around with my shirttails hanging out. I'm pretty sure everyone else thought I was just a casual sort of guy. They didn't know I was

continues

continued

embarrassed by the roll of fat that plopped over the waist of my pants. Finally, I found myself standing naked in front of a three-way mirror and being absolutely astonished at what I saw. I didn't have any idea how much I weighed, but what I saw in the mirror wasn't me. At least, it wasn't a me I'd ever seen before. I didn't like who I'd become, and I was angry for allowing myself to be so lazy and so lackadaisical about my health. I didn't want to go the way of my father and grandfather, dying young from heart attacks. But clearly I was heading in that direction.

"So a few days before my thirty-eighth birthday, weighing close to 240 pounds and standing just shy of 6 feet tall, I decided I'd had enough. I set a very reasonable goal—drop 40 pounds before my fortieth birthday. I called it my "40 by 40" plan. I knew it would take time, and I knew I couldn't do it on my own. I needed a plan—and someone to be accountable to—to keep me honest.

"When I joined a medically supervised program at a local hospital, I didn't just join a weight loss program. I joined a program designed to help improve my overall health and well-being. The program included mandatory weekly education meetings with a registered dietitian. I joined a gym and found a workout partner who gave me a great deal of encouragement and support.

"I'm writing this story seven months after I started the program, and I feel almost like a completely different person—or at least a new and improved version of the person I was a year ago. I've lost more than 60 pounds, and that's great, but I've learned that the numbers on the scale don't really matter.

"The most important thing I've learned is that how I feel about myself is what matters most. When I entered the program, my self-esteem was pretty low. No one had to tell me I was fat or lazy because I was very good at telling myself. Now, because I like what I see in the mirror, I'm not as hard on myself as I was before and I believe in my ability to enact inner change.

"Right now I'm accountable to a lot of people—to the other members of my weekly counseling group and the dietitian we report to, and to my family, friends, and co-workers who have watched me get back in shape. Initially, those accountabilities helped propel my drop in weight. Now I have to learn to be accountable to myself and respect myself enough to stay in shape and maintain a healthy relationship with food on my own, for the rest of my life. That's the part that will take some time." *—Mikal B.*

Are You a Food Addict?

To answer this question, ask yourself the following questions and answer them as honestly as you can. These are the "20 Questions" of Food Addicts in Recovery Anonymous (FA), a 12-step program of recovery for persons suffering from any form of food addiction, including overeating, undereating, and/or obsession with food.

1. Have you ever wanted to stop eating and found you just couldn't?
2. Do you think about food or your weight constantly?
3. Do you find yourself attempting one diet or food plan after another, with no lasting success?
4. Do you binge and then "get rid of the binge" through vomiting, exercise, laxatives, or other forms of purging?
5. Do you eat differently in private than you do in front of other people?
6. Has a doctor or family member ever approached you with concern about your eating habits or weight?
7. Do you eat large quantities of food at one time (binge)?
8. Is your weight problem due to your "nibbling" all day long?
9. Do you eat to escape from your feelings?
10. Do you eat when you're not hungry?
11. Have you ever discarded food, only to retrieve and eat it later?
12. Do you eat in secret?
13. Do you fast or severely restrict your food intake?
14. Have you ever stolen other people's food?
15. Have you ever hidden food to be sure you have "enough"?
16. Do you feel driven to exercise excessively to control your weight?
17. Do you obsessively calculate the calories you've burned against the calories you've eaten?
18. Do you frequently feel guilty or ashamed about what you've eaten?

19. Are you waiting for your life to begin "when you lose the weight"?

20. Do you feel hopeless about your relationship with food?

If you answered yes to any of these questions, you might be a food addict. You are not alone.

(Copyright 2003–2004 Food Addicts in Recovery Anonymous. Reprinted with permission.)

What You Can Do

The first step to changing unhealthy eating patterns is to learn all you can about the nature of food addiction. Then you can begin to examine your own attitude and behavior to determine if you have a food addiction and what you can—and can't—do about it.

- ☐ Decide where you fall on the eating behaviors continuum.
- ☐ Think critically about the information you've received here and elsewhere about food addiction.
- ☐ Examine your own beliefs about the nature of food addiction.
- ☐ Look for patterns and traits in your behavior that might mean you have a food addiction.
- ☐ Answer FA's 20 Questions to find out if you have a food addiction.
- ☐ If you feel you have a food addiction, think about what it means to you and how it affects your life.

Your Psychological Relationship with Food

Everyone has two different relationships with food: a physical relationship and a psychological relationship. Your physical relationship is based on the types of foods you eat and your individual eating habits (see Chapter 3 for more on this relationship). Your psychological relationship with food is how you think about food and the effect it has on your weight and body image. A food addict often looks for love in the refrigerator, using food to diffuse her emotions, fill gaps in her life, and block out emotional problems. Food addicts often feel sad, guilty, afraid, and confused when they think about food. It's not usually a happy relationship.

Your Emotional Appetite

Sometimes we eat to satisfy hunger, and sometimes we eat to satisfy our appetite. There's a big difference between the two. Hunger is a physical need to eat and supply your body with nutrients. Your appetite, on the other hand, is your desire for food. It's a psychological need that has nothing to do with true hunger.

Your appetite is at work when someone puts a to-die-for dessert in front of you and you eat the whole thing, even though you've just finished a big meal and you're actually full. At a time like this, you're indulging your appetite and eating for sheer pleasure rather than to satisfy hunger.

Sometimes a specific food arouses a memory or an emotion and you'll want to eat it even though you're not really hungry. It can be a good memory or a bad memory, a positive or negative emotion. If it triggers your appetite, you'll eat. Likewise, an emotional situation can trigger your appetite, and if you don't recognize or acknowledge the trigger for what it is, you'll eat.

you're not alone

Food and the Single Mom

"I consider myself an intelligent woman and knowledgeable about health issues, especially my own. But even though I've been diagnosed as hypoglycemic and have high cholesterol levels, all warnings about what I'm not supposed to eat fly out the window around 9 P.M. every night.

"After an hour spent putting my reluctant seven-year-old to bed; after singing the lullabies, playing the games, talking, cajoling, promising, threatening, and bribing her to go to sleep, visions of cookies dance in my head. I dash into the kitchen to grab whatever looks good. If I don't see anything ready-to-eat, I put together some weird concoction like mozzarella and grape jam, or fruit loops on a buttered bagel.

"In the morning, my daughter asks, 'Who ate my animal crackers?' I hang my head in guilt and shame. Yes, I did it, and I promise I'll never do it again. Not only do I feel remorse and embarrassment for having eaten all my daughter's snacks, I feel physically awful as well. Because of my hypoglycemia, I react to all the sweets and wheat with itchy eyes, rashes, bloating, and dizziness. And ultimately, I gain weight. When it gets to the point that I can't get into some of my clothes and I can't hide my bigger waist with longer jackets, I go on a diet. Within a few weeks, I lose the extra pounds. But the nights feel longer, and I can't handle the deprivation. And so the next binge begins.

"Like a lioness seeking its prey, I graze my apartment at night, looking for the perfect food that will comfort me, award me, appease me, and satisfy my cravings. It has to be sweet, chewy, and of course, loaded with carbs. I pass up all the healthier food in the kitchen and go straight to the real stuff—cake, cookies, and candy. When you've got a child in the house, there's always a good supply of binge food around.

"As a single mom, I have complete responsibility for my daughter. I can't say to a partner, 'Please deal with her. I can't handle it right now.' I am often frustrated and exhausted and left at the end of the day with a deep need to be comforted, to be fed. So I eat. It's hard to get off the merry-go-round. I don't stop bingeing until I feel really awful. And that hiatus usually doesn't last long. As soon as I'm feeling better, I think, 'What harm can a little cookie do?' Before the night is over, I've eaten the whole box.

"I never gain more than 5 or 10 pounds, so I never do anything about my fixation on junk food other than try to take the extra weight off by dieting. I know that's not a real solution because I'm always dieting and always feeling miserable about it. I know I need to find a healthier outlet to deal with the emotional situations that trigger my overeating. The answer for me is to reconnect with who I was before I became a mother. I was an artist first; I need to reclaim myself and find a creative outlet." –*Natalie E.*

Alone in a Crowd There are two types of loneliness, and both can lead a food addict to overeat. Situational or social loneliness is what you feel when you don't know many people in a new town, a new school, or a new job, or when you walk into a room full of strangers. Internal or emotional loneliness is what you feel when you don't have anyone in the world to talk to or think no one understands how you feel when you have a problem. This is the type of loneliness you can feel even when you're surrounded by family or friends.

College counselors often hear stories of isolation, loneliness, and self-doubt from students with dysfunctional eating habits. As their eating issues intensify, many of these students avoid going to parties, joining clubs, or getting involved in any social situations. Loneliness, isolation, and depression flow together. Self-defeating thoughts and unhealthy eating behaviors only perpetuate these feelings and bring on another binge. For a food addict, dealing with isolation becomes a vicious cycle of eating to handle the stress of loneliness, then avoiding social gatherings because he's feeling bad about himself and his weight, then eating again to cope with the loneliness.

There are many solutions to loneliness—reaching out to a friend or relative, getting involved in a hobby, joining a club, going for a drive, window shopping at the mall—but if you're a food addict, you'll comfort yourself with food rather than look for a positive solution.

Nancy McReynolds, C.E.D.S., a counselor in the Eating Disorder Program at the Menninger Clinic in Houston, Texas, says the first step toward a solution is to determine which type of loneliness you are experiencing. If it's situational, the answer is to deal with the immediate situation in obvious ways, such as getting involved in social activities and finding new ways to meet people. If what you're feeling is a more profound internal loneliness, finding a solution will be a more complicated process. You've probably been feeding your loneliness for a long time, and the answer won't be so obvious or come as quickly. To get to the root of your lone-liness, you might first have to figure out the true role food has been playing in your life.

Nothing to Do, Nowhere to Go Boredom will always get the best of a food addict. When you can't think of anything else to do with yourself, you start thinking about food. The answer to bore-dom seems obvious: find something to do. But for a food addict, it isn't that simple. *Food* is what you do.

If you constantly tell yourself, "I'm bored," you'll always feel bored. It's become part of your belief system that you get bored easily, before you even try to find something to occupy your time. A food addict eats for the pleasure of it, but soon discovers it's only a temporary pleasure. It's over quickly, and you're bored again, so the only thing you can do to alleviate the boredom is eat more.

Life quickly gets boring when you feel no sense of purpose. For some people, it's simply a matter of finding the things in life that give you pleasure and then doing them. The key is to find pleasure in doing something other than eating, something longer-lasting and more satisfying.

Sometimes boredom is a mask for fear. All you can do with that type of boredom is stay with it. Examine your boredom until you discover your underlying fear. You might find that you're afraid of change, of trying new things, of rejection or failure. You're sticking with boredom because it's much safer.

The Heat Is On Stress and anxiety are common triggers for overeaters. Some stressors come from within yourself, such as the stress you put on yourself to have a perfect body or the self-doubt you feel when you want to ask your boss for a raise you know you deserve. Other stressors come from outside you. These include day-to-day job stress, anxiety over family medical problems, and other people's behavior that is simply out of your control.

Even positive situations in your life can cause stress. Getting married, getting a promotion or a better job, buying a house, and giving birth are all happy events, but change comes with all them, and with any change come new problems and new sources of stress.

Whether or not a situation is stressful depends on how you respond to it. You might rise to a challenge that someone else will go out of his way to avoid. Even though the word *stress* has a negative connotation, a little stress can actually be a good motivator because it helps signal a need for change in your life. It might also give you the push you need to make that change.

Both positive and negative events can stir your emotional appetite and create the perfect environment for overeating. Managing stressful situations can be difficult, especially when stress is coming from family, friends, or your job. If you respond to stress by overeating, giving up on yourself, or acting out some other self-defeating behavior, the first thing to do is identify your stressors and find a way to change your response.

The best way to deal with a stressful situation is to address it head-on. Quickly find something—other than food—that will take the edge off the stress so you can get to a direct and realistic solution.

But what if you find that no matter what you do, your positive attempts to resolve a stressful situation just aren't working?

Sometimes the most positive response might be to stop trying to fix an unfixable situation and let it go. It's always okay to give up on an impossible situation—but never give up on yourself!

you're not alone

Taking Control

"I've always known that stress is behind my overeating, but it's taken thirty-seven years to figure out that it's only a particular type of stress that affects me in negative ways. I can handle work stress, deadline stress, emergency stress, and all types of stress that might send another person straight to the cake box. Not me. The only thing I can't handle is the pressure of being with my family.

"When I was a kid, eating was a contest in our family. My aunts and uncles would brag about eating ridiculous amounts of food. I can still hear my uncle saying, 'I ate 15 ravioli. How many did you eat?' Eating was a way of being recognized, whether it was for the good or for the bad. It got attention. Our family had a food motto: quality and quantity. That meant good-tasting food—and lots of it. We didn't eat; we feasted. I learned to eat enormous amounts of food. And it showed.

"I never let being overweight get in the way of taking gymnastics classes or ballet lessons or joining the swim team. But I was teased mercilessly about my size. We had to buy 'special order' bathing suits because nothing in the normal range of swimwear would fit me. When I got to high school and went for cheerleading tryouts, I could split wider and cartwheel, round off, and flip higher than anyone else. But I still wasn't picked because I didn't fit the mold.

"It wasn't until I escaped to college that I could lose weight and keep it off, at least for a while. There was no one around to overstock the fridge and few opportunities to overeat. I was the only one among my friends who didn't gain the proverbial 'freshman 15,' those extra pounds first-year college students always seem to put on because they're away from their families and finally free to eat whatever they want, whenever they want. For me, being away from my family meant being free to *not* eat. It was the only time in my life I wasn't overweight.

"These days, the family gatherings and tables laden with food that once seemed so festive cause me nothing but anxiety and grief. I walk into a roomful of overweight relatives and see the buffet table warping from the weight of so much food, but there's not a vegetable in sight. My first thought is, *None of these people take care of themselves.* Then the fights start and the tears come, and I realize they have nothing left but their food.

"I can't avoid my family, but now I know I also can't use them as an excuse for not taking care of myself. I still overeat when I see my relatives, and not just during the few hours I spend with them. Sometimes I binge for days, even weeks after they're gone. And then I start to feel sluggish. Clothes start to feel tight. I feel depressed. That's when something clicks in my head and my internal regulator goes on. I start exercising again, which gets me feeling good about myself. I write down everything I eat so I can keep track of everything that's going in my mouth. I take charge of the situation before it gets out of control. And that's the key word: *control*. I can handle other types of stress because I feel I have control over them. I don't feel control over my family, and I never will. But I have control over myself, and I know I'm the only one who can stop my own madness." –Meryl B.

Eating Anger Anger is often a response to fear, frustration, or pain. It's a tough emotion to deal with because in many situations, it's socially unacceptable to express it. A food addict who is angry with himself or someone else uses food to suppress an emotion that's too difficult or too painful to express. Think about it. Someone did something you didn't want him or her to do. Or someone said something that made you angry. You've been hurt, and the way you're coping with it is to hurt yourself even more by overeating.

For many people, all it takes to arouse anger is a phone call from a relative or a fight with a spouse. Your immediate thought is of food. For one thing, food is a distraction. Once you start focusing on food, you stop focusing on your anger and you feel better. You eat, and your anger moves to the back burner, at least for the time being. But then different emotions set in. You feel guilty or ashamed or perhaps angry with yourself for eating. How will you cope with these additional feelings? You'll use food again to distract yourself and push away the feelings. The cycle continues until you stop it by learning to deal with your anger head-on.

Some people scream out loud when they're angry, while others rage quietly, holding in their anger out of fear or a need to avoid conflict. But holding in anger only intensifies your feelings. The way out of the cycle is to not turn your anger back on yourself. Internalized anger usually leads to depression. A better way to deal with anger is to let it out in healthy ways. Speak your anger. Be very clear what you're angry about and why. If you can't address your feelings directly to the person who made you feel angry, write down your feelings in a letter or in your journal. The goal is to release your feelings rather than suppress them or ignore them by overeating.

Feeling Blue Everyone feels sad at times, especially when we experience the death of someone we love, a personal trauma, or the end of a meaningful relationship. If depression doesn't go away with the passing of time and the help of friends, and if it interferes with normal daily activities, this can be a sign of a more serious problem. People who suppress their emotions, have perfectionist tendencies, have survived physical or sexual abuse, or have a family history of depression are among those at risk of experiencing depression.

Depression is often at the root of food addiction. You eat because you're unhappy, then you're even unhappier because you ate. Studies show that people are more dissatisfied with their bodies when they are feeling sad and are more likely to see themselves as heavier than they are.

Exercise is one of the best coping tools for depression because it raises levels of "feel-good" brain chemicals known as *endorphins* that help improve your mood. (You'll learn more about the positive effects of exercise on your body *and* your mind in Chapter 15.)

What Are You Afraid Of? Although you might not recognize it, fear could be the underlying emotion that drives your unhealthy eating behavior. Before you can face your fears, however, you have to figure out what they are. Are you afraid of hunger? Or are you afraid of facing the emotions you're trying to cover up by overeating or not eating? What scares you the most when you think about developing a healthier relationship with food?

Perhaps you're afraid to eat a normal amount of food because you think you'll get fat. High school students in their junior and senior years have been known to go to dieting extremes in anticipation and fear of gaining the "freshman 15" when they get to college. Unfortunately, this type of dieting behavior can lead to years of bingeing and purging behavior or other forms of disordered eating or a even a full-fledged eating disorder.

Anyone who recognizes fear knows that it can be paralyzing. But the first step to overcoming fear is to recognize it and stare it in the face so you can become desensitized and move on from it. Some common fears of food addicts include the following:

- **Fear of fat.** If you're careful about the amount of fat in your diet, that's healthful eating. If you obsess over every little bit of fat in your diet, that's a fat phobia. Understand that you do need *some* fat in your diet. (For more on eating without fear, see Chapter 8.)

- **Fear of success.** You might say you want to lose weight, but you might actually be afraid of becoming a thin person. What if you lose weight and you don't like the way you look? What if others don't like the way you look? How will you act when you're thinner? How will it change your life? If you've been overweight for a long time, your weight is familiar to you and comfortable in its own way.

- **Fear of failure.** What if you don't reach your weight loss goals? What if you reach them but can't maintain them? Maybe you've promised someone you'll lose weight and you're afraid you can't live up to the promise. Some of the best lessons are learned the hard way, by falling down, picking yourself up, and trying again.

- **Fear of hard work.** It's not easy for a food addict to develop and maintain a healthy relationship with food. Whatever you've been doing up to this point hasn't been working for you, so something has to change. You have to work on physical and psychological changes. Change is always difficult. You might have to ask for help.

Measuring Up

Some food addicts aren't overweight, but they're obsessed with their own bodies and, as a result, have a miserable relationship with food. They're constantly on a diet, or they just don't eat enough food. They weigh themselves all the time, count fat grams, and constantly compare themselves to other people, especially people whom they think are skinnier, better-looking, or more successful because of their appearance. Food addicts are often perfectionists who are overly critical of themselves and the people around them. Food addicts who don't eat enough aren't happy people because they're hungry all the time.

Sound familiar? If this is you, you can improve your relationship with food and the way you think about your body. First of all, silence your inner critic. Stop comparing your body to others, and learn to view yourself more realistically. If possible, take a look at blood relatives on both sides. You have inherited genes that influence your basic shape and size, your bone structure, and to a certain degree, your weight. Look at family members with similar body types as you and who are at a healthy weight, and you'll see what you can realistically expect from your own body.

What Do You See in the Mirror?

Research shows that at least 80 percent of women over eighteen are unhappy with what they see in the mirror. When surveyed, an equal number of women overestimated their size. They look in the mirror and see someone who is fatter than she actually is.

Even thin women want to be thinner. Women who suffer from eating disorders often dissect themselves in front of the mirror. They mentally section off their bodies and simply refuse to look at certain parts because they are so disgusted by what they see.

Distorted body image is by no means confined to people who suffer from eating disorders. Because women are judged more harshly on their appearance than men, and because standards of beauty have always been higher for the "fairer sex," women tend to be more critical of their appearance, food addicts or not.

I know I'm at a healthy weight for my height and age, but when I look in the mirror, all I see are chunky thighs and fleshy arms. I'm a size 10, which isn't very big, but all I see is a fat person. How can I change the way I see myself?

Sometimes your body image gets so distorted it's like you're looking in a fun-house mirror. Nancy McReynolds, who runs body image workshops at the Menninger Clinic in Houston, says to try to look at yourself through honest eyes and appreciate your body's strengths. Rather than focusing on your shape and size, appreciate the fact that you have strong legs to walk on or strong arms to hug a child. And think about this: a size 10 isn't what you *are;* it's what you *wear.* Many people make the mistake of saying "I'm a size this or a size that" as if they were describing a personality trait or an innate characteristic. Try to change the way you talk to yourself. Don't let your clothing size become a permanent part of your belief system about who you are.

Sports researchers studying the relationship between perfectionism and body image in competitive skaters found that perfectionist skaters were more concerned with thinness and at higher risk for developing disturbed eating behaviors than skaters who were not perfectionists. If you are a perfectionist—as many food addicts are—you will never be happy with what you see in the mirror because the standards you've set for yourself are impossibly high. You will always be unhappy with your weight and body shape, and your sense of self-worth will be tied up in what you see reflected in the mirror, not in who you actually are.

GET PSYCHED

"Perfectionists let unrealistic expectations get in the way of self-acceptance. No matter how much weight you lose or how fit you look, it's never good enough. Before you can change perfectionist behavior, you have to recognize that something is wrong with the way you treat yourself. That recognition is the first step to change." *—Vivian Roy, M.A., M.S.W., psychotherapist, New York City*

Some of the stress perfectionists put on themselves manifests as good or bad, all-or-nothing thinking. You're good if you don't eat, bad if you do. Stay away from all fats, or you'll get fat. One way to challenge your own perfectionism is to listen carefully for these types of thoughts and replace overly critical, black-and-white thinking with something more positive. For instance, you could replace "You're good if you don't eat, bad if you do" with "Eating healthful foods is good for me" and spare yourself some unfair judgment. You'll find more information about monitoring your internal dialogue and changing the way you think about yourself at the end of this chapter.

Food and Mood

No one doubts that food affects mood, but at the same time, no one knows exactly why it's true. Although it was once a far-fetched idea, researchers now know that carbohydrates such as bread, pasta, potatoes, and sweets provide the brain with the raw materials it needs to synthesize and release serotonin, a brain chemical that plays a role in mood regulation.

Low levels of serotonin in the brain are associated with both depression and aggression. Many antidepressants work by increasing serotonin levels. Carbohydrates can help boost serotonin levels, and researchers say carbs could have a mild but very real antidepressant effect. Studies performed at Massachusetts Institute of Technology (MIT) by food-and-mood pioneer Judith Wurtman showed that women who suffer from premenstrual syndrome (PMS) could relieve symptoms of depression and anger by eating carbohydrates. This, in turn, might explain why some women with PMS experience uncontrollable cravings and binge on carbohydrates in the weeks prior to their menstrual periods. When the brain needs serotonin, Wurtman says, people self-medicate with carbohydrates.

Serotonin is actually manufactured from the amino acid tryptophan, which is found in high-protein foods such as turkey and milk. Interestingly, however, eating high-protein foods does nothing to boost serotonin levels in the brain. When the proteins are broken down to amino acids in the body, those that are involved in neurochemical production, including tryptophan, have to compete to get into the brain. Tryptophan doesn't make it in. When you eat a meal rich in carbohydrates, however, insulin is released into the blood. Although its main job is to gather carbohydrates, insulin also picks up any amino acids that are roaming around in the blood—except tryptophan. With no competition, tryptophan is free to move into the brain, where it is converted to serotonin.

Although the protein in fish won't boost your mood, omega-3 fatty acids found in oily fish just might. There is substantial evidence that omega-3's are effective at easing the symptoms of depression.

At the same time, other types of fat might cause some cases of depression. Researchers at the Cholesterol Center of The Jewish Hospital in Cincinnati, Ohio, have reported that high levels of triglycerides in the blood are associated with depression. Once the triglyceride levels are normalized by treatment with a low-fat diet, medication, and fish oil supplements, symptoms of depression usually disappear.

Many individual nutrients, particularly the B vitamins, have also been found to boost both mood and mental performance and reduce stress and anxiety. The subjects of

GET PSYCHED

"If you're being evaluated for clinically significant depression, have your fasting triglyceride level checked. If they are over 1,000 mg/dl (about five times normal), they may be associated with your depression." –*Charles Glueck, M.D., medical director, Cholesterol Center of The Jewish Hospital, Cincinnati, Ohio* most of this research, however, have been people with nutritional deficiencies. Although B-vitamin deficiencies have profound effects on mood and memory, there's no evidence that these same vitamins can elevate mood, reduce anxiety, or improve memory in people who aren't deficient.

Masking Shame

Overweight food addicts often talk about the deep sense of shame they feel, as if they are to blame for the failed diets, out-of-control behavior, depression, and emotional hunger that defeat their attempts to lose weight and develop a healthier relationship with food. If you are overweight, you might have faced prejudice or felt discriminated against in a way that left you feeling rejected and ashamed.

You have the power to change some things in your life, including your relationship with food, but admittedly, it takes much more than an assertion of will to move beyond a food addiction. As you learned in Chapter 1, experts in this field now know that eating behavior and weight, to a certain degree, are governed by a complicated network of genetic, neurological, and psychological systems. The experts still don't know exactly how these systems work together, and until you understand how those systems are operating in your own life, there's no way you can be held entirely responsible for your eating behavior or the results of that behavior.

Not a lot is known about the nature of shame in food addicts. A recent Yale University study looked at how shame affects men and women with binge eating disorder. In keeping with the results of earlier research looking into gender differences, women in the Yale study felt most ashamed of their weight, while men felt most ashamed of the way they looked. Women were no more likely to be ashamed than men, however, and shame had nothing to do with how often a person binged or a person's degree of overweight. Further studies along these lines might help researchers determine if shame is an emotion inherent to people with binge disorders or if it is simply a temporary reaction to their bingeing behavior.

Emotional Self-Talk

What are your first thoughts when you wake up in the morning? Do you feel good about yourself, full of positive energy, and determined to move on from food addiction? Or do you lie there, kicking yourself for eating too much last night or not losing enough weight this week? Self-talk is the way you communicate with yourself; it's your internal dialogue. It can be positive or negative, but it's rarely neutral. Much of the time, you might not even be conscious of your self-talk, but it's always with you and always has a profound effect on your life.

Negative self-talk includes all the not-so-nice things you say to yourself throughout the day that kick at your self-esteem and make you feel bad about yourself. It includes thoughts such as *I'm so fat, I'm an idiot,* or *I have no self-control.* If you constantly put yourself down for every mistake or blame yourself for everything that's wrong with your life, you're swimming in negative self-talk.

The problem with all these negative thoughts is that they turn into an overall negative opinion of yourself. Thinking *I'm so stupid* when you make an ordinary mistake turns into *I'm no good at anything. I didn't lose enough weight this week* turns into *I'll always be fat.* The more you think negatively, the more you'll believe it. The lower your self-esteem drops, the more you start to think that you don't deserve anything better than what you have. Ultimately, you might start to think that you don't deserve to have a healthier relationship with food, and you'll stop trying. Negative self-talk is nothing more than a self-destructive tool.

It takes a concerted effort to stop a cycle of negative self-talk because after a while, these types of thoughts become automatic. They're hard to stop. The good news is, you *can* change the way you think and feel about yourself. The first step is to pay more attention to your thoughts. Listen carefully to yourself until you start to hear negative self-talk as it happens. When you have a negative thought, stop what you're doing. Try to replace the negative thought with a positive thought—*any* positive thought. For instance, if you hear yourself think *I'm a fat pig,* stop and immediately say to yourself, *I have great legs* or *I look 10 years younger than I am* or even something like *I'm going to eat more vegetables today.* Say anything that's positive and true about yourself or your behavior. Keep this up until positive self-talk becomes as automatic as any other habit.

The following table lists some more examples of how you can turn negatives into positives.

Instead of Saying ...	Say ...
I knew I couldn't do it.	I'm doing my best.
Other people are better than me.	I'm going to work at my own pace until I reach my goal.
It doesn't really matter.	I care enough about myself to take steps to get healthier.
It's never going to work.	I will conquer my food addiction, one step at a time.
I can't eat.	I can eat so many wonderful foods.
Healthful food doesn't taste good.	I love eating food that makes me look and feel better.
I'm still fat.	I've made great progress so far.
My body is ugly	My body is getting stronger and healthier every day.
I hate to exercise.	I love how I feel after a good workout.

What You Can Do

Everyone eats for emotional reasons from time to time. Emotional eating only becomes a problem when it interferes with your health and the quality of your life. You can improve your psychological relationship with food.

- ☐ Think about the different reasons why you eat.
- ☐ Learn to recognize the difference between physical hunger and psychological, or emotional, hunger.
- ☐ Come up with nonfood ways to cope with emotional situations such as loneliness, anger, stress, and boredom.
- ☐ Acknowledge the fact that your unhealthy eating behavior might be based on fear.
- ☐ Stop criticizing yourself and comparing yourself to others.
- ☐ Know that you have nothing to be ashamed of and that you are not entirely responsible for the relationship you've developed with food.
- ☐ Practice talking to yourself in positive ways.

Your Physical Relationship with Food

Unlike your psychological relationship with food, which is driven primarily by your emotions (see Chapter 2), your physical relationship with food is determined mostly by your biology and the eating habits you've established over time. Outside factors, such as the makeup of your diet, availability of food, and even the weather also help determine what and how much you eat.

Healthful eating means eating when you're truly hungry and stopping when you feel full. It means responding to your stomach's appetite, not your emotional appetite. Normally, your body sends out signals that let you know when you're truly hungry and when you're full and should stop eating. Food addicts often lose touch with these signals. Establishing new eating habits will help you learn how to listen to your body and reconnect with your internal hunger cues.

Hunger and Eating

Normal eating is a response to internal cues that signal true biological hunger. We're all born with the ability to recognize when

GET PSYCHED

"We all came into the world knowing how to eat. With patience, you can relearn what you once did naturally." —Katy Kram, M.P.H., R.N., R.D., Freedom From Dieting, a professional counseling program for food, weight, and body image issues in Columbus, Ohio

we're physically hungry and when we've had enough to eat. For the most part, when you have a healthy relationship with food, you recognize and respond to these cues and eat only when you're hungry. Often, however, this relationship is sabotaged by "clean plate" messages we get as children, "gulp and run" eating habits we develop, years of following diets that encourage us to ignore our natural eating instincts, and so on.

Many factors affect hunger and how you respond to it, including the following:

- **Your diet.** The macronutrients you get from your diet—carbohydrates, fat, and protein—interact in your body to help regulate how much you eat and let you know when it's time to stop eating. After you eat and digest a meal or snack, the amino acids from protein, fatty acids from fat, and glucose from carbohydrates are absorbed into your blood, causing a feeling of fullness. Over the next few hours, as these nutrients are absorbed into your cells and used for energy, your hunger signals return.

- **Your central nervous system.** As you know from Chapter 1, brain receptors involving serotonin and other neurochemicals are linked to feelings of hunger and fullness. Glucose (from carbohydrates) increases serotonin levels in the brain, which, in turn, increase the production of the amino acid tryptophan. Tryptophan decreases your desire to eat carbohydrates. To keep the cycle going, your brain monitors glucose levels and triggers hunger when glucose is low.

- **Other body systems.** Different body systems send out different signals to indicate hunger and fullness. When your stomach is full, stretch receptors in your stomach wall signal fullness. Enzymes that are active in your fat cells communicate with your brain to say "I'm full" so you'll stop eating, or "I'm empty" to signal the need for energy in the form of food. Your hormones also regulate how much you eat. As you finish eating, your feelings of fullness and satisfaction rise along with the rise of certain hormones. Later, other hormones signal increased hunger as nutrients leave the bloodstream and are taken up by body cells.

- **Your environment.** External factors, such as the immediate availability of food, will affect how much you eat. You'll have a harder time controlling how much you eat if you're surrounded by all your favorite foods. Even the weather can affect how hungry you feel. Cold weather increases hunger; hot weather diminishes hunger.

- **Your eating patterns.** In the process of developing your own personal eating habits, you train your body to feel hungry at specific times throughout the day. For instance, if you're a "grazer" who eats every hour or two, you've trained your body to feel hungry more often than someone who eats regular meals spaced three to four hours apart.

- **State of your health.** If you develop a medical problem, such as diabetes or low blood sugar, or an emotional problem, such as depression, you might feel hungrier or less hungry than normal.

- **Your emotional appetite.** Feelings of boredom, anger, frustration, and loneliness make you think you're hungry; stress and sorrow can cause an increase or decrease in appetite. Although these aberrations in appetite stem from your psychological relationship with food, they ultimately affect your true sense of hunger.

Are You Hungry? It can be very difficult to differentiate between true physical hunger and emotional appetite or cravings because the feelings are similar and your response is usually the same: you eat. One way to tell why you're eating is to look at the types of food you eat. Usually, when you're physically hungry, just about any food will satisfy you. When you're eating for emotional reasons or giving in to a craving, however, you usually want to eat very specific foods or food from very specific food categories.

Basic hunger is driven by a number of biological systems. In your brain, hunger signals come from the *hypothalamus,* or the feeding center. Within the hypothalamus are two nerve centers that help control eating behavior. The *lateral hypothalamus* responds to any stimulation—internal or external—that causes you to feel hungry. Some of these stimuli include low blood sugar, nutrient deficiencies, and the sight or smell of food. Even the mere thought of eating can stimulate the hypothalamus to tell you you're hungry. Once you've eaten, the *ventromedial hypothalamus* tells you that you've had enough.

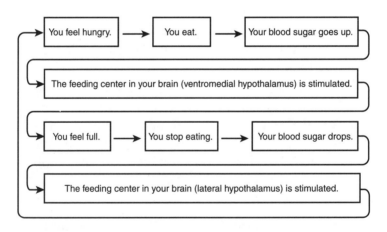

Although there's no real measure of true hunger, hungry people who were studied at the Monell Chemical Senses Center in Philadelphia, Pennsylvania, reported some common and perhaps obvious signs of hunger, including an achy, empty feeling in their stomachs and grumbling stomachs. When you're learning to recognize your own internal hunger cues, those are the sensations to look for. Study participants also reported headaches, dizziness, weakness, fatigue, and loss of concentration—all clear signs you've waited too long to eat.

When Susan Dopart, a registered dietitian and exercise physiologist in Santa Monica, California, talks to new clients about reconnecting with feelings of hunger and fullness, she says a surprising number of them have no idea what she's talking about. They are used to eating a certain amount of food throughout the day without thinking much about whether or not they're actually hungry or stopping to respond to sensations of fullness. Susan says that everyone's stomach has "muscle memory"; the wall of your stomach is used to holding a certain amount of food before it distends enough to send out signals of fullness. When you eat, your stomach waits to be filled by that amount of food. By practicing different eating behavior, you can begin to retrain your stomach's memory so it will begin sending "I'm full" signals much more quickly.

GET PSYCHED

Using a hunger scale to rate your feelings of hunger and fullness can help you learn to sense when it's time to eat and when it's time to stop. It will also help you learn the difference between physical hunger and emotional hunger.

One classic method used by nutritionists and other health experts to teach people how to reconnect with true feelings of hunger and fullness is the hunger scale. The scale ranges from 0 to 10, with 0 being ravenously hungry and 10 being overstuffed and uncomfortable from eating too much food. A food addict's goal is to stay away from either of these extremes. Never let yourself get to 0, a state of ravenous hunger that Dopart calls "the point of no return." At the same time, you don't want to eat until you get to 10, where you're overstuffed and actually feel sick. Her advice is to eat when you get to 2 or 3, when you just begin to feel hungry. Stop eating at 5 or 6, when you feel comfortably satisfied, just before you feel completely full.

The Hunger Scale

0	Ravenously hungry
1	Seriously hungry
2	Hungry; stomach grumbling
3	Slightly hungry
4	No longer hungry but not yet satisfied
5	Comfortably satisfied
6	Just starting to feel full
7	Beginning to feel uncomfortably full
8	Very uncomfortable
9	Great discomfort; possible stomachache
10	In great pain

If you eat when you're truly hungry and stop when you feel satisfied, you're allowing your built-in regulatory systems, which enable your body to make sure you get enough, but not too much, food to do their job. You stop interfering with nature and reconnect with your body's innate ability to maintain its normal weight.

How can I learn to eat only when I'm hungry and stop eating when I'm full?

Start by learning to recognize your own personal patterns of hunger and fullness. To do this, nutritionist Susan Dopart advises the following:

- Start by eating balanced meals at regular times, spacing those meals no more than four hours apart. If you feel hungry when it's time to eat, then that's a good time for you to sit down to a meal. If you don't feel hungry, it's probably not necessary for you to eat yet and you probably can hold off for another hour.

- Use a hunger scale to determine if you're actually hungry before you decide it's time to eat. Try to stay within the range of 2 to 6, eating when you just begin to feel hungry and stopping when you are satisfied but still feel comfortable.

you're not alone

Who's in Control?

"For thirteen years, I was obsessed with what I ate and what it would do to my body. It started when I went away to college and, for the first time in my life, I could eat whenever and whatever I wanted. I was average size when I was growing up and never thought much about my weight or the food I ate. But at school, I ate more often and I ate a lot more junk food than I ever did before, and as a result, I gained almost 30 pounds that first year. When I went home for spring break, my father made a comment about my weight, and for some reason, his words just stayed in my head. From that time on, I was always on a diet, always trying to control my weight. I felt happiest when I was doing something to lose weight, but at the same time, I started hating myself because I thought I was fat, ugly, and weak.

"The fact is, I never gained much more than those 20 pounds, but I always looked at myself as if I'd gained 100. I would lose some of the weight one way or another and then I would quickly gain it back. When I felt I couldn't lose weight fast enough, I started throwing up after meals whenever I could get away with it. I took laxatives. I was always being sneaky about food, and it got to the point where I felt guilty eating a piece of fruit.

"All those years, I thought my food addiction was my secret, but I found out later on I wasn't fooling anyone. Even if they couldn't pinpoint the problem, everyone who knew me knew something was wrong. When you have a food addiction, it's impossible to imagine life any other way. It just becomes part of you, part of who you are. It becomes your entire world, and you get lost in it. I knew my food addiction was pushing away the people who cared most about me, but I didn't really care. It takes a long time to understand that addiction is all about control. I realize now that dieting, not eating, and throwing up were all ways I tried to keep my life in control because whenever I was doing something to lose weight, I felt more powerful. I was in charge, or so I thought.

"When I was in my early 30s, I finally realized something was wrong with my thinking, I was not in charge of my life at all, and it wasn't going to get better by itself. I joined a weight loss program but soon quit because it really wasn't for me. A friend recommended a therapist who finally helped me understand the control issue. It took a while, but the more I learned, the more I was able to let go of my obsessive thoughts. It's been several years since I stopped going to therapy, and I still have some issues with my weight. But I can honestly say I'm no longer obsessed with being thin and I'm able to eat without feeling guilty. I look in the mirror and I accept what I see." —*Barbara W.*

Likes and Dislikes Humans are born with a preference for sweet foods and soon after birth develop an aversion to anything bitter. We are even genetically programmed to prefer high-calorie, high-fat foods as a means of survival.

We learn through personal experience which foods we like, and which we don't. If you have an early, positive association with a certain food or flavor, it might always be a favorite—you might even crave it. On the other hand, if you associate a particular food with something unpleasant, you probably will feel a sense of revulsion for that food.

For instance, you might be disgusted by the idea of eating meat, or you might simply dislike the taste of meat. Maybe you like the taste but are disgusted by the trim of fat that comes with some cuts. And even if you eat meat and enjoy it, you might be disgusted by the idea of eating certain types of meat that are not typical foods for your culture. Most Americans are turned off by the idea of eating insects, rodents, and dogs, but these are important sources of protein in other parts of the world. If you become ill after you eat a particular food, you probably will develop an aversion to that food, even if it wasn't the food that made you sick. Likewise, if you are allergic to a specific food, you won't want to eat it because you know it could make you sick or even kill you. You feel a sense of danger when you see or smell that food.

Research shows that most people will eat almost anything if you put a little sugar on it. That's one of the reasons we like so many high-fat foods. The flavor of fat in baked goods, ice cream, and other sweet dessert foods is masked by sugar. In turn, fat gives the food a better "mouth feel," making it more pleasant to eat. You don't always realize you're eating fat.

Most taste preferences are learned, so they can be modified, if necessary. Research at the State University of New York at Buffalo found that once you reduce the sugar, fat, or salt in your diet, your taste buds adapt to the change, making it easier for you to not go back to eating sweet, fatty, or salty foods. But it's a learning process that requires time and a great deal of patience. You have to train yourself to prefer something different. Eventually, you will like the new flavor, but it takes time to get to that point.

Take, for example, making a switch from whole milk to skim milk. At first, the flavor of skim milk might seem weak, watery, and unsatisfying. But if you continue to drink skim milk, whole milk starts to taste too rich, almost like cream. Likewise, when you start to cut back on salt, after a while, foods such as potato chips and other snacks that once tasted normal to you will taste too salty.

GET PSYCHED

"You can regulate your taste receptors up or down to get used to different levels of saltiness or sweetness. At first, lower-salt and lower-sugar foods won't taste good, but soon you'll be able to get the same taste satisfaction at lower levels." *—Alan Hirsch, M.D., neurological director of the Smell and Taste Treatment and Research Foundation in Chicago, Illinois*

Feeling Full Your brain and stomach constantly communicate while you eat. Your stomach sends a signal to your brain that it's getting full, and your brain responds by letting you know that it's time to stop eating. If something interferes with that communication, you might overeat. In laboratory experiments with blowflies, when the connection between the brain and stomach was cut off, the blowflies ate until they exploded. Happily, although we might often feel as if we're going to explode, humans rarely do. But many of us do allow ourselves to overeat to a point of extreme discomfort and ultimate injury to our bodies.

Dietitians promote well-balanced meals that contain a variety of foods because different types of food are digested and absorbed into your bloodstream at different rates. That means some foods stay in your stomach longer than others, helping to maintain a feeling of fullness. Sugary foods, including candy and low-fat baked goods made with refined flours, provide quick energy but leave your stomach quickly. If that's all you eat, you're hungry again within two to three hours. Foods that are high in protein and fat can help you feel full longer because they stay in your stomach for up to six hours. High-fiber foods, especially fresh fruits, vegetables, and whole grains, may be even more effective at helping you feel full longer because your body takes longer to process the fiber.

Most people start to feel full within ten to twenty minutes after they start eating. That's how long it takes for your stomach to send a signal to your brain that it's full. Studies at the University of Florida's College of Medicine have shown, however, that very overweight people experience a delayed feeling of fullness and might take almost twice as long to get the message to stop eating. Dr. Mark S. Gold, Chief of Addiction Medicine at the University of Florida's McKnight Brain Institute, says the brain works differently in heavy people than it does in thin people, although no one knows exactly why. It's as if your brain conspires to keep you overweight, he says. Something breaks down in the normal communication process between brain and stomach. Your brain doesn't recognize that you're eating, even after you've been eating for fifteen or twenty minutes. The question researchers are still contemplating is: What breaks down?

Eating slowly helps everyone, heavy or thin, receive fullness signals by allowing time for the message to get through before too much food has already been eaten. If you eat your entire dinner in five minutes, you will still feel hungry and be tempted to eat more food than you need, because your brain doesn't yet know that you've filled your stomach.

> **GET PSYCHED**
>
> "If you're overweight, it's especially important to eat slowly because otherwise you'll overeat before your brain gets the message that your stomach is full."
> —Mark S. Gold, M.D., Distinguished Professor and Chief of Addiction Medicine, University of Florida's College of Medicine

How Hormones Help and Hurt

Hormones are chemical messengers produced by body cells that move through your blood from organ to organ. They communicate changing conditions in your body that require some sort of action or response. Using hormones, your body is able to regulate normal body processes, including hunger and appetite.

Many different hormones play a role in regulating when you eat, how much you eat, and when you stop eating. Leptin, one of the hormones normally produced by fat cells, travels through the bloodstream to the hypothalamus in the brain and to other body tissues, suppressing appetite and promoting fat loss. As discussed in Chapter 1, a small number of overweight people might be deficient in leptin due to a genetic abnormality. Others might have sufficient leptin in their bodies, but might still have a tendency to retain fat. Some say this is due to a condition known as leptin resistance, wherein fat cells are producing leptin, but the hormone is not reaching the brain where it would normally help signal an increase in metabolic rate and a decrease in appetite.

Ghrelin, an appetite-stimulating hormone secreted by the stomach that sends "Feed me, I'm hungry" messages to the brain, is another recently discovered piece of the obesity puzzle. Research suggests that undereating and yo-yo dieting can cause an increase in ghrelin production, which, in turn, causes increased hunger and decreased metabolism.

Cholescystokinin (CCK) is a hormone that has many jobs during the digestion process. It has also recently been identified as a satiety hormone. When it is released during eating, CCK apparently sends "Stop eating, I'm full" messages from the vagus nerve in your stomach to your brain.

Numerous other hormones have recently been identified as having a role in the regulation of hunger and digestion, and others might still be discovered. When researchers fully understand which hormones play the most important roles in weight regulation and how they work, they can develop medications to get the faulty hormones under control. Medical experts concede, however, that hormones are just one part of the weight control picture, and even when the time comes that hunger-related hormones can be regulated, many people will continue to overeat for other social and psychological reasons.

The hormone that continues to get the most scientific attention for its role in food and weight regulation is insulin. Under

WEB TALK: For more information on hormones, search The Hormone Foundation's site at:

↑ **www.hormone.org**

normal circumstances, when you eat a meal—or even sometimes when you see or smell food—insulin is released from your pancreas into your bloodstream. Insulin's job is to carry glucose (sugar) and amino acids (protein) from your blood into the muscle and fat cells. In this way, insulin also regulates hunger. When there's a moderate amount of insulin in your blood, you know you're no longer hungry and you stop eating. Both high and low levels of insulin, however, can make you feel hungry.

People with diabetes mellitus (DM) have a hard time controlling their weight because their bodies can't produce enough insulin. Without enough insulin, none of the glucose in their blood is carried into the muscle and fat cells. Until insulin becomes available, the cells think they're starving, and the individual feels hungry, even after a meal.

Some people develop a condition called insulin resistance syndrome. They have a problem with too much insulin production. They, too, feel hungry and overeat, but for different reasons. Normally, insulin helps convert some of the glucose from the food we eat into fat. Unlike other body parts that can use glucose or fat or even protein for energy, your brain can use only glucose. When there's excess insulin in the blood and most of the glucose is being converted to fat, there's none left for the brain. As a result, hunger signals are sent out, and the person eats more to try to get sufficient fuel to the brain.

Scientists are investigating how insulin acts on other hormones to regulate eating behavior and body weight. They are particularly interested in insulin's effect on ghrelin and leptin. Other interesting research delves into hormones that stimulate preferences for high-fat foods and hormones known as opioids, which are involved in the reward and motivational aspects of eating. Understanding exactly how these hormones work, alone and in tandem, helps researchers figure out the physiology of weight control. With a better understanding of how hormones control eating habits, more effective treatments for obesity can be developed.

How you eat affects your hormonal balance, which, in turn, affects the state of your health. For instance, fat in the diet is known to increase the production and activity of the female hormone estrogen, which has been linked to breast cancer and other hormone-related diseases. Low-fat diets have been shown to lower levels of estrogen and related hormones, but there is no evidence that these hormones, in turn, affect what or how much we eat. Although hormone imbalances sometimes can contribute to weight gain or loss, they usually are related to unusual conditions and are not often the primary reason why people gain weight.

Fighting to Stay Fit

When you're trying to lose weight, nothing works against you more than a low-calorie diet regime. Eating actually helps you burn calories because it keeps your metabolism moving; not eating enough lowers your metabolic rate so you burn calories less efficiently. The less you eat, the more your metabolic rate drops. Your body reacts to a lower metabolic rate by holding on to its fuel supplies in anticipation of not having enough energy. This built-in protection system makes it very difficult to lose weight and maintain weight loss.

When getting fit means losing weight, experts recommend losing no more than 2 pounds a week. At that rate, you lose mostly excess fat. If you lose weight at a faster rate, you lose both fat and lean tissue (muscle). Anyone who has repeatedly gained and lost weight knows the results of losing too much lean tissue. Every time the weight comes back, it comes back as fat first, and you end up with a higher proportion of fat to lean tissue.

If you were raised to overeat, you might have developed a surplus of fat cells in your body when you were young, causing you to struggle with weight control your entire life. As a child enters puberty and the teen years, their bodies produce a rapid growth of fat cells. An overweight child experiences a greater growth of fat cells than an ideal-weight child, and by the time he's a teenager, that child might have as many fat cells as an adult.

Once they develop, fat cells never go away; they simply shrink and enlarge in response to how much they are fed. That's one of the reasons it becomes so much more difficult to lose weight when we get older. When individual fat cells expand and reach their maximum size, they split in two. Then you have even more fat cells, and they are also permanent.

When you take in calories from food, your body "spends" those calories on its own maintenance and on energy production. If you take in about the same amount as you spend, no more and no less, your body's energy budget is balanced. When you consume more energy than you spend, that extra energy is saved as body fat. When you consume less energy than you spend, your body draws from those stored fat reserves.

The genes you inherit might also play a role in determining whether you have a fast or slow basal (resting) metabolic rate. If you have a low metabolic rate, you burn calories more slowly than someone with a higher metabolic rate. Regardless of genetic predisposition, exercise is the best way to speed up a sluggish metabolism.

The Balancing Act

Maybe you eat too much or too little. Maybe you don't get regular exercise. These lifestyle choices certainly play a role in how you look and how you feel about your body. But other factors play a role in weight control and body satisfaction. Attitudes and habits that have nothing to do with eating or exercise can skew your own perception of yourself.

WEB TALK: For information on nondieting approaches to weight control, check out:

www.healthyweight.com

Love Changes Everything

"When you're short, any weight gain is a lot. I'm 4'11" and, based on the charts, my ideal weight is somewhere between 105 and 110 pounds. When I graduated college, I weighed 140. For more than ten years, I tried to lose weight. I dieted, saw a nutritionist, took diet pills, dieted again and again and again. I got to my early 30s and still weighed 140. Then I went through infertility treatments that helped me gain an additional 20 pounds. I wanted to lose weight for my husband so I tried dieting again, but it didn't work any better than it did when I was in my 20s. I could never stand the restrictions; I got bored, never enjoyed 'diet' food, and fell off the wagon very quickly.

"As far back as I can remember, my mother, who was overweight, was always telling me to be careful what I eat because I had inherited 'fat genes' from my family. So as much as I have always enjoyed food, especially the Persian food I grew up on, I have also always felt guilty about eating. I've spent my whole life putting delicious food in my mouth and then promising myself I wouldn't do it again.

"Everything changed when I adopted my daughter. There I was at 37, 50 pounds overweight, and trying to keep up with a 4-year-old. I felt I owed it to her and myself to get back in shape. It was no longer for my mother or for my husband. It was for me and for the one person I love most on this earth. I wanted to be able to run after her and stay 'young' for her.

"I went to see a doctor about weight loss medication. After listening to my diet history, he told me nothing is worse for my health than yo-yo dieting. He felt that, instead of dieting my way down to 110 pounds and then bouncing back to 140 pounds six months later—something we both knew was a strong possibility—I should stop worrying about losing weight and start exercising to get fit. When I agreed to exercise, he agreed to prescribe a new weight loss medication. I took the medication for one year, and during that time I lost an average of $\frac{1}{2}$ pound a week until I lost a total of 35 pounds. At that point, I was exercising two days a week for an hour each day and I decided not to depend on the medication anymore. I knew I'd probably gain a few pounds, so I just allowed myself that.

"It's been $2\frac{1}{2}$ years since I stopped taking the medication, and I've maintained most of the weight loss. I'm now in my 40s, wear a size 10 dress, and feel perfectly at peace with myself and my body. I no longer wear big baggy clothes to hide my fat. I no longer care how my body compares to anyone else's. There are occasions, like when I go on vacation or I'm having a particularly hard time emotionally, that I'll eat more and gain a few pounds. But I'm still motivated by love, so I nip it in the bud and within a week or two get back down to my own personal 'ideal' weight of 133 pounds." —*Naz V.*

One big, positive step you can take immediately is to put away the bathroom scale and stop weighing yourself for now. When you step on a scale, the number you see doesn't tell you how fat or thin you are; it tells you how much you weigh. That number is the combined weight of your bones, organs, muscles, blood and other body fluids, the contents of your stomach, *and* fat. More than half your weight is from water.

No matter how much you try to control the amount and types of food you eat, you might not be able to control the numbers on the scale. Your age, metabolism, genes, the number of fat cells you have, your brain chemistry, your psychological state, and even your past dieting habits all play a role in how much you weigh. When you learn to bring your mind and body back into balance and become more attuned to your own eating habits, you won't need a scale to tell you if you've gained or lost weight.

Changing your attitude and your behavior requires unlearning old, ingrained habits and learning or relearning new ones. It took many years to develop the unhealthy eating habits, negative attitudes, and impulsive behavior that led you into an unhappy relationship with food. These practices are deeply entrenched in your memory. You can change them, but it can't happen overnight and you might not be able to do it alone.

Balance is something you have to strive for and work toward. It doesn't come naturally for most people. Whether you're thinking about your diet or your life as a whole, you have to learn what it takes to find your own individual balance.

What You Can Do

Begin to reestablish healthy eating habits by learning to slow down and pay attention to your own internal hunger cues.

- ☐ Use the hunger scale to help determine if you're hungry enough to eat.
- ☐ Eat only when you're physically hungry.

- ☐ Balance every meal with foods from different food groups to help you stay satisfied and feeling full longer.
- ☐ Consciously eat more slowly. Take at least twenty minutes to finish a meal.
- ☐ Use the hunger scale as a reminder to stop eating just as you begin to feel full.
- ☐ Eat before you get too hungry, and stop eating before you get too full.

Dieting and Disordered Eating

Millions of men and women suffer from eating disorders. Some people overeat and become grossly overweight, some don't eat enough and starve themselves, while others eat too much and then purge by vomiting or using laxatives.

One thing all eating disorders have in common is that they can become serious enough to cause permanent damage to your health. Extreme eating disorders such as anorexia and bulimia are diseases that can and do kill people. It's important to recognize when you or someone you know shows signs of an eating disorder and get professional help. People with eating disorders can be very good at hiding them from family and friends, so pay close attention when there's even the slightest hint of a problem.

Disordered eating—when someone routinely diets, binges, and even purges but not as often or as severely as someone with a *bona fide* eating disorder—is more common and usually less serious than diagnosable eating disorders. Although many of the symptoms are similar, disordered eating is often temporary or clearly circumstantial and rarely requires treatment. It might just be a bad habit, a temporary response to an unhappy event or change, or the result of following a trend. But if disordered eating goes on for a long time, causes emotional and physical distress, or starts to get in the way of normal everyday activities, professional help might be necessary. Excessive dieting and other forms of disordered eating can eventually turn into full-fledged eating disorders.

A Lifetime of Dieting

As a registered dietitian, I talk with a lot of people about their dieting history. After years of on-again, off-again dieting, some people are still confused about weight control. They can't figure out why it's so easy for them to gain weight and so hard for them to lose it. Sometimes, I have to point out that they've actually lost weight as often as they've gained it. The problem for most chronic dieters is that they never permanently lose their excess weight.

The truth is, there's no simple way to lose weight and keep it off. Diet alone, even a relatively healthy diet, won't do it for most people. Diets are short-term solutions, and short-term solutions are temporary. But weight loss diets, as they are so often presented in magazines and best-selling books, continue to fool people into thinking *This will be the one that works.* Truth be told, it's not likely that anyone else's one-size-fits-all diet plan will work for you.

Why Diets Don't Work Dieting to lose weight means restricting calories, depriving yourself of food, eating certain foods while avoiding others, and following someone else's rules for what and when you should and shouldn't eat. The biggest problem with restricted diets, besides the fact that they don't work as a means to permanent weight loss, is that they don't promote normal eating behavior or healthy attitudes toward food. Instead, many diets promote the same abnormal preoccupation with food seen in people with clinical eating disorders.

Dietitians and other credible nutrition experts have long been trying to convince people to stay away from fad diets. Before there was evidence of genetic and neurochemical influence on weight and eating behavior and before there was any real understanding of the psychological motivations driving that behavior, simple biological truths explained why extreme diets don't work for long-term weight loss or weight maintenance.

When you cut back substantially on the amount of food you normally eat, your body doesn't know you're on a diet. For all your body knows, it's being starved. It doesn't know if or when it will get more food, so being a smart body, it goes into "starvation mode." Your metabolism slows down the rate at which you burn calories. It's a natural survival tool in the event you actually are starving. Everybody has this survival tool—handed down to us from our cave-dwelling ancestors, who used it to keep from starving when food was scarce.

That's why dieting often causes weight *gain,* not weight loss. When you stop dieting and your body no longer thinks it's starving, your metabolic rate goes up again—but not to where it originally was. Repeated dieting means more and more drops in your metabolic rate until your body can no longer burn calories efficiently. That makes it extremely difficult—and sometimes impossible—to lose weight.

People with medical problems often have to go on restricted diets because certain foods are no longer good for them. If you have heart disease, your doctor might recommend a low-fat diet. If you have kidney disease, a low-protein and sodium-restricted diet might be in your future. People with diabetes must be very careful about the types and amounts of food they eat at every meal, and they don't get to enjoy fabulous desserts. But a healthy person doesn't have to live with these food restrictions. A healthy person shouldn't have to live with *any* food restrictions beyond the confines of a reasonably well-balanced diet.

For most people, dieting is only a temporary weight control solution. Most dieters regain the weight they lose within five years because they haven't made lifestyle changes or chosen a diet plan they can stick with for the rest of their lives. Once they go off their chosen regimen, the weight comes back. Also, a dieter's overeating is often a symptom of underlying emotional problems or bad eating habits that need to be resolved before the weight will come off and stay off. No diet can do that for you.

From a psychological point of view, dieters can be overly pre-occupied with their weight and appearance. Counting calories, counting carbohydrates, worrying about the fat content of every dish, and thinking constantly about eating or not eating is nothing short of obsessive behavior. The way to lose weight is to stop thinking so much about food and eating, not to obsess on it. In fact, more serious eating disorders often follow years of strict dieting and obsessive thoughts and behavior.

you're not alone

The Dark Side of Dieting

"My first experience with feeling fat and being self-conscious about it was when I was ten years old. After that came years of struggle, dieting, hating myself, working out, dieting, hating myself. I couldn't stop overeating, and I never felt good about myself. It wasn't long before I found myself shopping for clothes in Fashion Bug Plus and having trouble feeling comfortable in their biggest size, which was a 30/32. But even that didn't stop me from overeating.

"Many nights, I would eat a pint of ice cream, and then some. I was always looking for more food—sweet, salty, crunchy—I had no preferences and I never felt satisfied. The worst part was how I felt about myself after a binge. I always hated myself afterward. There were times when I would eat so much at night that I would wake up the next morning feeling like I had been on a drinking binge. My face was puffy, my eyes were tired, and I had a headache. It all made me feel so depressed. I felt ashamed of myself. But it didn't stop me from overeating.

"I lost my mother and grandmother to colon cancer and thought that if nothing else, that would be motivation to start eating better and living a healthier lifestyle. I didn't stop overeating. When I needed gall bladder surgery, the doctors told me it was probably a result of all those years of liquid diets, starvation diets, and other forms of abusive dieting. It still didn't stop me from overeating. I just hated myself more for what I had done to my body.

"Food was a drug for me. It comforted me when I was down, calmed me when I was feeling stressed, kept me company when I was lonely, and tasted especially good when I was feeling happy. There was never a time when I wasn't tempted to overeat and rarely a time that I didn't give in to the temptation. Eventually, I had gastric bypass surgery. I lost 123 pounds as a result, but the struggle continues.

"Years of psychotherapy have taught me that damaged self-esteem and other emotional problems are at the root of my food addiction. I eat instead of dealing with emotional pain. Even though I can cross my legs, fit in chairs I would get stuck in before, and am wearing a dress size that I haven't seen in more than fifteen years, I still tend to be hard on myself and put myself down. I talk to myself in ways that I would never talk to anyone else. The more I pick on myself, the more I find myself slipping back into old habits and looking for comfort in food instead of dealing directly with my feelings.

"Does it ever end? I believe it does. I don't lose faith. I put out my last cigarette thirteen years ago and haven't touched one since. I know if I could overcome that addiction, I can overcome this one. I just have to keep struggling to work with my feelings, not against them, and find other outlets to replace food. It'll happen. It's just a matter of time, and I'm not about to give up now!"
—*Dorothy C.*

Diets Come, Diets Go In this world where marketing rules, we are continuously bombarded with TV commercials, magazine displays, book promotions, pop-up ads, and infomercials promising the perfect weight loss plan. Some say low fat is key; others insist on counting calories. When carbohydrates are hot, protein's not. When protein is fashionable, carbs get a bad rap. It's not easy to sort through all the mixed media messages to find out the truth about weight loss.

Some weight loss plans rise to such celebrity status they get more attention than a presidential election. Others quickly fall from grace, only to reappear a decade later, sometimes under another name. A handful of diets have stood the test of time and are still with us; they've actually helped people learn more about healthy food, develop better eating habits, and, sometimes, lose weight. But that's not true for most weight loss diets. Most diets don't work.

Some interesting diet fads have come and gone over the last few decades. You might have even followed some of them. Do any of these sound familiar?

- **1963** Weight Watchers came out with its first programs, which were based on "exchanges" of similar foods and included support groups and behavior modification workshops.

- **1972** The first edition of Dr. Atkins's *Diet Revolution* was published. It ultimately sold more than 10 million copies, even though most health experts at the time advised people to stay away from this high-protein, low-carbohydrate plan.

- **1975** The Grapefruit Diet (also known as the Mayo diet, although it is neither associated with nor condoned by the Mayo Clinic) had many people believing that if they ate half a grapefruit before each meal, they could burn calories more effectively.

- **1978** Dr. Herman Tamower came out with a high-protein, low-carb plan known as the Complete Scarsdale Medical Diet. This plan promised a 20-pound weight loss in two weeks by eating lots of steak and no starch.

- **1979** The Pritikin diet plan introduced its high-fiber, very-low-fat diet with no added sugar or salt to heart patients and dieters alike.

- **1981** The Beverly Hills Diet allowed nothing but fruit—and only very specific types of fruit—for the first ten days of the diet.

- **1983** Jenny Craig introduced its counseling services and line of food for people who want to lose weight.

- **1988** Optifast got a huge endorsement from Oprah Winfrey, who lost 67 pounds on the plan.

- **1993** Dr. Dean Ornish's *Eat More, Weigh Less* plan reduced fat to less than 10 percent of total calories and promoted weight loss on a vegetarian diet.

- **1995** *The Zone Diet* by Barry Sears brought back the high-protein diet. Promoted not as a diet but as a "lifelong hormonal control program," this plan included vegetables and fruits but excludes breads, pastas, and other grain foods.

- **2003** As Dr. Atkins's high-protein revolution rose again, the *South Beach Diet* swept the nation. This weight loss plan promoted a higher-protein diet, discouraged starchy vegetables and foods made with white sugar or flour, and eliminated all fruit for the first two weeks. It claimed you would lose weight and never go hungry. Sound familiar?

Q & A

How can I tell if I'm following a sound diet plan?

The National Institutes of Health (NIH) recommend you look for several features when you choose a weight loss program. First, the diet should be safe and include the Recommended Daily Allowances (RDA) for vitamins, minerals, and protein from food. It's all but impossible for any diet that provides fewer than 1,200 calories to meet the RDA. Choose a program aimed at slow, steady weight loss. You should expect to lose no more than 1 or 2 pounds a week unless you are in a medically supervised program and your doctor feels you can safely benefit from faster weight loss. A sound weight loss program also includes an educational component such as group meetings or one-on-one counseling, exercise recommendations, and a plan for weight maintenance. If you have any health problems, take any medications on a regular basis, or plan to lose more than 15 or 20 pounds, see your physician before you begin any weight loss program. And if you plan to use a very low-calorie liquid formula diet that provides fewer than 800 calories, you absolutely must be examined and monitored by a medical doctor.

Riding the Roller Coaster Many people who eat in response to their emotional needs rather than their physical needs are caught on a perpetual roller-coaster ride of deprivation and bingeing, weight loss and weight gain. This diet cycling is called yo-yo dieting for obvious reasons: not only is your weight continually going up and down; so are your emotions.

Yo-yo dieting makes weight loss difficult, even impossible, in the long run. With on-and-off dieting, your body learns to maintain its weight on fewer calories. That means someone who weighs 180 pounds and who would normally lose weight easily on a reduced-calorie diet will eventually find it impossible to lose weight at any calorie level. Some overweight people stay overweight for this reason, despite the fact that they're not eating more food than average-weight people.

GET PSYCHED

"The only way to break the destructive cycle of yo-yo dieting is to accept the healthy weight you can achieve and maintain by eating well, exercising regularly, and working out any underlying psychological issues that are getting in your way." —*Mindy Hermann, R.D., co-author, Change One: The Breakthrough 12-Week Eating Plan*

Most dieters learn from hindsight. It's not until you look back over years of dieting that you begin to realize none of the diets you tried really worked. How do you know? You're still overweight. You might even be heavier than you were before you started dieting. The reason is simple: all those diets were temporary solutions. They didn't help you find a way to make lasting changes in your lifestyle and eating habits.

To stop weight cycling, you have to get off the dieting roller coaster once and for all. Instead of following fad diets or joining and dropping out of programs, you have to find the one-time, lifetime eating and exercise plan you'll be able to stick to for life.

If you're overweight and frustrated by years of dieting failures, your self-esteem has probably gone down the tubes. As you've lost and regained weight, chances are you've gathered a lot of emotional baggage along the way. If you've been trying to lose weight on your own and it hasn't worked, this might be a good time to seek individual counseling or to reach out to others who have had the same struggles.

Overweight people with medical concerns might need to go on reduced-calorie diets to help them lose weight and decrease their risk of serious health problems. For those people, and anyone else considering a weight loss plan that includes a reduced-calorie diet, the message is clear: be sure you're ready to make a real commitment to permanent changes in your eating habits before you go on a diet.

Where It Begins

Five-year-old children can tell you who is fat, who is skinny, and who is average weight. Within the next couple years, they begin to sense that being overweight is unattractive. It's not long before some children look in the mirror and are unhappy with what they see. Even at this early age, physical attractiveness is something to strive for, because beauty is thought to be indicative of other positive and desirable traits such as intelligence, good social skills, and self-confidence. If a child is teased about her size or weight, she might develop distorted ideas about her appearance that last a lifetime. Studies have found significant numbers of girls as young as six and seven years old who think they're bigger than they actually are and who are dieting to lose weight.

Children become especially self-conscious about their body size and shape when they reach puberty. A Harvard University study showed that up to two thirds of underweight twelve-year-old girls thought they were too fat. When young boys are observed, however, they tend to be less critical of their own appearance. Even obese boys often have fewer concerns about their size than average-weight girls. When adolescent boys do have concerns, they are more likely to consider increasing their weight or muscle tone.

Parents are role models and influence their children's attitudes about eating, dieting, and body size just as they shape attitudes and behavior in other areas. Studies show that girls are more likely to learn weight loss strategies from their mothers, while boys are more likely to learn from their fathers how to use exercise strategies for losing weight or changing their body shape.

The heavier the child, the more they report getting messages from their parents encouraging them to lose weight or get fit. This is particularly true for girls.

Teenagers get similar feedback from their peers. When it comes to losing weight, both girlfriends and boyfriends are more likely to encourage teenage girls to lose weight than boys. But when it comes to gaining weight and building muscle, they encourage both girls and boys.

Research also suggests that body dissatisfaction among both girls and boys increases with age. As they move through their teenage years, girls are increasingly likely to use weight loss supplements, and boys are more likely to use supplements for weight gain.

you're not alone

Turning Myself Inside Out

"When I was in elementary school, my nickname was 'Skeleton.' My mother died of cancer when I was five, and I basically stopped eating when she got sick and went into the hospital. A year later, our house burned down. The one parent I had left started falling apart, losing his mind. He never got over my mother's death. He was raising eight children by himself. He was angry most of the time. He often became mean and physically abusive. It's no wonder I didn't eat. All I remember wanting to do was crawl under the covers and sleep.

"As a teenager, I was still a 'skeleton.' I started to like being skinny. I was a rather superficial and naive adolescent. I was pretty, and I loved the attention I got for the way I looked because deep down I didn't believe it, and I needed constant confirmation.

"When I was eighteen and living near a ski resort, I was almost raped by a couple of tourists. One of them pulled me into a room while the other drove my friend miles away and left her on a roadside to walk home. Then he came back and the two of them attacked me. Although I was all of 107 pounds, I fought back and was able to stop them. But it was a humiliating experience, and I blamed myself. I was ashamed and wondered what I'd done to make it happen.

"But for years, well into adulthood, I never gave much thought to my feelings about anything. Then I turned thirty-four, the age my mother was when she died. I felt guilty for outliving her. I had children of my own at that point and realized what it must have been like for her while she was sick and what she missed by dying so young. Around this time, my brother-in-law also died at a young age. I became pregnant, and after I had my son, I developed severe postpartum depression. Soon after, I developed medical problems, and something inside of me snapped. I couldn't cope anymore, and I started overeating. I kept it up until I gained 60 pounds. That's where I'm at now.

"I know my weight problem has nothing to do with food. I'm using food to fill a void that's been there for a long, long time. I just never let myself think about it. Psychotherapy has helped me open up, find my feelings, and talk about my history for the first time in my life.

"I have mixed feelings about being overweight. I sometimes question why my husband stays with me. He's younger than I am and very attractive. I don't feel worthy. I feel bad about myself and guilty for not being a better role model for my children. My twelve-year-old daughter has started mimicking my eating behavior and using food as an emotional tool.

"But I've also gained something valuable from gaining weight. For the first time in my life, I've had to use what's inside of me because no one is paying attention to the outside. I've learned that the people who matter the most accept me for who I am, at any weight. I've begun to work through the loss of my mother, the shame I felt about being molested, and the resentment I didn't even know I felt toward my father. I believe that as I get closer and closer to these feelings, I will move further and further away from my emotional need to overeat." —*Tammy G.*

Impossible Standards

Men and women have always been concerned with appearances. Every culture and every period of time throughout history has had its own standards for ideal beauty. Today, thanks to advances in technology and mass media, we are more concerned with appearance than ever before.

Thin, beautiful women and buff, handsome men fill our TV and computer screens and adorn the pages of the magazines we read. We see so many images of people with exceptionally good looks on billboards and in advertisements, they start to seem real and achievable to the average person. Anyone we see who falls short of this ideal seems unattractive and undesirable, including ourselves. It is no wonder that we've become so preoccupied with appearance and that so many of us end up frustrated and dissatisfied with the way we look. Most of us will never have model-perfect bodies. It's simply not possible.

Several decades ago, models weighed about 8 percent less than the average woman. Today, they weigh as much as 23 percent less. Studies have shown that many women feel depressed, guilty, ashamed, and insecure when they are shown pictures of ultra-thin models in magazines. What a surprise!

Signs and Symptoms of Eating Disorders

Until the late 1960s, eating disorders were relatively unknown in Western cultures. Suddenly, physicians and media were reporting on young female patients from middle- and upper-class families who were literally starving themselves. Anorexia nervosa was soon recognized as a psychological disorder and, along with bulimia, a binge-and-purge syndrome that emerged in the next decade, was listed and described in the *Diagnostic and Statistical Manual* (*DSM*) *of Mental Disorders* used by psychiatric professionals to diagnose and treat patients.

PsychSpeak

True eating disorders are illnesses with emotional and physical symptoms that can make you very sick and even prove fatal.

The National Institutes of Mental Health (NIMH) estimate between 5 and 16 million people in the United States suffer from anorexia and bulimia and that young women account for 90 percent of these cases. The majority of eating disorders start to develop before the age of twenty. However, anyone, at any age, can develop an eating disorder. Adolescent girls are at particular risk because they are more likely to be concerned about their weight and are more easily influenced by the appearance of models, dancers, athletes, actresses, and pop stars.

Anorexia Nervosa People with anorexia always think they're fat, no matter how much they weigh. They refuse to maintain a healthy body weight for their age and height and don't acknowledge being underweight as a potentially serious medical condition. Women with anorexia stop getting menstrual periods, and their periods only resume following hormone administration. People with anorexia …

- Pretend they're not hungry.
- Are extremely afraid of getting fat.

- Spend more time "playing" with their food than eating it.
- Refuse to eat.
- Lose large amounts of weight in short periods of time.
- Complain of nausea or bloating after eating a normal amount of food.
- Think they're fat when they're thin.
- Eat only low-calorie, low-fat foods.
- Binge and purge.
- Tend to be perfectionists.
- Dress in layers to hide their weight loss.
- Exercise excessively.
- Suffer from constipation and missed menstrual cycles.
- Become withdrawn and secretive.
- Can and do starve themselves to death.

Q&A

What causes eating disorders?

There's no simple or single answer to that question. Biological factors; social and cultural pressure to be thin; family dynamics; dieting; genetic predisposition; personality traits; distortions in thinking such as perfectionism, obsession, and low self-esteem; and negative emotions such as depression and anxiety all appear to play a role in the development of eating disorders. But these are *factors* associated with eating disorders, not necessarily *causes*. Some of these factors have underlying causes themselves that might be more directly related to the development of an eating disorder.

Personal experiences such as trauma, abuse, and teasing are most often associated with the development of eating disorders. Over the past twenty years, Nancy Reynolds, a certified eating disorder specialist at the Menninger Clinic in Houston, has observed that in her practice, more than 90 percent of people with anorexia have a history of sexual abuse, incest, rape, or molestation. Research also shows a connection between childhood sexual abuse and the symptoms of bulimia. But thousands of eating disorder studies haven't helped researchers understand why some people develop eating disorders while similar people in similar situations do not.

Bulimia People with bulimia binge frequently and then vomit or use laxatives to purge. They feel out of control during an episode of bingeing, as if they cannot stop eating or control the amount of food they're eating. Sometimes people with bulimia fast or exercise excessively in lieu of purging. Bulimics may ...

- Be normal weight or overweight.
- Eat secretly.
- Eat large amounts of food but not gain weight.
- Act compulsively in all areas of life.
- Spend a great deal of time thinking about food and planning their next binge.
- Feel out of control while eating.
- Feel depressed and ashamed after overeating.
- Be sexually promiscuous.
- Feel relieved once they've emptied their stomachs.
- Steal food or hoard it in strange places.
- Abuse alcohol or drugs.
- Have dental problems as a result of vomiting stomach acid on their teeth.
- Become dependent on diuretics, laxatives, emetics, or diet pills.
- Disappear after eating (to a bathroom to vomit).

Binge-Eating Disorder People with binge-eating disorder have recurring episodes of binge eating wherein they eat abnormally large amounts of food in a relatively short period of time. Their binge eating occurs at least two days a week for at least six months. As with bulimics, they sense a lack of control over their eating habits, but they do not feel the need to purge. People with binge eating disorder frequently ...

- Eat huge amounts of food in one sitting, even when they're not hungry.
- Spend a great deal of time thinking about food and planning their next binge.
- Fear gaining weight.
- Eat quickly.
- Eat until they are uncomfortably full.
- Eat alone to hide the amount of food they are eating.
- Feel ashamed, guilty, depressed, and disgusted with themselves after a binge.
- Become withdrawn and avoid family and friends.
- Become overweight.

Unspecified Eating Disorders The term the *DSM* uses for an eating disorder that doesn't quite fit into one of the preceding categories is *Eating Disorder Not Otherwise Specified (EDNOS)*. A person with an EDNOS shows signs of disordered eating behavior but doesn't have all the symptoms required to be diagnosed with anorexia or bulimia. For instance, a person might have all the characteristics for bulimia except that their binge eating and other typical bulimic behavior occurs less than twice a week or goes on for fewer than three months. Someone with an EDNOS might be of normal weight but show signs of anorexic behavior such as self-induced vomiting after eating just a small amount of food. Another person might chew and spit out large quantities of food without swallowing, but not have other characteristics typical of someone with anorexia.

WEB TALK: For more information on eating disorders, visit the Harvard Eating Disorders Center website at:

➤ www.hedc.org

No Laughing Matter

People with eating disorders are at risk of developing a wide variety of medical problems. Someone with anorexia might become severely dehydrated or develop anemia, experience brain shrinkage, or have irregular menstrual periods, irregular heartbeats, low blood pressure, slow pulse, and heart failure. Anorexia might also hinder normal growth and development in teenagers.

People with bulimia often suffer from swollen glands, an inflamed esophagus, and worn tooth enamel from the acid in their vomit. Vomiting causes excessive loss of essential minerals, so people with bulimia are also at risk of heart failure. Some people with bulimia use a medication called syrup of ipecac to induce vomiting. When used regularly, syrup of ipecac can cause severe damage to the nervous system or the heart. Overuse of laxatives can lead to intestinal problems.

Binge eating puts people at high risk of obesity, which then increases their risk of developing heart disease, diabetes, and other medical conditions associated with obesity.

Eating disorders can be treated successfully, but treatment is never simple. It can take a multidisciplinary team of professionals— including an internist, an endocrinologist, a psychotherapist, and a dietitian or nutritionist who specializes in eating disorders— to bring someone with an eating disorder to full recovery. Medications, including antidepressants, often are used to help adjust the abnormal brain chemistry that plays a role in eating disorders.

The sooner an eating disorder is treated, the better, because in most cases, early intervention increases the chances of successful treatment. Of anorexics who are treated, approximately 40 percent recover completely, 40 percent partially recover, and the remaining 20 percent have ongoing problems. For people with bulimia who seek treatment, approximately half recover completely, 35 percent partially recover, and 15 percent continue to have problems.

If you think you or someone you know has an eating disorder, the first thing to do is make an appointment with a family physician to be sure there are no urgent medical problems. A good physician should be able to recommend a licensed psychotherapist and other specialists, if necessary.

What You Can Do

Dieting is big business, but for all the money people spend on weight loss books, videos, diet centers, and diet pills, there are more failures and disappointments than there are success stories. Dieting doesn't work for most people and can lead to serious physical and psychological problems for others.

- ☐ Examine the different ways you've tried to lose weight in the past.
- ☐ Make a list of weight loss strategies that seemed to work best for you in the past.
- ☐ Decide whether or not you're ready to give up dieting and change your relationship with food in healthier ways.
- ☐ Learn to recognize the signs and symptoms of eating disorders.
- ☐ If you think you or anyone you know has an eating disorder, arrange to get help.

Part 2

The Nature of Eating

If you've ever wondered why you eat the way you eat or why some people eat the way they eat, Part 2 has the answers. You'll learn the basics of good nutrition, and you'll begin to see why it's so important to step away from old, destructive eating habits and fearlessly enter a new world of healthy living.

Why We Eat

We eat first and foremost for survival. But in modern times, we no longer eat just to satisfy biological and nutritional needs. Today we eat to satisfy our senses and sometimes to try to fulfill our inner longings. We eat for fun, and for many people, eating is a form of entertainment. We celebrate with food, and at the same time use food to cope with stressful situations. In the United States and other developed countries, most of us can afford to buy enough food to eat well for any occasion and often mark many moments in our lives with food.

Food and eating are promoted in ways designed to get us to eat more and more. Advertisers and marketing executives know what you like when it comes to food and food packaging, and they're very good at giving it to you so you'll buy their product. It's not a conspiracy; there's no evil intent. It's just part of the business of selling food in a free-enterprise system. But some advertising and marketing schemes can sabotage a food addict's efforts to develop a healthier relationship with food. If you are concerned about what and how much you're eating, you might want to make it your business to understand some of the promotional strategies that drive many of your decisions to buy and eat certain foods.

Survival

Early humans didn't enjoy the endless supply of food we have available to us today. There were times when they had plenty to eat, but there were also times of famine. The human body adapted to these conditions by making itself omnivorous, able to digest and use nutrients from both plants and animals. This gave humans a wide range of food choices and reduced their risk of starvation. Human bodies were also designed to store excess energy in fat tissues when food was readily available to provide reserves in case of future famine.

It is part of our survival instinct to eat almost the same way our ancestors in the Stone Age did. Our bodies work nearly the same today as they did then. We are able to digest and metabolize many different types of food, and we are able to store excess energy as body fat. But today, our food supply is much steadier and more abundant, full of foods that didn't exist in earlier times. There were no doughnut shops, hamburger chains, or ice cream parlors in the years B.C.E. So now, instead of traveling around on foot to search for hard-to-find food, all we have to do is open the refrigerator or drive a few blocks, and we're immediately well fed. The deposits of body fat that once helped humans thrive during famine stay with us longer and, unfortunately, can end up making us sick. Researchers think the average person living in the Stone Age consumed about 3,000 calories every day, yet was not overweight. Compare that to today's statistics, which show that many of us average fewer calories a day, yet more than half of us are overweight or obese.

WEB TALK: For an entertaining look at the many ways fast-food manufacturers promote their products, check out:

➤ www.junkfoodnews.com

Your body renews itself every day, building muscle, replenishing bone, recycling blood cells, and replacing old skin cells with new. This is how we stay healthy. It's how we stay alive. A diet that supports this growth and renewal process by providing all the necessary energy and nutrients also helps prevent nutrition-related diseases that can profoundly affect your long-term health. A steady diet of junk food does the opposite.

From a biological perspective, the chief goal of healthy eating is to get the most nutrients for your calories. To achieve the biggest nutritional bang for your calorie buck, most nutritionists promote a variety of nutrient-dense foods such as deeply colored fruits and vegetables, low-fat dairy products, whole grains and legumes, and lean meats and seafood. These foods are the best sources of all the nutrients that are essential to life. If you avoid specific food groups or don't eat enough of the right types of foods, you can become malnourished even if you are consuming a large quantity of food.

Although you might not think of yourself as someone who could ever become malnourished, the term covers a wide range of conditions. If you are grossly overweight, underweight, or you have nutritional excesses or deficiencies that negatively impact your health, you might be malnourished. Over time, the effects of any type of malnutrition take their toll, compromising your health and quality of life.

Primal Urges

When we eat, we are responding to a natural, primal urge to stay alive and stay connected to our natural surroundings. The psychology and biology of how and why we eat what we eat have always existed, but we are only just beginning to explore and understand them.

At one time, hunger was a simple need satisfied by finding and eating food, but today we use food and drink to satisfy ourselves on many other levels. Our basic drives are still at play, but technology and other products of the modern world have turned our relationship with food into a much more complicated affair.

Feeding Your Senses Our taste buds help us perceive five different taste sensations: bitter, salty, sweet, sour, and a more recently identified taste called *umami,* which responds to the salts of glutamic acid found in monosodium glutamate (MSG) seasoning and processed meats and cheeses. Humans have an inborn preference for sweet and salty foods because in nature, sweet or salty means the food is edible. At the same time, we have a natural aversion to bitter flavors because bitter often means poison.

According to Dr. Alan Hirsch, psychiatrist and neurologist at the Smell and Taste Treatment and Research Foundation in Chicago, Illinois, you don't taste your food so much as you smell it. When you think you taste your food, you're actually responding to your sense of smell. When you chew your food, vapors are released and float through the passageway connecting the back of your mouth to your nasal cavity. Once there, the vapors land on odor receptors that recognize different smells and tell your brain what you are eating. That's an easy concept to grasp when you think about how tasteless food is when you have a cold or how much easier it is to swallow bitter medicine if you pinch your nose shut first. Without your sense of smell, you might be able to tell whether your food is sweet or spicy; you'll know if it's hot or cold, creamy or grainy; but you won't actually be able to "taste" it.

Researchers report that people who lose their sense of smell often begin to gain weight. It's easy to see why. If you have chronic sinus problems or allergies, or if you take medication that interferes with your ability to smell or taste, you might try to find ways to get more flavor from the food you eat. You might knowingly or unknowingly add more sugar, salt, or fat when you prepare food at home to try to boost the flavor. You might seek out more flavorful foods to get more enjoyment out of eating.

Dr. Hirsch has published more than 100 articles on the psychological powers of scent. His research has shown that you can help yourself lose and maintain weight by satisfying your sense of smell. In one study, Dr. Hirsch instructed participants to eat whatever they normally eat but to first sprinkle their food with odor-enhancing sprinkles. Over a six-month period, participants lost an average of about 35 pounds. Dr. Hirsch recommends a similar approach to eating at home. Smell your food before you eat it, then chew it well to release as many vapors into your nasal cavity as possible.

GET PSYCHED

"The key to feeling full is smelling your food. The more you use your nose, the less you'll have to eat to feel satisfied." –*Alan Hirsch, M.D., author,* Life's a Smelling Success

The smell of food can evoke strong emotional reactions, and some of the food smells we like and dislike are associated with emotional memories. There is a biological reason for this. Our olfactory (taste and smell) receptors are connected to the brain's limbic system, which is thought to be the seat of our emotions. Before we even recognize a scent, a deeper part of our brain responds emotionally. Studies show that smells perceived as pleasant, such as vanilla, can lift your mood and improve your sense of well-being.

Fat is important to flavor because odor molecules dissolve in fat. Fat carries flavors, which is why most of us favor foods high in fat. They're simply more flavorful than low-fat foods. When you take the fat out of food, the aroma goes with it, and so does much of the enjoyment. That's one reason why it's difficult for most people to stay on a low-fat diet.

Some experts believe overweight people crave more taste and smell from their foods than thinner people, possibly because their senses have adjusted to more intense flavor input. Dr. Susan Schiffman, professor of medical psychology at Duke University Medical School in South Carolina, calls this a high-flavor set point. To make low-fat food products more palatable to those who want more flavor in their food, food manufacturers and recipe developers add as much natural and artificial flavor as possible, along with salt and other flavor enhancers. Although that won't make low-fat foods healthier or more satisfying in the long run, it does help make some of them more enjoyable in the moment.

Comfort Foods Hot chocolate. Fried chicken. Mashed potatoes. Warm apple pie. Potato chips. These are foods that are well known to soothe the soul and help calm an anxious spirit. They're comfort foods—the foods you eat when you're searching for psychological comfort. Different people become attached to different types of foods, although it's well documented that sweet, fatty, and salty snacks and desserts top the list of comfort food favorites. Comfort foods offer solace during stressful times, but many people also turn to comfort foods when they're happy.

GET PSYCHED

It's probably safe to say that more people drown their sorrows and celebrate their successes with chocolate pudding than with chicken livers. Chocolate gives most people pleasure because it tastes good and often triggers a positive emotional connection to childhood. It's a classic comfort food. Any food you associate with people or circumstances that made you feel safe, loved, or empowered in some way can become a source of comfort as you get older. At the same time, a food that carries negative connotations or experiences will most likely cause an aversion. For instance, foods you really disliked but were forced to eat as a child might never again grace your plate when you're old enough to make your own decisions about what to eat.

When researchers at the University of Illinois Food and Brand Lab surveyed Americans about their favorite comfort foods, the results yielded many surprises. As they expected, potato chips, ice cream, cookies, and candies topped the list, but nearly 40 percent of the respondents mentioned foods normally eaten for lunch or dinner. Steaks, burgers, pizza, pasta, fruits and vegetables, and soup are all popular comfort foods. Ice cream tops the list of favorites for men and women. After ice cream, however, women's favorites were sweets such as chocolate and cookies, while men preferred soups, pizza, and pasta. Age also plays a role in comfort food preferences. People between the ages of 18 and 34 preferred ice cream and cookies, those age 35 to 54 preferred soup and pasta, and those age 55 and older favored soup and mashed potatoes.

Even more interesting than the types of comfort foods chosen as favorites were the reasons why people sought out comfort foods. Many people head to the kitchen when they're sad or stressed or bored, but more people actually reported eating comfort foods when they were happy or wanted to reward themselves. The type of comfort food people chose often varied with their moods. More often than not, people who felt sad or bored went for ice cream, cookies, or potato chips. People who were happy chose more nutritious foods such as steak or pizza.

Although the foods you turn to for emotional comfort might have a pleasurable and calming effect in the moment, they can also have a weighty effect on your waistline in the long run. That's when comfort foods stop being warm and fuzzy and become a danger to your health. In animal studies, chronic stress resulted not only in overeating but also in weight gain, specifically around the abdomen. Researchers speculate that comfort foods might have a soothing effect on humans during times of acute stress by calming down a brain system associated with anxiety, but these same foods might also cause some chronically stressed people to overeat and gain weight around the middle—the type of weight gain associated with higher risks of developing heart disease and diabetes.

If you are an emotional eater and you're constantly under stress, seeking out other ways to cope and relax can help put the brakes on overeating. Medical research confirms that mind-body exercises, aerobic exercises, meditation, or even a hot bath can sometimes take the place of emotional eating because all these activities stimulate the same neurochemicals that activate the pleasure centers in your brain.

you're not alone

Notes from a Chocoholic

"I am obsessed with chocolate. I know that too much isn't good for me because it's high in fat. Even though I've read that the type of fat in chocolate is a 'good fat,' one that won't necessarily raise my cholesterol, I have high cholesterol and a family history of heart disease so I have to watch the total fat in my diet. I have all this knowledge, but it never stops me when I need a chocolate fix.

"I know if I don't eat chocolate, I can survive, but it doesn't feel that way when I want it. When something stressful happens in my life—and because I'm divorced with two sons to raise and a full-time job that takes up most of my time, something stressful is *always* happening—I cave in and have a piece of chocolate. That wouldn't be so bad except once I give in, I can't stop eating it. I don't keep candy bars around the house if I can help it, but somehow there's always a bag of semi-sweet morsels in

continues

83

continued

the cabinet. I justify it, of course, by telling myself that I'll bake chocolate-chip cookies for the kids. But most of those chips never make it into cookies. They're as good at stress-busting as any other type of chocolate, so I find myself reaching into the bag on a regular basis.

"I turn to all kinds of junk food whenever I'm stressed out or bored, but eating a bag of chips or a pint of frozen yogurt doesn't give me the same pleasure as eating chocolate. I think I'm drawn to chocolate because it has a soothing effect as it melts in your mouth, almost as if it is washing away the hurt.

"My obsession with chocolate clearly stems from my childhood. Growing up, I had weight issues from the eighth grade until I was about twenty-five years old. This had a big, negative effect on my self-esteem, and I turned to chocolate for comfort. All candy was banned from our house, so I went to great lengths to sneak it into my diet every day, often hiding while I was eating. (I still closet-eat chocolate in the morning so my kids don't see me.) Somehow, eating chocolate made me feel more secure. I think I felt more in control because I found a way to do something I wasn't supposed to do.

"I'm turning forty and still turn to chocolate for comfort. The good news is I don't beat myself up psychologically when I go on a chocolate binge. With age and a lot more self-confidence about my body and the woman I have become, I simply allow myself to indulge in chocolate-eating frenzies. Other than my kids, I can't think of too many other things that give me as much pleasure. I can't see giving up something that makes me feel so good and doesn't ask for anything in return. I do think about my children, and I realize that if reducing my chocolate intake will help reduce my risk of developing heart disease, I owe it to them to do that. But that's where there's more good news: Chocolate manufacturers are now making trans-fat–free chocolates with 15 to 20 percent fewer calories and up to 75 percent less fat than other choco- lates. So it looks like I will still be able to depend on chocolate to help me get through life without worrying so much about its effect on my health!" *—Stacey J.*

Living Rich

Although there are serious pockets of poverty in our country, on the whole, we in America are wealthier and better fed than most. We have what global analysts call "food security." Unlike China, India, and other countries around the world, we have access to enough food to feed our entire population and then some, and our food supply is comparatively safe and inexpensive. We have the natural resources and agricultural technology necessary to produce great quantities of food that can be sold at affordable prices. The more money you have, the more food you can buy, and we have the disposable income to spend on food and pay less for it than do consumers in any other country. In 2001, American families spent almost $740 billion, or 10 to 11 percent of our disposable income, on food.

Just think about all the different types of stores where we buy food, then think about the size of some of them! In addition to traditional neighborhood grocery stores, which still exist in many parts of the country, we have larger standard supermarkets, convenience stores, superstores, warehouse stores, hypermarkets, wholesale clubs, and retail supercenters—department stores with as much as 40 percent of their space devoted to supermarket items. Even some of the larger discount drug stores devote as much as 20 percent of their floor space to food. And more and more people are staying home and doing their grocery shopping on the Internet. Why not? Why leave home when you can have food delivered to your door for not much more than it would cost to carry it back from the market yourself?

It's not just an issue of money. Our population is wealthy compared to many others, but we are also very pressed for time. We turn to convenience foods at home and rely more than ever on restaurants, including fast-food chains, for many of our meals. Compared to years past, we spend less of our income on eating in and more of it on eating out. Of the more than $740 billion we spent on food in 2001, $365 billion was spent in restaurants.

The problem with eating out is *over-eating out*. Having someone else do the cooking is convenient and easy, but we also want to get our money's worth. As a result, many restaurants, especially fast-food chains, provide high-calorie, high-fat foods in supersize portions for little more than you would pay for normal-size portions. If you eat out often and consistently choose supersize foods, those calories add up.

WEB TALK: The Center for Science in the Public Interest provides consumer information about food and health at:

▲ www.cspinet.org

An enormous and powerful food industry helps drive the American economy and influences what and how we eat on a daily basis. Food is big business in America. As Marion Nestle, Ph.D., M.P.H., professor in the Department of Nutrition, Food Studies, and Public Health at New York University, says in her landmark book, *Food Politics,* we are bombarded by messages from the food industry to "eat more." Unfortunately, many of us are getting that message and eating it up, often at the expense of our own health. According to Dr. Nestle, too many of the decisions we make about what and how we should eat are based on food industry propaganda and pure hype. Ultimately, we are responsible for our own food choices and for controlling our own weight, says Nestle, but it is getting harder and harder for consumers to make sound, wholesome choices about food because there is a lot of confusion about what is healthful and what isn't.

While we can be grateful that few of us die of starvation, we need to recognize that many more Americans are dying from diseases related to unhealthy eating. The richness of the American diet, the types of food products available to us, and the promotion of food as something more than simple sustenance all contribute to the high rates of heart disease, diabetes, hypertension, and stroke that plague our nation.

you're not alone

Having It All

"I've always associated plentiful food with having access to the bountifulness of life. We didn't grow up poor, but my family didn't live the rich lifestyle our cousins and other relatives seemed to have.

"My parents made a decision to raise my brother and I on a farm so we could grow most of our own food and live a more 'wholesome' life. My school lunches were always different than the other children's. I didn't mind the difference because I had a pretty stable sense of myself, and I knew the food represented my mother's special care for me. I did sometimes mind the portion sizes, though. My mother controlled my portions at all meals, and I remember sometimes wanting more food than I was allowed to have, especially at dinner or dessert. Even though I understood and appreciated the way we ate at home, I always looked forward to going to my grandmother's house because I knew I would get to eat all different kinds of food and lots of it.

"As I got older, I began to question my parents' beliefs and choices and, like most kids, wanted to start making my own decisions about what and how much to eat. I began to find ways to sneak in some of those forbidden processed foods. When I had money, I would buy snacks in the school cafeteria, rather than eat my lunch from home. By the time I got to college, I was ripe for rebellion. I wanted as much of those forbidden foods as I could get my hands on.

"When I got to law school, food became my reward for hours upon hours of studying. My boyfriend and I only had enough money to eat and no time to do anything else, so food was our entertainment. Later, when we graduated, started working, and eventually married, we ate out often. We moved to New York City, and going out to all the great restaurants made us feel like we were successful and, finally, part of that bountifulness of life I'd always associated with eating well.

"Food has had a starring role throughout my entire life and, like many people, I use it as a reward. But I think that because I've developed a positive attitude toward food and allow myself to eat well, I don't gain a tremendous amount of weight. I'm not afraid to eat, I work out pretty regularly for my health, and I can live with a few extra pounds. I think about food a lot, but I'm not obsessed with eating or my body image. Giving myself permission to eat what I want and as much as I want made all the difference. I have nothing to rebel against anymore.

"All in all, I'm quite comfortable in my own skin, and if I didn't live in New York City, where the standards for 'healthy weight' are so much higher, I probably wouldn't give a thought to the 10 or 15 extra pounds I carry around these days. I am who I am, the same person I've always been. My clothes are just a little tighter now." —*Carrie S.*

The Image Makers

More thought goes into the size, shape, and color of food packaging than you could ever imagine. Price promotions, packaging, and marketing are all designed to entice you to buy more food. Food manufacturers and packagers know that most customers make split-second decisions in the supermarket about buying one brand or another, so they invest a great deal of time and money learning what motivates people to choose one product over another.

Advertising and marketing professionals know when you shop, where you shop, and what you buy when you go food shopping.

They know who does the food shopping in your household and how much money you spend on food. They know how you respond emotionally to the color of food packaging as well as the color of the food itself, because they understand the subliminal meaning and associations different colors have for most people. Of course, marketing professionals don't know your every personal preference, but consumer surveys and focus groups have given them enough general information to enable them to package and promote foods in ways almost guaranteed to appeal.

According to reports from the U.S. Department of Agriculture (USDA), American food manufacturers spend billions of dollars each year advertising their products on television and in print media, and most of this money is spent on promoting processed convenience foods such as canned soups and frozen dinners. After convenience foods, the products backed by the most advertising dollars are snack foods such as candy, cookies, crackers, and chips. Comparatively little money is spent to promote fresh or natural foods such as fruits, vegetables, grains, fish, or meat. It is well documented that most Americans don't eat the amount of fruits and vegetables recommended by nutrition experts, and at the same time, we eat more than the recommended amount of junk food. Statistically, then, the foods we don't eat enough of are the ones that aren't being promoted.

WEB TALK: Download an illuminating study on food advertising in America from the USDA's Economic Research Services at:

www.ers.usda.gov/publications/aib750/aib750i.pdf

Fun and Games Celebrity endorsements, catchy refrains ("Betcha can't eat just one ..."), and stylish or comical logos are just a few of the strategies food manufacturers use to convey the idea that their products are sexy, desirable, or fun.

Many food companies work hard to establish what is known as *brand identity*. They hire marketing executives and advertising teams to be sure consumers develop strong positive associations between the products they're selling and an appealing lifestyle.

We identify with some of these products because they seem part of a lifestyle we have or wish we had. If we believe what some advertisers tell us or imply, then we believe at some level that we will be happier, healthier, skinnier, sexier, brainier, more popular, or more successful if we eat or drink those products. When marketing executives are successful at their jobs, they have convinced us that we cannot live a complete life without their products.

Brand identification is also a food-shopping shortcut. When we recognize and identify with a familiar brand, we don't have to think about whether or not it's something we want to buy or eat. The confidence we feel in the brand name makes the decision process that much easier. Through brand identification, food manufacturers build brand loyalty. That means we always go back for more.

And just like wearing expensive, brand-name sneakers can make you feel more athletic and help convey a message to the world that you're serious about fitness, buying and eating foods with labels that declare "low-fat" or "sugar-free" can make you feel like you're following a healthful diet and making an attempt to control your weight.

Media and Marketing Next time you pick up a package of food in the supermarket, notice what color it is. Just as the color of food affects how we perceive its flavor, the color of the package can influence its appeal. Marketing executives know red, green, white, and brown are more likely to whet your appetite than are black or blue. They know most consumers want food packaging to reflect what's inside the package. By packaging specific types of food products in specific colors, they are sending silent messages about the supposed quality, healthfulness, and flavor of the product itself. These messages might or might not be true.

The goal of advertising and promotion is to get you to choose and use a particular product, whether it's a specific brand name or a general category of food such as milk or potatoes. The strategy might be to get you to switch brands or to suggest ways you could use a product more often, such as eating soup for breakfast or eggs for dinner. You rarely see discount or "free food" promotions such as "buy one, get one free" on unprocessed foods such as fruit, vegetables, or meat unless those foods are past their prime. Most of these types of promotions are for packaged and processed foods—including products that aren't considered the most healthful.

Consumer surveys have indicated that people who "stockpile" foods they like eat more of those foods. In another study, Dr. Wansink found that the bigger the package, the bigger the portion used. He found that consumers took more spaghetti from a medium-size box than from a small box and poured more oil from a medium-size bottle than a smaller one. Free food comes at a high price for a food addict when the result is more food on the plate and more calories consumed.

GET PSYCHED

"Promotional tools used in supermarkets, such as price discounts or '30 percent more' promises on the label, cents-off coupons, and '2-for-1' sales, can be hazardous to a compulsive eater because they encourage you to buy more food than you might normally buy, and that means extra food in the house to tempt you to eat more."
—*Lisa Adler, M.S., R.D., nutrition consultant, New York City*

What You Can Do

Many factors play into the decisions you make about which foods you choose to buy and eat. Although some of these factors are out of your control, how you respond to them *is* in your control.

☐ Think about the different reasons why you choose specific foods when you decide to eat. Are you influenced by brand names, health claims, packaging, or implied promises on labels?

☐ Use your sense of smell to help you feel more satisfied when you eat.

☐ Make a shopping list before you go food shopping and stick to it when you're in the store.

☐ Pay attention to packaging and think about why some packaged foods appeal to you more than others.

☐ Consider the effect advertising has on your food choices and your self-image, whether you're eating at home or at a restaurant.

☐ Analyze the foods you choose to determine if they live up to their packaging promise. Are you getting good value in terms of quality, taste, and healthfulness for the price you paid?

☐ If you're someone who eats just because food is there for the having, avoid "stockpiling" food products just because they're on sale.

The Way We Eat

Dieting has become an American way of life—that isn't working for many overweight Americans. There is a real solution, however. Instead of alternating between overeating and undereating, focus on healthy eating. When you stop dieting, you can start to make peace with food and with your body and take more positive steps toward being fit and healthy.

Your individual food choices and your eating style are influenced by many factors. Personal preference, which might be determined in part by genetics, is probably the surest predictor of what and how you eat. Everyone likes food that carries positive associations, such as comfort foods and foods our families traditionally served at holiday gatherings. Your values, heritage, and ethnic background all play into the types of food choices you make as well.

For many people, eating style is dictated by habit. You eat the same thing for breakfast almost every day because that's what you've always done. Convenience plays a bigger role in most people's food choices than ever before. More and more, people are affected by the availability and affordability of food.

Gaining and Losing

It's not breaking news that Americans are heavier than ever. Six out of ten adults—more than 120 million people—are overweight, and almost half of America's heavyweights are considered obese.

Approximately 9 million children ages six to nineteen are also overweight. These numbers are particularly distressing because, percentage-wise, they're so much higher than they were twenty years ago, *before* we became a nation of fitness fanatics. After all these years of jogging, spinning, stepping, juicing, supplementing, and eating low-fat foods and lean meats, we're heavier than ever. The reason might be that although we talk a lot more about eating well, exercising, and maintaining a healthy weight, we don't actually follow through. It's just as likely that our attitudes toward ourselves and our bodies, our expectations about who and what we should be, and our overall approach toward fitness and weight control have all been moving in the wrong direction. Now we know that a complex combination of biological, environmental, and genetic factors also work against our best efforts to lose and maintain weight.

Q&A

How do I know if I'm obese or simply overweight?

When you hear the word *obese,* you might think it means truly huge, but an *obese* person can be as few as 30 pounds overweight. According to Carla Wolper, M.S., R.D., a nutritionist at the New York Obesity Research Center at St. Luke's–Roosevelt Hospital, *overweight, obese,* and *morbidly obese* are medical definitions used in relation to standard height/ideal weight charts. They are as follows:

- **Overweight** is 10 to 20 percent higher than ideal weight. If your ideal weight is 135 pounds, you could be considered overweight if your weight is between 13 and 26 pounds higher.
- **Obese** means 20 percent or more above ideal weight.
- **Morbidly obese** means double ideal weight, or sufficiently overweight to cause severe problems or interfere with normal functioning.

Keep in mind that these are standards used by physicians and researchers to provide information about the general population. They don't necessarily have anything to do with you as an individual. For a more accurate idea of the meaning of your own weight, use the body mass index (BMI) formula and waist-to-hip ratio described in Chapter 15.

For many years, medical authorities and individuals alike attacked weight problems with restrictive diets. Finally, in the mid-1990s, health experts decided once and for all that dieting is the wrong approach. Diets absolutely don't work in the long term, the experts proclaimed. In spite of this announcement, the weight loss industry is booming, and plenty of people are still dieting. And as always, very few people who lose weight on restrictive or calorie-controlled diets are successful at keeping it off and maintaining a healthy weight.

Why is it so hard to lose weight and even harder to keep it off? Most medical experts now agree that obesity is a chronic condition, not unlike diabetes or heart disease. It doesn't just go away by itself, and there's no quick-fix pill or one-size-fits-all diet that will treat it. Because so many factors contribute to obesity, the condition can be resolved only with specific solutions.

Everyone is different when it comes to gaining and losing. It's harder for some people to lose weight than for others. You might have a family history of obesity, but if you're active and make healthy food choices most of the time, you might never become dangerously overweight. You might have emotional problems that are causing you to have an unhealthy relationship with food, but if you resolve those issues, you might well resolve your eating issues at the same time.

If you're very overweight or obese, you probably have good reasons for trying to get to a healthier weight. As nutritionist Carla Wolper points out, your risk for developing weight-related diseases increases dramatically as weight goes up. People with diabetes and high blood pressure can often control their conditions without medication simply by losing weight. In some people, being overweight appears to contribute to the development of other medical conditions, such as breathing disorders, heart disease, and certain types of cancer. Being overweight can also exacerbate certain medical conditions such as arthritis, asthma, and sleep disorders.

But this doesn't mean you should ever go on another self-imposed starvation. The health risks associated with being overweight are not

WEB TALK: For reliable information and facts on being overweight and obesity, check the Centers for Disease Control (CDC) site at:

www.cdc.gov/nccdphp/dnpa/obesity/

crystal clear, and they don't necessarily apply to everyone. Many medical experts believe that a vicious cycle of gaining weight, losing weight, then gaining it back again can, over time, be more detrimental to your health than staying overweight.

No matter what you weigh right now, if you're overweight and not already in a weight control program, the best thing you can do is stop focusing on losing weight and instead focus on not gaining any more. Then you can start to make positive lifestyle changes such as building a support base of family and friends or finding a group that specializes in weight issues, developing healthier eating habits, and increasing your activity. These types of changes you can make on your own, and they will help you get fit and take off weight in a more sensible and long-lasting way.

Cultural Influences

For many people, culture has a greater influence than biology or psychology on eating habits and their attitude toward food and body weight. If you grew up with eating habits based on ethnic, religious, or other cultural traditions, those practices could be strongly imbedded in your thinking today. The types of foods you choose, how you prepare them, the flavorings you add, when you eat, and how much you eat can have great social meaning if you strongly identify with your culture.

Your culture includes where you live, your family size and composition, your age, your gender, your ethnicity, your marital status, your family's emphasis on education, your own education level, your family's income, and your occupation or the occupations of family members. Research done at Cornell University's Division of Nutritional Sciences confirms these are all social characteristics that can affect your attitudes toward food and eating. Your culture permeates every aspect of your life, including what you eat, how you eat, how much you eat, how much physical activity you get, and how you view your own body.

Statistics show that in the United States, being overweight is more prevalent in the South and Southeast than in other regions, although no one is sure why. This might soon change, however, because as our weight "crisis" reaches epidemic proportions, it is spreading to all areas of the country. Urban values emphasize thinness, so city dwellers might be more likely to try to control their weight, but statistics show only a slight difference in calorie intake and weight between rural women and those who live in urban areas. However, working women tend to be thinner than unemployed women, and women who have had children tend to be heavier than women who haven't given birth.

Your occupation can have a strong influence on your eating and activity habits, as well as your weight, especially if your job involves taking clients out to eat or if you work around food. More likely, your job affects your activity level, especially if you are sitting or standing still most of the time and don't have the flexibility to go out to a gym or squeeze some other type of physical activity into your workday.

Your income can also affect your eating and exercise habits, and statistics show that higher-income women tend to be thinner than lower-income women. Money gives you more control over your life and affords resources such as gym memberships, spa visits, personal trainers, nutrition counseling, and specially prepared foods—all of which can help with weight control.

Just as your personal culture affects your attitude about food and eating, cultural values and norms affect how you think about fatness and thinness. Some groups of people are more accepting of higher body weights than others. Traditionally, most cultures have valued a certain amount of heaviness over extreme thinness, and at one time, a little bit of extra weight was thought to provide protection against wasting diseases. But social ideals change over time, and thinness is in vogue, especially in the United States and Europe. America's obsession with dieting clearly shows that we value thinness. The prevailing cultural attitude toward size and shape affects our self-esteem and influences how we feel about our bodies and our places in society.

Body weight is a social and cultural issue as well as a potential health issue because, as any heavy person knows and research confirms, overweight people face discrimination when traveling, shopping, looking for jobs, getting promotions, seeking admission to colleges, and trying to get health care. This prejudice only adds to the feelings of guilt, shame, and self-contempt so many overweight people experience.

WEB TALK: The National Association to Advance Fat Acceptance website can be found at:

🔺 www.naafa.org

From a psychological point of view and, quite possibly, a medical standpoint as well, there's a lot to be said for accepting yourself at whatever weight you are. Although research shows that, for some people, there are serious health risks associated with being overweight, it doesn't hold true that weight is a health problem for everyone. The fact is, there isn't enough research on the general population of overweight people to make blanket statements or give clear-cut advice to individuals. That's where your own personal biology, genetics, and lifestyle choices come in. The participants in most of the studies done on the psychological and biological aspects of weight control have been people who sought professional help for obesity or clinical eating disorders. That's a relatively small number of people and not representative of the entire overweight population.

you're not alone

Happy to Be Me

"I am certainly aware of my weight problem; I've had it all my life. I was a chubby girl shopping in the big-girl section of the department store, and today I shop in the plus-size section. Here's the thing, though … I don't sneak or avoid food. I'm not compulsive about it, nor am I obsessed by my body image. I eat what I like, when I like, and that's my only food story. I'm very comfortable with myself, but it hasn't always been that way.

"When I was kid, being overweight was tortuous. It's not easy to grow up being called Fatty Patty. My mother, who was often critical of my weight, sent me to a weight loss program when I was ten years old. It wasn't easy for me because she was very thin and stylish. My brothers were also slim and taller than me. I struggled physically and emotionally with my weight throughout all my childhood and teenage years.

"Once I was out of high school, however, I realized that I didn't have to hide behind my weight. Somewhere, deep down, I knew that my self-acceptance shouldn't be based on my physical appearance, and because I was out there enjoying life, and meeting men, I guess I was able to get confirmation of that. But I think the most important event was when I met my husband, John. Somehow, we are just a great fit. He met me when I was overweight, but he has never been critical, loves my curves, and really adds to my self-esteem. My mother, who is still a tough critic, lives 3,000 miles away, so the effect she has on me is minimal.

"What's most important is that my daughters see me as someone who accepts herself. I want them to know their mom is okay with who she is so they will follow my example in that respect. I feel great, I'm healthy, I walk for thirty minutes every day, and even though I wear a size 18, I consider myself pretty stylish." —*Patty S.*

Personal Style

Your *eating style* isn't the same thing as your *diet*. Your diet means the specific foods you choose to eat. Your eating style, on the other hand, refers to the eating habits you've formed over time, such as how often you eat, how quickly you eat, where you eat, and whether or not you stick to a rigid eating plan. For instance, your diet might include a lot of vegetables, but your eating style might or might not be vegetarian. Your diet might be high in sugar or high in fat, but either way, your style is to eat a lot of junk food. Like your actual diet, however, the eating habits you form might be a conscious choice on your part or they might be a result of your family heritage and environment. Some researchers think there might even be a genetic link to eating patterns.

When it comes to eating style, we all have our idiosyncrasies. Regardless of your weight, you might or might not have a tendency to overeat. If you do overeat, your overeating style can be very different from the next person's and might have different causes. Analyzing your individual eating style is important when you want to change your eating habits. For instance, if you over-eat simply because you love food, you'll need to take a different approach to modifying your eating habits than someone who compulsively overeats to fill emotional gaps or someone who gives little thought to food but mindlessly overeats.

Here are some examples of eating styles that can interfere with your ability to have a healthy relationship with food:

- **Eating foods that are inherently high in calories or fat.** If you grew up eating fatty foods, and you're still eating those foods, you've developed a habit that's hard to break.

- **Eating a lot of junk food.** If lunch or dinner routinely means fast food, and snack time is all about doughnuts or chips, this habit will also be hard to change.

- **Eating all the time.** Munching all day or "grazing" works for some people but generally doesn't work for anyone who is struggling to maintain a healthy weight. The reason is that when you graze throughout the day, it's difficult to keep track of what and how much you eat. Most people who are trying to lose weight or maintain a healthy weight usually benefit from the structure of three regular meals eaten around the same time every day and spaced three to five hours apart, perhaps with a snack between some meals.

- **Overeating at every meal.** Some people simply have no idea what a normal portion size of food looks like.

- **Eating quickly.** The faster you eat, the more you'll eat before you feel full.

- **Snacking constantly.** If you snack on healthy foods such as fruits and vegetables, this might not be a problem; however, if you snack on junk food, you're filling up on foods that contribute a lot of calories and nothing else to your diet.

- **Mindless eating.** You might be totally unaware of the eating behavior that's affecting your weight because you're not thinking about what or how you're eating. When you're not paying attention to what you're eating, you can mindlessly shovel food into your mouth all day and never really realize that you are overeating.

- **Eating too many foods from one food group.** A diet that emphasizes or eliminates a particular food group often lacks nutritional balance.

- **Weekend overeating.** Some people eat well during the week, then blow it on weekends by eating and drinking in excess.

- **Random eating.** If you have a choice, sitting down to regularly scheduled meals is physically and psychologically healthier than grabbing a meal wherever and whenever you can.

- **Frequently eating on the run.** When you grab food on the go, you're not paying attention to how much you're eating. It's easy to forget about food you eat on the run, and that can lead to overeating.

- **Frequently eating out.** The problem with eating out often is that you have little or no control over what you eat and how it's prepared. But if you have control over the amount of food you eat, the type of food doesn't matter as much.

- **Eating in front of the television.** It's not a good idea for a food addict to participate in any other activity while having a meal, because you won't be paying attention to what you're eating.

- **Chronic dieting to lose weight.** Deprivation and semi-starvation are never conducive to developing a healthier relationship with food.

- **Skipping meals.** If you don't eat every 3 to 5 hours, you're likely to overeat at your next meal or grab the first food available, whether it's good for you or not.

- **Emotional eating.** Emotional eating has little or nothing to do with actual hunger, so if you're eating in response to your emotions, you're not eating for the right reasons.

Some obesity researchers theorize that there is an obese eating style. That is, people who are obese eat larger portions, choose higher-calorie foods, chew each mouthful of food fewer times, are more inclined to eat between meals, and might eat less often but eat more food at one sitting than people who are at a healthier weight. This theory is highly controversial, however, because other experts believe this approach is too simplistic, and there's no real evidence that such a distinct eating style exists. In fact, some studies have shown just the opposite; that overweight people often show more restraint in eating than underweight people.

Some overweight people—as many as 10 million, according to some reports—suffer from night eating syndrome (NES), a condition first identified in 1955 by psychiatrist Albert Stunkard, an obesity researcher at the University of Pennsylvania. People with NES eat more than half their food after dinner and before breakfast the next day, often getting up from bed at night to snack. They have no appetite in the morning and usually have their first meal after noon. People with NES are often tense, anxious, moody, and nervous, especially at night.

WEB TALK: To find out more about night-eating syndrome or to participate in ongoing NES studies, go to:

www.uphs.upenn.edu/weight/nighteating.html

In the years since NES was first identified, researchers have discovered that people with NES experience consistent and abnormal hormonal changes. Normally, night brings on an increase in the hormone melatonin, which helps us fall asleep and stay asleep. Night eaters do not show the same rise in melatonin or in the hormone leptin, which suppresses hunger. At the same time, the stress hormone cortisol is elevated throughout the day and night in people with NES, indicating that this is a combined eating, sleep, and stress-related disorder. If you're overweight, eat more than 50 percent of your food at night, have trouble falling or staying asleep, and don't eat breakfast, you might have night eating syndrome.

Night eating syndrome is not to be confused with nocturnal sleep-related eating disorder (NSRED), or sleep-eating, a rare condition that affects only a small subset of sleepwalkers. People with NSRED often eat and sometimes binge in their sleep. They are usually overweight and typically choose high-fat, high-sugar, and high-calorie foods. They are unaware of their behavior while it's happening, and in the morning, have no recollection of their sleep-eating episodes. As a result, sleep eaters might not be fully aware of their problem. Not much is known about the causes of NSRED, but it is considered a reflection of an underlying psychological problem, such as depression, that is not necessarily related to sleep itself.

Fast Food

In an ideal weight control world, there is always time to shop for fresh food and cook all your meals from scratch so you can have better control over what you eat. But you might have no choice but to rely on convenience foods and fast-food restaurants for many of your meals. Or maybe you just like fast food, and it's your favorite quick indulgence. After all, fast food is tasty, inexpensive, and very convenient.

Fast foods might not directly cause weight gain, obesity, or chronic disease, but because most fast foods are especially high in calories, fat, cholesterol, and salt, they can surely play a role in the development of any of these conditions.

According to Kelly Brownell, Ph.D., professor and chair of the Yale University Psychology Department and director of the Yale Center for Eating and Weight Disorders, fast-food restaurants are part of a toxic food environment that has contributed to the obesity epidemic in America. Fast food, Brownell says, limits our personal control over our weight and health. You can have fast food wherever you are—at home, in your car, or at a restaurant. In his book, *Food Fight: The Inside Story of the Food Industry, America's Obesity Crisis and What We Can Do About It,* Dr. Brownell argues that fast foods are popular because they're convenient, accessible, processed with fat and sugar to be especially tasty, heavily promoted, and inexpensive, while healthier foods are less popular because they are less convenient, less accessible, less tasty, more expensive, and not as well promoted.

According to the National Restaurant Association, however, fast-food restaurants across the country have started responding to consumer requests for healthier food by providing nutrition information about the food they serve, adding special menu items, and by developing educational campaigns to help customers live healthier lifestyles. Some examples include Applebee's teaming up with Weight Watchers International to develop a special line of menu items that list "point" totals, which are part of Weight Watchers' Winning Points program; McDonald's creating lighter adult meal combinations that include pedometers and instructions on beginning a walking program; Ruby Tuesdays now uses healthier oils for cooking and provides nutrition information to help consumers make smart menu choices; Pizza Hut now offers lower-fat pies; and Taco Bell will substitute salsa for cheese on any menu item ordered "Fresco style."

GET PSYCHED

"Sometimes it helps to have an almost militant attitude about the food industry—believing on one hand that they offer healthy options but knowing that what gets pushed are foods high in sugar, fat, and calories. Resisting the pressure to eat these foods is an especially powerful tool for parents who wish to create a positive nutrition environment for their children." *—Kelly D. Brownell, Ph.D., director, Yale Center for Eating and Weight Disorders*

Even if you don't choose special menu items, if you can practice moderation, you can eat fast-food fried chicken and fish fillets, hamburgers, cheeseburgers, tacos, and pizza without giving your weight a second thought. Fast food becomes a problem only when you eat too much, too often.

Here are some suggestions for eating healthfully at fast-food establishments:

- **Order only regular-size portions.** Skip large, super-, or deluxe sizes, even if they're the same price.
- **Drink water in place of a soft drink.** If tap water is unavailable, most fast-food restaurants sell bottled water.

- **Order just one.** One burger, one slice of pizza, one hot dog, one small sandwich, or one taco is a healthy portion.

- **Don't go overboard when it comes to calories and fat.** Skip the "meal deals," and instead choose one higher-fat item such as a burger and surround it with lower-calorie and lower-fat side dishes such as soups and salads.

- **Order a kid-size meal.** In some restaurants, kid-size meals mean kid-size portions of adult food. If that's the case, you can save fat, calories, and money, too!

- **Have a balanced plan.** Try to go to fast-food restaurants on days when you know your other meals are going to be leaner, lighter, and higher in fiber.

WEB TALK: Find out what restaurants are doing to make their menus healthier at the National Restaurant Association site at:

www.restaurant.org

A Little History When Nathan Handwerker opened Nathan's Famous Hot Dogs in Coney Island, New York, in 1916, he probably didn't know he was starting a restaurant trend that would become a hotly debated health topic almost one hundred years later. Just for fun, here's a timeline showing the history of fast-food restaurants over the past century:

- Fast food began in the 1920s with Orange Julius and A&W in California and White Castle Hamburgers in Wichita, Kansas.

- In the late 1930s, Krispy Kreme doughnuts opened in Salem, North Carolina, and Bob Wian's Big Boy debuted in Glendale, California.

- Dairy Queen, Shoney's Big Boy, McDonald's, and Bob's Big Boy appeared on the fast-food scene in the 1940s.

- The 1950s saw the arrival of Whataburger, Dunkin Donuts, Jack in the Box, KFC, Church's Chicken, Fatburger, Burger King, IHOP, Sizzler, Pizza Hut, Sbarro, Little Caesars, Round Table Pizza, and Taco Time.

- With the 1960s came Domino's Pizza, Hardee's, Taco Bell, Blimpie, T.G.I. Friday's, Chick-fil-A, Red Lobster, Wendy's, Red Robin, Long John Silvers, and Old Spaghetti Factory.
- In the 1970s, Starbucks, The Cheesecake Factory, Godfather's Pizza, Subway, Chili's, and Chuck E. Cheese opened their doors.
- When the 1980s rolled in, so did Applebees, TCBY, Olive Garden, Papa John's Pizza, Hooters, Miami Subs, Boston Chicken, Outback Steakhouse, Hogi Yogi, and Jose's Taco Shop.
- The 1990s brought Baja Fresh, Juice Club, Kenny Rogers Roasters, Teriyaki Stix, and more juice bars.

For Your Convenience At the same time fast-food restaurants were taking off in the 1950s, convenience foods were becoming the favored fare at many dinner tables. Canned, frozen, and refrigerated processed foods were designed to be quick, tasty, and easy to serve, but not necessarily wholesome.

In 1951, the Duncan Hines company introduced the first cake mix. A year later, when Lipton introduced dehydrated onion soup mix and a recipe for using it in a dip, home party fare was changed forever. Fast forward to 1959, when Häagen-Dazs ice creams were first loaded into frozen-food cases in supermarkets. By that time, Swanson had served up its first frozen dinners, Eggo frozen waffles and Cheez Whiz had become kitchen staples, the first sugar-free soft drink had been introduced, and millions of people were sweetening their coffee with little pink packets of Sweet'N Low.

Mass-production techniques and food technology have made it possible for food manufacturers to make more and more convenience foods available at a lower price. The advent of these modern food-processing techniques coincides with the rise in obesity in this country, and many health experts and researchers believe that's no coincidence. Harvard economists who studied the consumption of fast foods and the use of canned and frozen entrées and other convenience foods at home found what they consider a clear association between easy access to convenience foods and the rise in obesity. The excess calories that have made us all heavier are coming more from meals eaten at home than from fast foods eaten outside the home.

Convenience food sales are growing by about 15 percent every year. Manufacturers know from market surveys and focus groups that consumers are willing to pay two or three times more for foods packaged for convenience. As a result, manufacturers create more tasty and convenient products, often at the expense of good nutrition. Almost half of Americans surveyed by the Food Marketing Institute in 2002 said they eat boxed, frozen, or canned meals at least once a week.

But there is hope. Surveys also show that consumers are gobbling up a new type of convenience foods—fresh foods prepared and packaged for convenience. Forty percent of those surveyed said they use premarinated meat, precleaned vegetables, and bagged salads. Many people are back in the kitchen cooking homemade—or at least semi-homemade—foods that can be prepared in a lot less time.

Supersizing and "Free" Food Top health experts agree that the obesity epidemic in America and around the world is complex, due to combined environmental, biological, and genetic factors. Together, these factors work against most people who are trying to lose or maintain weight. We live in an environment that provides us with easily accessible, tasty foods that are often served up in supersize portions. At the same time, we have a natural impulse to eat as much food as is available, whenever it's available, and we are genetically inclined to store fat in our bodies. Add to this a sedentary lifestyle, and the result is a supersize generation.

Supersize food items that contribute little more than excess calories and fat include oversize buckets of popcorn, larger-than-life–size cups filled with soft drinks, huge candy bars, and entrées and side dishes that are double or triple the size of a normal portion. We're tempted to buy extra-large servings of these foods because we get a lot more food for just a little more money so we've gotten a good deal.

The real deal, of course, is that we're getting a lot more calories, sugar, and fat than we need. Studies show that most of us, when given more food, are inclined to eat it—even when we know it's not good for us. The economic cost of these supersize foods might be low, but the nutritional price you pay can be very high.

Data collected by the Prevention Institute in Oakland, California, and the National Alliance for Nutrition and Activity in Washington, D.C., revealed some good examples of what you can spend and what you can get in terms of calories when you choose larger portions over regular-size or buy "value combo meals" rather than just the basic item. Here are some highlights from their 2002 report, *From Wallet to Waistline: The Hidden Costs of Super Sizing:*

- **Movie theater popcorn.** Seventy-one cents buys 500 more calories when you go from a small- to medium-size unbuttered popcorn.
- **Fries from a fast-food restaurant.** Sixty-four extra cents buys 330 calories when you switch from a small serving to a large. That means that for a 62 percent increase in price, you get 157 percent more calories.
- **Combo value meals from fast-food restaurants.** You add 600+ additional calories when you buy the "special" meal," rather than settling for just a quarter-pound burger with cheese or a double cheeseburger.
- **Extra-large chocolate candy bar.** Thirty-three cents more buys 230 more calories, most of which are from fat.

It's interesting to note that since the 1970s, the increase in supersize portions closely parallels the national increase in obesity rates. It seems easy to blame supersize portions for our overeating and overweight problems. But when Harvard researchers concluded that fast foods are, in part, responsible for the obesity crisis in America, they didn't blame it on huge servings. We're not eating that much more at meals than we did before, researchers say. In fact, most of those extra calories are coming from snacks and sodas consumed between meals. But as consumer complaints and media attention have focused attention on enormous "value meals" and high-calorie fast food, the large fast-food chains have begun to respond, removing some oversize items from their regular menus and offering healthier fare for adults and children.

Never Say Never

you're not alone

"By the time I was twenty-six, I was about 40 pounds overweight. I didn't really know how overweight I was. I just thought of myself as a big girl who could carry more weight than my friends because I'm very tall. I also thought I had pretty good eating habits because I ate a lot of vegetables, chicken, and fish. But I never thought about how my food was prepared. I used to eat in fast-food restaurants at least three times a week. I love fries and always ordered the large size—that was my vegetable, alongside fried fish or chicken sandwiches. I didn't realize that by the time I ordered a drink, I was ordering more than 1,000 calories. And sometimes that was just an after-work snack! I would eat dinner a couple hours later.

"I was closing in on my thirtieth birthday when I realized I had to do something about my weight, so I made a resolution to start eating better. I'm an all-or-nothing type, so I had to stop going to fast-food restaurants altogether for a while. That was hard because it meant cooking more often. But I learned how to make oven fries at home, and as long as I put enough salt on them, they were a pretty good substitute. I made similar changes in my diet, not so much in the types of food I ate, but more in preparation. By my thirtieth birthday, I'd lost 23 pounds. I lost another 30 pounds in the next six months, and I've kept all that weight off for two years. The best part is, I eat fast food again. I just don't eat as much or as often. I go with a friend or my cousin maybe once a month. We order one meal and one salad for both of us and end up splitting the same amount of food I used to eat by myself in one sitting. I still love fast food, but since I've lost weight, I'm satisfied with less." —*Elizabeth M.*

What You Can Do

Repeatedly gaining and losing weight can be more harmful to your health than simply being overweight. There are many things you can do to help stabilize your weight as you figure out how to change your eating habits and make healthier food choices.

- ☐ Instead of focusing on losing weight, focus on not gaining any more.
- ☐ When you're trying to change your eating habits and looking for areas of improvement, look at your personal eating style as well as the food choices you make.
- ☐ Think about how your personal culture—the way you grew up and the way you live now—affect your food choices and eating style.
- ☐ If eating at fast-food restaurants is part of your food addiction, learn to make healthier choices so you can eat out and not overdo it.
- ☐ Avoid "value meals" and oversize containers of food that seem like a good deal for the money. All you're really getting for free is excess calories.

Healthy Eating

This chapter could be called "Food and Nutrition 101." Here we forget about fad diets and alternative eating plans and go back to the basics of eating well. You'll learn how the foods you choose affect your body and help it run more or less efficiently, depending on your choices. You'll find out how your body uses nutrients from the food you eat and which foods are nutritional superstars when it comes to maintaining a healthy weight. You'll learn what it means to eat mindfully and why mindful eating is essential to developing a healthy relationship with food.

Some people who are trying to get to a healthy weight benefit from weighing and measuring food, learning standard portion sizes, and knowing how many calories are in the foods they eat. You can use these tools initially to help you gauge just how much you're eating from day to day. But because this book is designed to help you change your psychological and emotional relationship to eating, the techniques in this chapter go beyond those basic physical tools. Ultimately, to develop a healthy relationship with food, you need only remember three words when you sit down to eat: *balance, variety,* and *moderation.*

You Are What You Eat

You're not the cheeseburger you had for lunch today or the pint of ice cream you ate last night and, hopefully, that's not how you identify yourself. You are, however, a body full of nutrients. In that respect, you are very much like a cheeseburger or a pint of ice cream—or any food. The nutrients you get from the food you eat are broken down by your body's digestive system into their respective component parts. The parts are then absorbed into your body and used to make energy and perform a variety of other jobs that help replenish your body's nutrient stores and keep you healthy.

Food consists of three macronutrients—carbohydrates, proteins, and fats—all of which can be used to make energy. Although we often refer to an individual food as "a carbohydrate" or "a protein," most foods contain a mix of macronutrients. For example, bread, which is considered a carbohydrate, also contains significant amounts of fat and protein. Some obvious exceptions exist, such as cooking oils, which are 100 percent fat, and egg whites, which are pure protein, but most foods are a mix and earn their label by being higher in one macronutrient than the others.

WEB TALK: For reliable information about food and nutrition, visit the Food and Nutrition Information Center (FNIC) at:

↑ www.nal.usda.gov/fnic

Here's how your body uses the macronutrients you get from your food and why you need all of them:

All *carbohydrates,* except fiber, are broken down into a sugar known as glucose that your body uses immediately to make energy. If you eat more carbs than your body needs at the time, some are stored in your liver and muscles, and some are converted to body fat. Carbohydrates are your best source of physical and mental energy. Glucose is the only fuel your brain can use. Some excess glucose is stored in your muscles as reserved energy, but this sugar also is converted to body fat if you eat too much of it.

Proteins are broken down into amino acids, which then are reassembled into other body proteins such as muscle tissue and the carrier proteins that move fats and cholesterol out of your blood. Proteins form the mesh that mends broken skin when you cut yourself and make up the most important antibodies, enzymes, and hormones in your body. The body has no storage mechanism for proteins. Excess amino acids are sometimes converted to fat or carbohydrates, but most often they are simply eliminated from the body.

Fat from food is either used for energy or stored directly as body fat. As many overweight people know, it's easier to get fat from eating foods high in fat than from eating foods high in carbs or protein. Carbs and protein must be converted into fat first, whereas when your body stores dietary fat as body fat, it's practically a direct deposit. If there's one thing many people don't understand about fat, however, it's that everyone needs *some* fat in the diet. Fat is a nutrient that supports your skin, hair, brain, and nerves and also helps you absorb fat-soluble vitamins A, D, E, and K. If you don't get a little fat in your diet, your health will suffer. Your brain won't be able to function effectively.

When you eat a wide variety of foods, as most health experts recommend, you're not only getting what you need from all three macronutrients, you also have a better chance of getting all your micronutrients as well. These are the essential vitamins, minerals, fiber, and other substances your body needs to keep itself healthy.

Enough Is Enough!

Many weight loss programs recommend measuring, weighing, and portioning out food as strategies to help recognize how much food you're eating and understand the meaning of "portion control." These tools can also help you develop a better relationship with food.

Many people have no idea what it means to eat a reasonable amount of food. For example, a French toast breakfast platter at Denny's is meant to serve one person, and some people eat it all in one sitting. But that hearty plate, which comes with bacon and sausages, provides 1,146 calories (more than half of what most women need to eat each day) and 71 grams fat (well above most people's daily limit). So for most of us, it's not a bad idea to learn about weights and measures or to learn to recognize standard serving sizes to prepare reasonable amounts of food at home and recognize when we're getting double-size portions in restaurants. This knowledge will help you gain some perspective if you want to compare how much you eat to how much government and medical experts recommend you eat. And if, in fact, you can stick to standard serving sizes when you sit down to eat and still enjoy your meal and feel satisfied, that's half the battle for controlling your weight. It's easy enough to teach yourself what a standard serving size looks like.

- Use a standard $1/2$-cup measure for foods such as pasta, rice, and vegetables. Notice what $1/2$ cup (a standard serving) of each of these foods looks like on your plate. That way, whether you're home, at someone else's dinner table, or out in a restaurant, you'll have an idea of how much food you're eating just by looking at it.

- Use the same method for breakfast cereals. Measure one serving (according to the package label) into the cereal bowl you normally use. See what it looks like so you can measure it by sight in the future.

- Use visual cues. A 3-ounce serving of meat, which is considered to be one serving, is about the size of a standard deck of cards or a cassette tape. An ounce of cheese is equivalent in size to a standard pair of dice. A half cup of anything is about the size of a tennis ball.

Note that there are no standard serving sizes for desserts. That pretty much tells you how arbitrary the whole system is, doesn't it?

If you want to weigh and measure your foods, keep in mind that these are educational tools, not solutions for weight control. To develop a healthy relationship with food, you ultimately must learn to pay attention to your own body and let it tell you how much is enough.

Food addicts often worry about the number of *calories* in their food and which foods are high in calories and which are low. But even though many people make a big deal out of it, counting calories isn't a magic solution for weight loss. In fact, plenty of overweight people know the calorie counts for most foods, but they still can't shake their extra weight. That said, calories still count when it comes to weight control because you *can* have too much of a good thing, including energy. Excess food energy in your body ultimately turns into excess body fat. So even when you stop counting calories, you should still have some respect for them.

PsychSpeak

A **calorie** is a measurement of energy. Different foods provide different amounts of energy. Food addicts can become overly preoccupied with the number of calories in food. The healthiest approach is to balance higher-calorie foods with lower-calorie foods in your diet.

Paying attention to the calories in the food you eat can be helpful, as long as you don't get too preoccupied with exact numbers. If you're just learning about the caloric content of different foods and you want to set limits for yourself, do yourself a favor and set a range. If you want to eat enough food to provide, say, 1,800 calories a day, allow yourself a range of 1,600 to 2,000 calories. That gives you leeway on days when you feel hungrier than usual or want something special. Everyone's body handles food differently, and everyone maintains a healthy weight at different calorie levels. The range that works for you will be the range where you're not gaining weight and you feel comfortably satisfied with the amount of food you eat.

Ultimately, the goal of anyone who counts calories should be to *stop* counting calories. By having a good basic idea of the amount of calories supplied by the foods you eat, you'll be able to look at a plate of food and know instantly whether or not it's the right amount for you. You'll know what it means to eat within a calorie range that works for you without having to do any calculations or even think twice.

A Perfect Diet

To attempt to define the perfect diet, first we need to clearly define the word *diet*. When most people hear the word *diet*, they think of weight loss diets. But weight loss diets shouldn't be the focus when you are trying to escape a food addiction. "Being on a diet" implies that at some point, you're going to go back off the diet—and that's when you'll probably start gaining weight again. Instead, the diet we're talking about simply means the type of food you eat and your eating style. Good diets encourage lifelong, healthful eating habits. They aren't highly restrictive, nor do they emphasize one food group over another or encourage you to completely omit any food group. There is no one-size-fits-all diet. The majority of people who are successful at maintaining a healthy weight do so by following a personalized plan. The diet you ultimately can follow for life is one you've tailored to suit your own personal tastes and your own personal lifestyle.

Like many health and nutrition experts, Alan Lee, R.D., a nutrition consultant in New York City, recommends a high-volume, low-density diet based on plenty of vegetables, fruits, whole grains, lean proteins, and low-fat dairy products or dairy substitutes. The idea is not to eat a low-calorie diet but to eat a lot of low-calorie foods. Foods that have a high water and/or fiber content fill you up for comparatively few calories so you can eat them in relative abundance without worrying about measuring or counting calories. That's why you'll find salads, yogurt, vegetable soups, and bran muffins on almost every plan for healthful eating. From these food groups, choose foods you really enjoy so that whenever you eat, you're eating for pleasure. Lee recommends eating this way 85 to 90 percent of the time so the rest of the time you can indulge in what he calls "recreational eating." For some people that means fast-food hamburgers and fries once in a while. For others, it means dessert. Whatever it is, it's no longer forbidden food. Reserve a space in your diet for indulgences and give yourself permission to eat them now and then.

When it comes to recreational eating, Lee divides people into two categories: all-or-nothing people and moderation people. Most of his clients who identify themselves as food addicts admittedly have all-or-nothing personality types. In that case, it's best to keep indulgence foods out of the house, regardless of your commitment to healthy eating. If you won't be able to eat only 1 serving of ice cream when there are 14 servings in the container, why tempt yourself? But again, don't deny yourself. Just make it a point to limit recreational eating to those times when you're eating outside your home. Buy a single serving of ice cream at a deli or order, say, one killer dessert with extra spoons when you're at a restaurant and share it with your dining partners. If your indulgence is fast food, however, it might make more sense to order a reasonable portion of food, take it out of the restaurant, and eat it at home. If you stay in the restaurant, it's too easy to go back and order more.

> ## GET PSYCHED
>
> "Many weight conscious people aren't eating enough food. You need enough to satisfy both your senses and your psyche, to fulfill the craving to eat but still feel good about yourself. If you fill yourself up with larger quantities of lower-calorie foods, there's less room for the foods that get you in trouble." –Howard M. Shapiro, M.D., author, Picture Perfect Weight Loss

The perfect diet for you is a diet that keeps you mentally and physically fit. It must satisfy your hunger and at the same time create a happy, healthy food environment. If you're always counting calories, keeping track of fat, measuring portions, avoiding certain foods, and weighing yourself to measure the effects of eating, you're probably not having much fun with your food. The perfect diet focuses on healthy living, not on losing weight. If you're not enjoying your food, and you don't have a medical problem that requires you to avoid certain foods, then you're not following your perfect diet.

Tools for Healthful Eating

If health experts at the U.S. Department of Agriculture's (USDA) Center for Nutrition Policy and Promotion (CNPP) were clever, they'd hire a public relations specialist to develop a celebrity campaign to promote the Food Guide Pyramid. Any diet plan that's promoted by a superstar, or that hails from Miami or Los Angeles, is going to sound a whole lot sexier and appealing than the government's guidelines for good health.

But even if it's not that exciting, the government's plan makes sense. It promotes eating a wide variety of foods from different food groups to get all the nutrients you need to be healthy. The Food Guide Pyramid also recommends physical activity to maintain or improve your weight. From time to time, the Dietary Guidelines for Americans are updated by a committee of nutrition experts, but the general message is always the same and can be summed up in one word: *moderation*. It's not a bad message.

One problem with the government guidelines for healthy eating is that they're designed to be relevant to the entire population of healthy people living in the United States. In other words, they're very broad. The government's dietary guidelines also don't provide the structure and promise of quick results that weight loss diets offer. But you can take the government's dietary guidelines, which provide a sound foundation for most any diet, and narrow them down to create a lifetime healthy eating plan for yourself.

you're not alone

A Better Balance

"Everyone in my family is in pretty good shape, and so am I, but I've always wanted to be thinner than I am. It started for all the usual reasons when I was a teenager. I wanted to look like a model. I wanted to look sexy, and I thought skinny meant sexy. I started going on diets with my friends when I was in high school, even though none of us really needed to lose weight. By the time I was thirty, I'd been dieting and watching my weight for fifteen years. You name the diet, I've been on it. As an adult, I would make a point of telling everyone I was on the latest fad diet. It actually made me feel trendy. I thought it had cache, kind of like when people name-drop because they know someone who's rich or famous.

"Last year, after talking to a nutritionist at my gym about 20 pounds I couldn't lose, I had something of an epiphany when she talked to me about eating a balanced diet. I realized that dieting has never helped me lose weight, not even temporarily. I thought about diets all the time, was always on a diet, but I could never really stick to them. Most diets say 'eat this' and 'don't eat that,' and the minute I would tell myself I couldn't eat something, I wanted it desperately and always gave in quickly and ate more of it than I probably even wanted. I never realized how much I enjoy sandwiches until I went on a diet that said I couldn't eat any bread!

"Dieting only made me obsessive about food and ultimately caused me to gain more weight than I would have if I'd just eaten normally and not worried about it every time I gained 5 or 10 pounds. Whenever I was preparing to go on another diet, I would overeat the restricted foods in anticipation of depriving myself. I would go on the diet for a day or two, sometimes a week, until I couldn't stand it anymore. Then I would cheat big-time, not tell anyone, and start pretending to diet again the next day.

"I finally realized that even though it sounds boring and old-fashioned, eating a balanced diet actually works for me because I can eat all kinds of foods, anything I want. There are no restrictions on a basic balanced diet, just recommendations. I pretty much eat whatever I feel like eating at the time, although I do plan ahead to have healthy foods on hand and I give some thought to how much food I'm eating. But portion control is pretty easy when you're eating a lot of different foods at one time, because you naturally eat smaller portions of each.

"Now I eat all my favorite foods, including desserts and snacks. There's some self-control involved, but I've lost most of those 20 pounds and I feel good about the way I'm eating, so that keeps me motivated. Also, knowing I can make up my own rules and eat what I want makes me feel like there's no reason to overeat. I eat until I feel full. I don't feel like I have to eat a lot of food because I know there's always more coming and I can have whatever I want, whenever I want. And the best part of all? I've finally stopped talking and thinking about dieting all the time!" *–Amy C.*

Food Guidelines Every time a best-selling diet plan hits the stands, it seems as though the guidelines for healthy eating change. That's because every author has his or her own idea about how we should eat. Some say eat more carbohydrates; others say carbs are no good so you should focus more on protein.

Some say low-fat is where it is while others say pour on the heavy cream. If you jump from diet plan to diet plan, after a while you're bound to be confused about what it means to eat right and what it takes to get to a healthy weight.

Often, fad diets include nutrition advice that flies in the face of the dietary guidelines issued by government health experts and medical organizations. From a historical perspective, however, government guidelines have outlived most fad diets and, on the whole, have proved themselves to be a useful strategy for maintaining a healthy relationship with food. The USDA's 10 Dietary Guidelines for Americans are as follows:

WEB TALK: To view USDA's Food Guide Pyramid, go to: www.usda.gov/cnpp/pyramid.html

1. **Aim for a healthy weight.** Everyone has a range of healthy weights, and your healthy weight isn't necessarily the same as anyone else who is your same height. You can use the formulas you'll find near the end of this chapter to see if your weight is considered healthy. If you're not already in your range of healthy weights, you can set that as a long-term fitness goal.

2. **Be physically active each day.** The importance of exercise in maintaining a healthy weight and preventing chronic disease is becoming more and more evident. It doesn't matter what you do to stay physically active; what matters is that you do something.

3. **Let the Food Guide Pyramid direct your food choices.** The Food Guide Pyramid is a visual representation of the different food groups with advice on how much food you should have from each group, depending on how many calories you consume. It is based on the Dietary Guidelines. The Food Guide Pyramid is a tool that can help you plan a day's worth of balanced, calorie-controlled meals without actually counting calories. For some people, especially those who like structure or want to learn more about food groups and serving sizes, it can be a useful tool. For others, it might

be easier to simply fill a dinner plate with a variety of foods and not go back for second helpings.

4. **Choose a variety of grains daily, especially whole grains.** Whole-grain foods are emphasized because they are high in fiber and contain nutrients that are processed out of refined grain products and not always replaced.

5. **Choose a variety of fruits and vegetables daily.** Different fruits and vegetables supply different nutrients; choosing a variety of foods within each group helps ensure you get all the different nutrients they can provide.

6. **Keep food safe to eat.** Food safety at home means keeping your hands and work surfaces clean, keeping raw and cooked foods separate, cooking food to a safe temperature, and keeping hot foods hot and cold foods cold to prevent foodborne illnesses.

7. **Choose foods low in saturated fat and cholesterol and moderate in total fat.** Cut back on foods that can raise your blood cholesterol and blood fats, such as high-fat dairy products, fatty meats and cold cuts, palm and coconut oils, organ meats, egg yolks, and hydrogenated vegetable oils.

8. **Choose drinks and foods without a lot of sugar.** Soft drinks, cakes, cookies, pies, fruit drinks, dairy desserts, and candy add a lot of sugar to your diet.

9. **Choose and prepare food with less salt.** The latest research says just about everyone should cut back on the amount of sodium (salt) they eat. Processed and prepared foods, including fast-food restaurant fare, are the main source of excess sodium in the American diet.

10. **If you drink alcoholic beverages, do so in moderation.** The government defines *moderation* as no more than one drink per day for women and two drinks per day for men. From a nutritional point of view, alcohol provides calories but no significant nutrients.

To know more about the nutritional value of foods you buy at the supermarket, especially processed foods, read the Nutrition Facts labels that are on every package, bottle, and can of food produced in this country and most others.

One good way to use the information on the Nutrition Facts labels is to compare different brands of the same types of foods while you're in the store. For instance, there are many different brands of frozen pizza. Have you ever compared the nutrition information from one to another? There might be big differences in the amount of calories, fat, and salt among different brands of similar types of food found in the supermarket. Comparing that information can help you make healthier choices.

WEB TALK: For more on food labeling, check out the Food and Drug Administration (FDA) site at:

www.cfsan.fda.gov

It also helps to read the ingredient lists on the labels of prepared foods to be sure you know what you're buying and eating. Fat, sugar, and salt sneak into your diet in many different forms, so if you're concerned about the overall amount of these substances in your diet, be sure to read the food labels on frozen, canned, and packaged foods very carefully.

Mindful Eating Mindful eating means nothing more than eating with awareness—being aware of what and how you're eating, paying attention to your food and how your body responds to it, and giving your food some calm attention. It is a Zen Buddhist principal that is part of a larger philosophy and practice of mindful living. Many Western health experts have borrowed the concept of mindful eating to teach people how to eat more consciously as a means to control weight.

Katy Kram, M.P.H., R.N., R.D., is a nutrition counselor at Freedom From Dieting in Columbus, Ohio, who teaches mindful eating to clients as a first step toward developing a healthier relationship with food. The object of mindful eating, she says, is not to get it right, or to eat a certain amount of food or a certain type of food, but simply to notice everything that's going on with your food while you're eating, without judgment or guilt. Her advice to anyone who wants to practice mindful eating is this:

- Prepare your food with care and attention.
- Turn off the TV and put away any other distractions.
- Place your food on the table with mindful attention.
- Relax, look at your food, smell it, sense your hunger for it, then eat it.
- As you eat, feel your food in your mouth, listen to the sound of it, and follow it as it goes down your throat.
- Eat slowly and consciously.
- If you're eating with others, avoid stressful conversations.
- Notice the feedback you get from your body as you are eating.
- When you finish eating, sit quietly. Ask yourself if you've had enough food, if the food was satisfying, if any feelings came up while you were eating, and how you feel now that you've finished eating.

Maintaining a Healthy Weight

To maintain a healthy weight, it's important to know your own healthy weight range. For different people who are the same height, there can be more than a 25-pound range that's considered healthy because different people have different amounts of muscle and bone that contribute to total weight. Men generally have more muscle and bone than women.

Dietitians and other health professionals sometimes use the following formulas to figure out weight goals for average men and women:

- **For women:** Start at a height of 5 feet and a weight of 100 pounds. Add 5 pounds for every inch of your height over 5 feet. Then give yourself a range of plus or minus 10 percent of that total. Subtract 10 percent for a small frame, and add 10 percent for a larger frame. For instance, if you're 5'7" tall, a healthy weight for you is 135 pounds, plus or minus 13 or 14 pounds.

- **For men:** Start at 5 feet and a weight of 106 pounds. Add 6 pounds for every inch of your height over 5 feet. Then give yourself a range of plus or minus 10 percent of that total. For instance, if you're 5'10" tall, a healthy weight for you is 166 pounds, plus or minus 16 or 17 pounds.

Note: There's nothing absolute about these formulas, and they sometimes give results that are lower than the figures given in most height/weight tables. These are simply figures to work from.

Whenever there's a sustained shift in the balance between how much food you eat and how much physical activity you get, your weight will start to move up or down. If your work schedule changes and you suddenly have no time to get to the gym, your balance shifts and eventually you'll start to feel heavier unless you also cut back on the amount of food you eat. At the same time, even if you work out consistently, if you also overeat consistently, you will probably start to gain weight.

you're not alone

I've spent most of my adult life going on and off diets, losing weight, gaining weight, losing weight, gaining it again. I am the epitome of the emotional eater—eating when I'm happy and eating when I'm upset—and once I start, I'm not able to stop, even when I know the next bite will make me ill. Until lately, though, I was always able to knock off the weight. I could always find a diet I hadn't already tried and some new exercise plan to help me get back in shape. Now, I work out three times a week and it makes me feel better, but it hasn't stopped me from eating. I feel trapped in a body that's 60 pounds overweight.

"When I was widowed ten years ago, friends kept bothering me to go out and meet new people. I wasn't interested, and all

When you're trying to maintain a healthy weight by eating a healthier diet, the secret to success is to remember what you've learned about healthy eating and not fall back into old, self-destructive eating habits. Some people don't eat often enough and by the time they sit down to a meal, they're so hungry they could eat a pound of rhinoceros meat. If you go more than five hours without a meal, you're likely to overeat when you finally do sit down. Other people eat all the time, even when they're not hungry. Think about why you're eating, and if you're not really hungry, try to do something different instead.

To maintain a healthy weight, you have to maintain your commitment to the lifestyle choices that helped you lose weight in the first place. That doesn't mean you have to spend the rest of your life doing the same things repeatedly. It means that the principals that applied to getting fit—maintaining a positive outlook, eating nutritionally balanced meals, getting some type of regular exercise, and never giving up on yourself—also apply to staying fit.

No matter how old you are, no matter how many diets you've been on, no matter how distorted your attitude toward eating has become, you can improve your attitude, get to a healthier weight, and stay there. For some people, that means getting off the diet merry-go-round and onto a treadmill. For others, it means joining

that pressure just added anxiety to an already stressful situation. So I ate and ate until I got much heavier. In retrospect, I realize I was eating my way to a 'safe weight,' a weight that I could hide behind. I wanted to be less attractive so people would leave me alone. It worked. But since then I've become active in my church and I've found a social life there. No one bothers me anymore about getting out. I finally feel it's safe to lose the weight, but I'm older now, and it's almost impossible.

"I still have stress in my life, and I still respond by eating. I know now that dieting isn't a real solution because my overeating has never really been about food. I need to figure out how to cope with stress without resorting to overeating. My next step is to find a good support group." *–Joan P.*

a support group or working with a counselor to get to the root of their emotional eating issues. For everyone, it means a life-long commitment to better health.

What You Can Do

When you're trying to develop a healthier relationship with food, that's the time to forget about fad diets and base your food choices on the Dietary Guidelines for Americans or a similar, conservative approach to eating that emphasizes variety, balance, and moderation.

☐ Calculate your healthy weight range. If your current weight is out of that range, consider making it a long-term goal to reach a healthier weight.

☐ Teach yourself what standard serving sizes look like so you'll always have a good idea of how much food is on your plate.

☐ Choose healthy, lower-calorie foods most of the time so you can eat indulgence foods at other times without feeling guilty.

☐ Respect calories, but don't obsess over them.

☐ Read the nutrition information and ingredient labels on packaged foods to become more aware of what you're eating.

☐ Create a relaxed environment where you can practice mindful eating.

Food Matters

When it comes to developing a healthier relationship with food, one secret to success is not being afraid to try. Fear can prevent you from making the necessary changes in your attitude and your eating habits. In this chapter, you will learn about the different fears that can prevent you from eating freely and enjoying the great pleasures of food. You'll find techniques for getting out of a food rut and suggestions for eating better with an open mind. Finally, you'll find additional techniques for simplifying your approach to food and establishing healthy eating habits.

Eating Without Fear

Some food addicts can find as many reasons *not* to eat as others can find reasons to *overeat*. Many people experience some type of eating disturbance based on fear. Experts believe one reason might be because we are so much more disconnected from the food we eat than ever before because our food is so far removed from its natural state. As a result, we fear the unknown. This is especially true of convenience foods and fast foods, because they go through so many stages of processing and handling before they end up in our mouths.

If you're overweight or obsessed with weight and body image, you might also suffer from a fear of social embarrassment, which prevents you from eating well. You might suffer from a fear of eating in public or doing your food shopping in public because you view what you're doing as potentially embarrassing behavior, and you're afraid you'll be judged by what's on your plate or in your shopping basket.

Restrictive dieting to lose weight or prevent weight gain triggers many irrational thoughts and false beliefs about food and food's effect on the body. You can end up being afraid of foods that won't harm you and are actually good for you. In addition to common fears of getting fat or getting thin, as discussed in Chapter 2, other types of fears that might guide your food choices and eating behavior are discussed in the following sections.

> **WEB TALK:** For information on diet and nutrition, see Columbia University's Health Internet Q&A Service at:
>
> ↑ www.goaskalice.columbia.edu

Fear of Carbohydrates Believing that starchy vegetables, grains, beans, or anything made from wheat flour or white sugar will make them fat, some people swear off pasta, rice, bread, potatoes, cereals, and most desserts. The truth is, you get fat by consuming more calories than you burn, regardless of where those calories come from. Eating carbohydrates in moderation as part of a balanced diet won't cause excess weight gain. Carbohydrates do cause your body to retain more water, so when you cut back on carbs, you immediately lose water weight but not fat.

Fear of Dietary Fat Although it's true that dietary fat is more easily converted to body fat than carbohydrates and proteins, some people become fat-phobic and avoid any food that contains any fat at all. But you can avoid fat and still be overweight because excess calories from *any* type of food—carbohydrate, protein, or fat—will make you fat. Many people also fear fat's effect on their health. That might be a more valid fear, but it can be taken to distressing extremes.

Fear of Unsafe Food If you listen to some news reports, you might start to believe the American food supply is hopelessly contaminated by microorganisms that can kill us or, at the very least, make us violently ill. And in fact, the Center for Disease Control estimates 76 million illnesses from foodborne disease each year and 5,000 deaths. That's considered safe compared to rates in many other countries. The sources of most foodborne illnesses are animal products, but bacteria can be transferred to other foods, so the illness itself could be a result of eating anything that's contaminated. Proper cleaning, storage, and cooking on the part of both the producer and the consumer help eliminate most of the risk.

When it comes to food safety, bacteria isn't our only health concern. Several years ago, many people panicked when Swedish scientists announced that french fries and other foods high in carbohydrates form *carcinogens* when they are fried, toasted, or otherwise cooked at high heats. These same toxins are also found in cigarette smoke. Since that initial announcement, government experts have recommended cooking these foods at lower temperatures while follow-up studies indicate that there is no danger. Stay tuned.

> **PsychSpeak**
>
> A **carcinogen** is a substance with the potential to cause cancer. **Food biotechnology** is the use of genetic engineering or traditional cross-breeding techniques to modify and create new foods.

Fear of Technology Chemical pesticides, irradiation, *food biotechnology,* and other modern agricultural systems supposedly designed to make our food safer and better can be scary to people who don't understand the technology or who simply don't want these methods applied to the food supply.

Most people get their information about food, nutrition, and health from magazines and other forms of media. When confronted with fearful news about food, keep in mind that what appears in the news is often either a diluted or exaggerated report of the

> **WEB TALK:** For up-to-the-minute news on food science and nutrition, check out:
>
> ↗ www.foodnavigator.com

actual research and findings. Even when a report about food is honest, the information usually is presented out of context. You're often not getting the complete story because most of the time, the full story is too long to print. If you have particular concerns, always consider the source of your information and be sure it's reliable and unbiased. Try to do more research and find the pros and cons of any food issue so you're not depending on one source for the advice you need to make diet decisions.

One would think that eating wholesome, natural foods can only be a good thing, but in fact, some people take healthful eating to such an extreme it becomes detrimental to their health. In a 1997 article written for *Yoga Journal,* Dr. Steven Bratman, a Colorado physician and alternative medicine expert, coined the term *orthorexia* to describe a pathological obsession with healthful eating and an avoidance of any food deemed unhealthful. Dr. Bratman himself had suffered from this condition at one time in his life, and he began to see that some patients in his alternative medicine practice displayed similar behavior.

GET PSYCHED

"Life is too short to spend it obsessing over healthy food. No one on their deathbed says, 'My one regret in life is that I ate too much ice cream.' Live a healthy life, yes, but don't obsess over it. Love, relationships, joy, creativity, service, play, spirituality: these matter infinitely more than what you put in your mouth." *—Steven Bratman, M.D., author of* Health Food Junkies *and many books about alternative medicine*

As he describes it, orthorexia begins with a normal desire to improve health or overcome chronic disease, but then the desire becomes an obsession. As the condition progresses, the act of eating pure, natural food takes on psycho-spiritual undertones and the orthorexic starts to devote more and more of his time to planning and eating meals. His internal dialogue is dominated by efforts to resist the temptation to eat foods, self-praise for success, self-condemnation for relapses, and feelings of superiority over others who have different eating habits.

The danger, Dr. Bratman points out, is not necessarily in the diet itself, but in the obsessive approach toward the diet. Even though the food is healthy, the attitude can become a source of psychological distress. In some cases, the obsessive need to avoid so many foods results in drastic weight loss, and at that point, orthorexia can become a serious, and potentially fatal, medical problem.

Climbing Out of Your Food Rut

In his book, *Out of the Box for Life,* psychotherapist Warren Berland says that fear, worry, and insecurity are not accurate reflections of our true self. These feelings have nothing to do with reality and keep us trapped in an emotional prison of our own making. Dr. Berland's metaphorical box represents that prison. We spend our lives climbing in and out of that box. For a food addict, hating your body, obsessing about food, eating for emotional reasons, and judging yourself and others because of weight are all examples of "in-the-box" thinking. When you're out of the box, Dr. Berland says, you know better and, therefore, make better choices. You stop looking for excuses not to change so you are able to set goals and move forward. When you're out of your box, you accept yourself and your body, you stop obsessing about food, and you don't subscribe to other people's ideas about what you should look like. You change your relationship with food by changing your relationship with yourself.

According to Dr. Berland, you have a choice. You can be stuck in the box of your old patterns and thoughts, or you can be out of the box. You do not have to stay trapped. You can make the choice to respond differently to emotional situations at any time.

First, you must recognize that you're in the box. Then, try to remember or imagine a time when you felt free of any doubts or fears. Ask yourself, "If I were out of the box right now, what would I do, how would I think?" From this perspective, it is easy to recognize what the most appropriate and healthful response to a situation would be.

GET PSYCHED

"It's important to update your old beliefs and images of yourself to prevent negative thinking and harmful and destructive self-talk from overwhelming your efforts to change."
—*Warren Berland, Ph.D., psychotherapist, New York City*

Out-of-the-box thinking can certainly be used to open your mind to new and different food choices. For a food addict, trying new foods can be a form of personal growth and a way of creating positive change, particularly if you have spent a great deal of time avoiding certain types of food. Climbing out of a food rut can be difficult for a food addict because it means climbing out of your comfort zone. It's important to remember, however, that growth and change only happen *outside* that zone.

Your first step out of a food rut might be to go shopping at a different grocery store and buy something new, something you've never tried before, or something familiar in a different flavor. Similarly, you could go to a restaurant and order something you've never eaten before. Taking a cooking class is also a great way to introduce yourself to new foods.

A Brave New World of Healthy Eating

When you understand how to eat well and healthier eating has become a habit, you can eat almost anything you want. More than ever, if you're healthy, there's no reason for you to eat processed and packaged "diet" foods that have been modified to remove fat or sugar. You might once have considered fat-free cookies, fat-free dressings, and other such products to be convenient "health foods" for dieters, but in fact, they are simply processed food products that often contain substances not found in any natural diet. They might not hurt your health, but there's very little about most of these products that's actually good for you. You might want to use some of these products occasionally, for the sake of convenience or for the sake of indulgence just as you use any other processed food, but they don't have to be—and shouldn't be—your mainstay. Now you can learn to strike a better balance between natural, wholesome foods and those convenience foods that make sense in your diet.

Researchers in the Department of Nutritional Sciences at Penn State University have studied practical ways people can incorporate high-fat foods into their diets and still keep their calories from fat at less than 30 percent. They found that a healthful diet can be realistic and include some of your favorite higher-fat foods such as cookies and french fries, as long as you balance those choices with foods such as lower-fat dairy products and lean meats. Because higher-fat dairy foods and cuts of meat supply such a large percentage of fat in so many people's diets, it's often more effective to make changes within these food groups than to give up regular cookies, chips, and other occasional treats. Generally, she says, when you decrease the fat in your diet, you decrease the calories. If you're trying to lose weight, you can lose a pound a week just by keeping your percentage of calories from fat at less than 30 percent.

Healthful eating means eating well most of the time and indulging some of the time. Once you trust yourself to make better choices overall, you can be more open-minded and creative about food and have more fun with it. When eating well becomes a habit, you become less concerned with the nutritional details of every food you put in your mouth, and you're able to look at the bigger picture of your diet and enjoy your food more. Here are several ways you can make healthy eating more interesting:

- Invest in some new cookbooks that contain appealing, wholesome recipes that call for mostly fresh ingredients.

- Buy some type of new food every time you go to the supermarket. With so many varieties of fruits and vegetables and so many different types of ethnic and imported products, it will be a long time before you run out of new ideas.

- Experiment with different types of cuisines, at home and when you're eating out. The cuisines of Japan, Thailand, Vietnam, and other Asian countries tend to be naturally lighter and healthier than typical American or European fare.

you're not alone

Off the Couch and Out in the World

"For most of my life I was thin. When I was a child, I didn't eat enough to gain any weight. We were pretty poor, and there were very few indulgences. Years later, when I had children of my own, I was very proud to hear my daughter's friend refer to me as 'the pretty mom.' I knew this was because I was in good shape, even after having three children. Kids know the difference between fat and skinny, and there were a lot of overweight adults on the suburban block where we lived.

"Before I knew it, my children grew up and left home, and I lost my husband at any early age. Up to this point I had always been pretty active. I never belonged to a gym, but I walked a lot and did yoga and other floor exercises at home. I had learned a lot about vegetarianism and ate that way most days of the week. But suddenly, it seemed I had lost interest in it all. I couldn't bring myself to do any exercises at all. I didn't want to cook. I didn't feel like going out for anything more than a trip to the supermarket, and when I did, what I mostly brought home was packaged and frozen dinners and snack food. All I wanted to do was watch TV. More and more I found myself sitting on the couch at night, watching television and eating snacks. As time went by, I would do this earlier and earlier in the day until at one point I found myself in front of the TV, in my pajamas and with potato chips in hand, at 3 in the afternoon. I laughed at myself, but inside I knew I couldn't go on this way. I had gained almost 30 pounds in eight months. I knew what I was doing was hiding away, feeling lonely and sorry for myself, and as a result, letting myself go.

"What worked for me was to get busy and rejoin the human race. I was very nervous, but with the help of a friend, I found an office job. That meant I needed some new clothes, and that made me face the fact that I had to lose weight. But once I started working and having more face-to-face contact with people, it wasn't hard to lose. My spirits lifted, and I began to take an interest in health again. I thought about going on a diet, but I knew that all I had to do was give up the TV snacks, go back to eating healthier foods, and get moving. Every day I ate lunch at the office and used up the rest of my lunch hour by going for a long walk. I didn't stop watching TV, but I did stop eating snacks at night. In less time than it took to put on the weight, I took it off. That was six years ago, and I haven't had a weight problem since." —*Julia T.*

Happy Meals

What used to be called *eating behavior modification*—taking real-life steps to change the way you respond to eating cues—is now sometimes called *mindful eating, rational eating,* or *conscious eating.* Regardless of what it's called, behavior modification is both a teaching process and a learning process. If you were to talk to a registered dietitian or another qualified nutrition counselor, that person would teach you techniques and strategies for developing better eating habits. If you're going it alone, you have to teach yourself. Either way, you have to go over these lessons again and again until your new behavior becomes second nature and a real change occurs in your eating habits. These classic behavior modification techniques can help you develop a happier, healthier relationship with food:

- Pick one place to eat, such as the kitchen or dining room table, and eat there whenever you have meals or snacks at home. The purpose of this exercise is to narrow down the places in your home that you associate with food and eating.

- Always set a complete table service, including a place mat and a pitcher of water, even if you're eating by yourself. This exercise helps you pay more attention to the fact that you're eating and to treat the food you eat with more respect. Try not to eat anything, not even a nibble, until the setting is complete.

- Whenever you eat, don't do anything else. Don't watch TV, read a magazine, pay bills, or talk on the phone. This exercise helps you focus on what you're eating and how much you're eating. It also helps eliminate some of the activities you might unknowingly associate with food.

WEB TALK: To download information on behavior modification and weight control, go to:

www.ilsi.org/misc/pkn82.pdf

- Make it a habit to drink a full glass of water when you sit down, before you begin to eat, and to drink water throughout your meal. This will help you feel fuller without adding calories to the meal.

- Use small plates, and serve yourself small portions. This exercise helps you get used to smaller portion sizes so that, in time, they will seem normal. (If you're still hungry, you can always go back for more.)

- Eat your food slowly, and put down your fork between every bite. Consciously chew every bit of food. The more slowly you eat, the more likely you are to eat a reasonable amount of food and to recognize when you're full.

- Extend the concept of mindful eating to include mindful food shopping and preparation. In other words, pay more attention to food when you buy it and cook it.

Keep It Simple Lack of time and busy, stressful schedules create a lot of tension in our lives, and as a result, preparing food and eating it can become just one more thing you have to do. You end up eating as quickly as you're doing everything else. When that happens, you lose all the pleasure of eating. It's one thing to simplify your life by having an occasional fast-food meal when you're out and using convenience foods at home, but if you're not taking the time to sit down, relax, and enjoy being with your food in a mindful manner, you're just adding more stress to your life. You're more likely to make poor food choices and overeat because you're not giving your meal your full attention. Eating on the run and eating while you're doing something else are quick-fix behaviors—the last thing a food addict needs! The way to develop a permanent, healthy relationship with food is to set aside time to do it right.

In addition to the mindful eating techniques and behavior modification strategies you've already learned, you can do several things to simplify your approach to healthful eating and improve the quality of your diet at the same time:

- Drink water with every meal.

- Snack on fresh fruits and vegetables.

- Collect recipes with short ingredient lists and simple cooking techniques.

- Try to prepare meals with what you have on hand to avoid the stress of running out for missing ingredients.

- Think color. Whenever you eat, fill your plate with a variety of (natural) colors and textures so you know you're getting a variety of nutrients.

Healthy Habits Every available statistic and most research reports point to the fact that restrictive weight loss diets discourage weight loss in the long run and can ultimately be dangerous to your physical and emotional health. Studies also show that restricting food causes the body to release stress hormones that can lead to health problems. Eating well, on the other hand, helps prevent health problems.

WEB TALK: For weight loss inspiration, tips, and support from others who've been there, check out:

www.3fatchicks.com

Resist the urge to go on the latest fad diet, and instead, come up with your own plan for making better food choices and eating mindfully. No one else's plan is going to work for you in the long run. You can also borrow whatever was sensible, inspiring, or appealing from old diet plans and incorporate that into your own plan that focuses on eating well. Some weight loss diets, even fad diets, do have their good points. They provide direction, require a certain amount of discipline, and often include good tips for changing eating behavior. But generally speaking, diets do not teach good eating habits. Most are not designed for long-term use, and so sticking to them for more than a few weeks or months is difficult. They also tend to emphasize good food/bad food messages, making you feel virtuous for eating some foods and sinful for eating others. That message is a real pitfall in escaping a food addiction. The idea that some foods are good and some sinful is a myth. Unless you have a medical reason for avoiding a particular type of food or food group, any food can fit into a healthy eating plan.

Another problem with dieting is that it's narrowly focused on losing weight. A more holistic approach will not only help you lose weight but also improve your overall health, mental health, and lifestyle. Your goal should be to become as physically and emotionally healthy as you can be, not as skinny as you can be.

Drinking plenty of water throughout the day is a must in any healthy eating plan because water is the single most essential nutrient in your diet. You can live for weeks without food, but you can only live a few days without water. Health experts encourage drinking plenty of water throughout the day because you need a constant flow to keep your blood flowing, your joints moving, your muscles working, and your lungs breathing. You need water to digest food, carry nutrients to all your body cells, and carry toxins out of your body. Every part of your body, even your bones, contains water and needs a continuous supply. Drinking plenty of water can also help you with weight control because it helps you feel full. In addition, sometimes when you think you're hungry, you might actually be thirsty. If you suspect your hunger might not be real, try having a glass of water and waiting twenty minutes to see if you still feel hungry.

you're not alone

My weight came on slowly, over a ten-year period. If there was a reason for it, it might have been work stress, but I think it was mostly because I never paid much attention to how much I ate. By the time I decided to do something about my weight, I was thirty-three and needed to lose 25 pounds. I'm very independent, not a "joiner," so I couldn't see myself signing up for a weight loss program or joining any type of group. I wasn't exactly sure what to do, but when I looked at diet books and magazine articles, I also couldn't see myself sticking to any of the plans for more than a day. So I just decided to figure it out on my own.

"The first week, I did use a diet I found in a magazine as a guide so I would know how much food equals 1,500 calories.

Here are some tips to help you develop a water habit:

- Whenever you see a water fountain, take a sip.
- Carry a water bottle with you wherever you go.
- Wake yourself up in the morning with a glass of water—before you have coffee or anything else to drink.
- Add a squeeze of fresh lemon or lime to your water to give it some flavor.
- If you're not automatically served water in restaurants, ask for it as soon as you sit down.
- Eat plenty of watery foods such as lettuce, cucumber, tomatoes, citrus fruit, watermelon, and yogurt.
- If you drink beverages that contain alcohol or caffeine, have a glass of water or seltzer between drinks.

You probably don't need anyone to tell you what's wrong with drinking alcohol to excess, but here's a reminder. In addition to packing on calories and interfering with your body's ability to metabolize fat, too much alcohol can raise your risk for high blood pressure, stroke, heart disease, certain types of cancer, accidents, and death. You could end up with cirrhosis of the liver and brain damage, not to mention malnutrition. If you're a heavy drinker, you might be filling up on calories from alcohol rather

I liberalized the menus to include foods I like to eat, and because I don't eat breakfast, I used those calories for desserts and snacks. The one thing I did that was very different for me was to pay attention to what I was eating, whenever I ate. In the past, I never gave food a second thought. Now, even though I've kept the weight off for several years, I still pay a lot more attention to food.

"My story is a little boring, and I probably don't qualify as a real food addict, but I did get rid of those 25 extra pounds and I don't have any worries about them coming back. I think my tip that will help some people is to trust yourself to do your own thing. I did, and it worked."
–Jennifer B.

than from food, and you might not be getting enough of the nutrients you need.

For many people, food is about much more than eating. How we cook and share food often reflects the love we feel for our families and friends; it is our connection to other people. For some people, food choices reflect personal ethics and politics; for others they reflect a social status. Some of these are very important, personal connections. If your eating behavior is unhealthy or your thoughts about food have become obsessive, however, you might have to put aside some of your personal beliefs to overcome your food addiction.

I'd like to forget about diets, but I still need to lose weight. Where do I start?

First, focus on not gaining any more weight by developing better eating habits. Here are some tips for taking a nondieting approach to weight control:

- Plan ahead to avoid random eating and to be sure you always have healthy food available at home and at work.
- Review or learn more about calories, portion control, and healthy eating.
- Collect healthful recipes—or better yet, take healthy-cooking classes.
- Develop schedules for eating and exercising that suit your lifestyle, and try to stick to them. Plan your meals around the times of the day when you're normally most hungry. That's when you should be eating full, balanced meals.
- Prepare as much of your food at home as you can and prepare it in healthful ways.
- Use the Internet or subscribe to fitness and healthy-cooking magazines so you will regularly be stimulated by new ideas.
- Think ahead. If you're having a hard time sticking to healthier habits, ask yourself, "Do I want to be in better shape or worse shape a year from now?"

What You Can Do

When you overcome your food and weight fears, you can begin to simplify your approach to diet, enjoy your food more, feel less stressed out about food and eating, and at the same time open your mind to new ways of eating.

☐ Begin to face any fears you have by collecting as much reliable information as you can about diet, nutrition, and food safety.

☐ Understand why small changes in your eating behavior can result in big changes in your relationship with food.

☐ Create your own personal plan for eating well.

☐ Be sure the information you collect about food and nutrition comes from reliable sources.

☐ Try to be open-minded about different types of foods so you can get more variety into your diet.

☐ To reduce the stress of trying to lose weight, wean yourself off dieting and try a more natural, long-term approach to eating.

Part 3

Breaking the Bonds

It takes a lot of hard work and courage to make the changes necessary to break free from a food addiction. Part 3 teaches you how to set goals, break old habits, identify your eating triggers, and move on to a healthier relationship with food. You'll also learn how to set personal boundaries and where to turn for help if you need it.

Making Changes

The more flexible you are and the more easily you accept change, the easier it will be to develop a healthier relationship with food and improve your lifestyle. As you feel your life improving, you will experience many changes in the way you see yourself and in the way you see the world around you. These might all be changes for the better, but they can be scary simply because they are different. You will learn to cope. You'll be thinking in new ways and doing many things differently than you've ever done them before. Remember, fear of change can prevent you from letting go of self-destructive habits and truly enjoying the rest of your life. You don't have to let that happen.

The Six Stages of Change

According to Dr. James Prochaska, professor of Clinical and Health Psychology at the University of Rhode Island, there are six stages of change we all go through before we completely work through any problem. Whatever type of food addiction you're dealing with, you're at one of the following stages. It might take some time to get to the next stage. Along the way, you might hit some bumps or even go backward before you're ready to move forward again. That's normal. Dr. Prochaska's six stages of change and what they mean to a food addict are described in the following sections.

Precontemplation In this initial stage, you're not even thinking about change. You might think it's impossible; you don't think you have a big enough problem; or you might be in denial, assuming the problem will resolve itself some day. You might even resent anyone else's suggestion that you have a problem. You've acknowledged the problem, but you're not intending to take action in the near future. You still need to muster up the courage it takes to make changes in your relationship with food.

Contemplation This is the period when you begin to acknowledge that you have an unhealthy relationship with food. You're weighing the effort it will take to solve your problem against whether or not it's worth the effort. This is a tough stage for many people because you intend to take action sometime in the near future, but you might still get stuck here for months, years, or even the rest of your life. If you're already feeling discouraged or demoralized and think you won't be successful, you might spend a very long time weighing whether or not it's worth the effort.

Preparation You've made the decision to act, and you're gathering information. You're making phone calls and searching the web. You're emotionally prepared to make lifestyle changes. In this stage, you're finding out exactly what you need to do to start developing a healthier relationship with food. You're making plans and setting goals. You might be openly discussing your plans with other people. You're laying the groundwork for change.

Action Now, you're actively doing something about your problem. You're trying out lifestyle changes. Maybe you've stopped buying trigger foods, joined a gym, or made an appointment to speak with a counselor or a

> **GET PSYCHED**
>
> "If you lose weight by diet and exercise alone and you don't change your mindset, you're probably going to gain it back. You have to look at why you overeat and find your own personal motivation for change. That's where the real solution lies." *—Anne M. Fletcher, registered dietitian and author of* Sober for Good *and the* Thin for Life *books*

dietitian. During this stage you might need a great deal of under-standing and support from family and friends.

Maintenance You've made real lifestyle changes, and you're sticking with them. You're learning to work through obstacles. For some food addicts, this is the final stage of change. You might spend the rest of your life here. If you have a lapse and find your-self going back to stage 3 or even stage 2 again, be careful not to fall back into old, self-destructive habits such as self-blame and negative self-talk. Backsliding happens to just about everyone.

Recycling/Relapse Some people with food addictions get to the maintenance stage and stay there, but for most, the first attempt at developing a healthier relationship with food doesn't work out as planned. You might have fallen back into old habits. This stage is a learning opportunity. You're learning about damage control. Let yourself go back to where you feel comfortable and move through the stages again.

you're not alone

To the Depths and Back Again

"These days, I can hold my head up high and feel good about myself and love and accept myself as someone with a food addiction. But it hasn't always been that way. I had to learn how to live a life that's free and happy, and it took a long time.

"I was morbidly obese most of my life. I ate compulsively and was bingeing out of control at a very early age. I weighed in at 160 pounds in third grade and was 270 pounds by the time I got to seventh grade. For thirty-seven years I struggled with food and weight. I went on many diets, lost hundreds of pounds over the years, and gained hundreds back.

"One day I decided to have just one piece of pie, and that started a binge that lasted six weeks. During those six weeks I gained 56 pounds. At that point I started seriously planning my own funeral because I knew I was killing myself and felt it was just as well because everyone around me would be better off if I were dead. I was thirty-eight years old, and that's when I went into a hospital-based

continues

147

continued

treatment center for five weeks, followed by a halfway house for another three months. That's where my transformation began.

"Learning to accept myself began with knowing who I am as a food addict and understanding that I'm not a normal eater. I learned that I ate for emotional reasons and that certain foods did for me what drugs and alcohol did for other addicts. I learned that I had to abstain from these foods.

"Once I was out of treatment, I had to make many big changes in my life. I had to look at my addiction as someone else would have to look at another type of disease. I had to build my life around what I needed to do for my recovery, rather than fit my recovery into the rest of my life. I had to find new friends, better role models. I started weighing and measuring my food. I realized I had to turn to help outside myself to get the support I needed to sustain my recovery and move on to a fuller life. I did a lot of self-educating and joined a 12-step program. I went to meetings every day. I spoke to my boss about the adjustments I had to make and changed my work schedule to accommodate my new needs.

"My top weight was 340 pounds. I once had a 63-inch hip measurement. Now, at 5'5", I weigh 145 pounds, and I've maintained that weight for fourteen years. This disease took me to the depths and back again. While I have a great deal of compassion for that lonely young girl who tried so hard and felt so bad about herself and blamed herself for so long, I have moved on from the shame and the self-blame. I know now that my food addiction wasn't my fault and that there are so many other people out there like me.

"In fact, I'm now trained as a relapse prevention specialist and work with people like me all the time, facilitating recovery groups and helping out at food dependency workshops around the country. The fact that I can now be of service to others is the gift my addiction gave me, because through my work I began to truly see wonderful qualities about myself that were hidden by my obsession with food." *—Mary F.*

Setting Goals

You can and should set goals in several different areas of your life. There are state-of-mind, or psychological, goals; behavioral goals; food goals; and exercise goals. All these goals for change are important to someone with a food addiction.

State-of-mind goals are the goals you set for changing the way you think about yourself, raising your self-esteem, and accepting yourself just as you are. They might include stopping all negative self-talk, working on your body image, or getting professional counseling. Behavioral goals are action-oriented goals, such as eating slowly, avoiding the vending machines at your job, reading nutrition labels on packaged foods, or not wearing clothes that are too big in an attempt to hide your weight. Food goals are about eating a healthier diet. They might include eating more vegetables, measuring your food to learn about healthy portion sizes, or eating healthy snacks. Exercise goals are all about increasing your physical activity. These might include taking a walk after dinner every night, taking a hike, learning to swim, or joining a gym.

WEB TALK: For more on goal-setting, visit the Partnership for Healthy Weight Management website at:

▲ www.consumer.gov/weightloss

All good goals have a few things in common. They should …

- **Be specific.** Rather than say, "I want to feel better about myself," say, "I'm going to improve my self-esteem."

- **Be realistic.** Be sure you can really do what you're setting out to do. If your goal is to get to a gym three times a week, be sure your schedule really allows for that time. If not, set your goal for twice a week until your schedule lightens.

- **Be as enjoyable as possible.** Reaching your goals might be hard work at times, but it shouldn't be downright painful. If one of your goals is to include more vegetables in your diet, learn how to prepare them in delicious new ways by taking a cooking class, asking friends or family for favorite recipes, or getting a recommendation for a good vegetable cookbook.

When you set goals for yourself, establish long-term goals and keep them in mind, but focus more on the shorter-term goals that will get you to your end goals. Don't spend a lot of time thinking about where you want to be six months or a year from now. For now, think about changes you want to make within the next couple weeks or even the next couple days. That way, your expectations will be reasonable, you're more likely to reach your goals, and you're less likely to be disappointed.

What Do You Want? To get what you want, you have to know what you want. You need a plan. When you know what you want, you can establish goals for the future. Your goals are the groundwork you lay for a healthier, more positive lifestyle. Setting goals helps you define and articulate the expectations you have for yourself and the plans you have for changing your relationship with food.

You might have experience setting goals at your job. "What are your goals?" is the one question that appears on all self-evaluation forms. Personal goals aren't much different from professional goals except that you establish them for your own personal use. They provide focus and direction. They're about growth. Goals are a way of measuring success.

Q & A

How can I be sure I'm setting reasonable goals for myself?
First of all, figure out where you are in the process of change and be sure you're committed to making changes. If you're not in the action stage, you're not ready to make changes. But you might be ready to start thinking seriously about the types of changes you want to make. Start off with short-term goals that are easy to accomplish. Set objectives that will improve your quality of life. Be sure to set achievable goals that include changes you can live with for the rest of your life.

Short-Term Goals Short-term goals are objectives you can expect to reach within a week or two. They are stepping stones to your intermediate- and long-term goals. For instance, if your long-term plan is to improve self-esteem and your intermediate goal toward that end is to stop negative self-talk, then your short-term goal might be to stop saying "I'm fat" every time you look in the mirror and instead say something like, "I like the way I look in black pants."

Short-term goals are useful when you're feeling impatient with yourself and need to feel like you're taking charge of the situation. Set a goal for today and think about what you need to do to achieve it. Here are some more examples of short-term goals for developing a healthier relationship with food and improving your lifestyle:

- Make an appointment for a complete physical checkup.
- Eat three vegetables with dinner.
- Carry a water bottle.
- Walk somewhere instead of taking the car.
- Buy a self-help book.

Intermediate-Term Goals Intermediate-term goals are where you want to be when you're about halfway to the finish line. In other words, these are mid-term ambitions that are closer to realization than your long-term goals. If your long-term goal is to change your eating habits for the better, one of your intermediate-term goals might be to learn how to cook healthier foods. Here are some other ideas for intermediate goals:

- Learn how to meditate.
- Build a healthy cookbook collection.
- Find volunteer work to fill extra time.
- Join a biking club.
- Walk 5 miles a day.

Long-Term Goals Long-term goals look at the bigger picture and help you define your end results. For instance, one of your long-term goals might be to improve your self-esteem. That's going to take some time. Another long-term goal might be to reach a healthy weight. That's going to take a lot of planning and a lot of small steps (short-term objectives) along the way.

Give yourself all the time you need to reach your long-term goals. Following are some other long-term goals you might set:

- Improve physical health.
- Reduce stress.
- Get back in shape.
- Expand social circle.
- Find diversions from eating.
- Accept myself as I am.

Keeping Track Setting goals, writing them down, and tracking them as you go are all helpful steps toward positive change. Writing down your goals and putting them where you will see them will help remind you what your goals are and what you need to do to reach them. You can write your goals on a scrap of paper in your wallet or in a separate section in your journal. You can hang your goals on a bulletin board or, better yet, on the refrigerator door. A goal organizer looks something like this:

Area	Goal	How to Get There	Progress
Psych.	*buy self-help food book*	*go to bookstore*	✓ *bought Intuitive Eating*
Psych.			
Behav.	*eat only at kitchen table*	*stop eating at desk*	
Behav.			
Food	*more vegetables*	*stop at farmer's market*	
Food			
Exercise	*walk more*	*drive less*	✓ *walked to dentist*
Exercise			✓ *walked to post office*

you're not alone

Getting There

"It's impossible to grow up in an Italian American household and not have a love-hate relationship with food. The little old lasagna-ladling grandma isn't just a stereotype. She really does believe that the more she cooks, the more she loves you—and the more you eat, the more you love her back.

"Along with an overabundance of food in our home came a family obsession with weight. During much of my childhood, my mother recorded her weight every day on our kitchen calendar for all to see. One younger aunt would swallow whatever the fad diet was that week and often enlist her nieces to join her. The summer I was seventeen, I was on her version of the Atkins Diet, eating salami omelets and other not-so-classic high-protein diet fare.

"This same aunt once held up a photograph of me and said, 'You look thin in this picture.' Of course, I really was thin; it wasn't just a trick of the camera. But my aunt didn't acknowledge it, and I started to question it. That began a cycle of my eating stringently. I would eat one meal a day. Soon I started bingeing on party-size bags of potato chips and full containers of ice cream. Thanks to early instruction from my aunt, I also 'binged' on protein, devouring the equivalent of four servings of meat at a time.

"I went on like this for several years until, eventually, I joined Weight Watchers. That's when my eating habits and attitudes began to change. I learned what a healthy portion size is and that carbohydrates are not evil. I figured out that I was using food to deal with almost every emotion. I realized that a phone call from almost any member of my family is a trigger that sends me straight to the kitchen.

"I also learned how to deal with cravings by avoiding trigger foods. I still crave the same foods I used to binge on—chips and ice cream. But because I'm lazy, I won't go out of my way to get my hands on whatever I'm craving. I simply eat whatever is in front of me. So to limit temptation, I don't keep any of my trigger foods around, and I rarely have any high-fat foods in the house at all. The mere thought of a salami omelet makes me gag at this point, so it seems I've tamed the protein monster inside me. But after a phone call from a family member, I do sometimes find myself standing in my kitchen with a mouthful of cashews wondering how they got there, and why. That's when it helps to have a sense of humor!

"The most important thing I've learned is that by setting goals and making a commitment to myself, I *can* make changes, both in my eating habits and in my attitude about my body and myself. I can finally say that I'm in charge now and I'm enjoying every minute of it. It's still hard sometimes not to use food to punctuate every mood— happy or sad, angry or insecure—but my desire to stay healthy is stronger than my need to overeat. For years, I've channeled my urges into t'ai chi exercises or meditation, which require control and concentration. They seem to calm my cravings and generally improve my mental well-being, and the feeling stays with me. Until the next phone call, that is!" —*Cheryl S.*

Breaking Old Habits

Habits, including eating habits, are behavior patterns acquired by repetition. Having dinner at the same time every day is an eating habit. Positive or negative self-talk is a habit you acquire by telling yourself the same thing over and over again. Bingeing on the same food again and again is a habit. To break the destructive habits that support an unhealthy relationship with food, you must be committed to making lifestyle changes. Otherwise, you won't be successful.

Unlike your brain chemistry, genetic background, and psychological makeup, your habits are something you can control on your own. Breaking habits isn't easy, however, because it involves change. Behavior modification is the method most often used to break old, self-destructive eating habits by replacing them with new, healthier habits. By creating new habits, you're teaching yourself to make changes in the way you think and act in your relationship with food.

Developing new and improved habits often means establishing new rules for yourself. Suppose you want to develop better eating habits at home. Your new rules might include not eating anywhere except the dining room table or not doing anything else—like answering the phone or watching TV—during a meal so you remain conscious of how much you're eating.

To break the habit of, say, stopping at a fast-food restaurant on your way home from work every day, think about your options. You could take a different route home, but you still need to eat. A better plan for finding a substitute habit might be to scout out healthier restaurants in your area.

Like goals, new habits must be realistic if you're going to stick with them. It's also important to introduce change gradually. Don't try to break all your bad habits at once!

GET PSYCHED

"Don't be afraid to develop healthier eating and lifestyle habits just because you've been unsuccessful in the past. It's another time, and you're at another stage in your life. You might be better prepared now to make the necessary commitment." –*Laurie Deutsch Mozian, M.S., R.D., nutrition counselor, Kingston, New York*

154

Remember to monitor yourself as you go along to be sure you're not slipping back into old habits.

Keeping a Journal

Anyone who has ever kept a personal journal or diary knows how therapeutic it can be to write down your innermost thoughts on paper. Although there's no science that explains exactly how or why journaling helps people, psychological studies have shown that most people who write about difficult events in their lives get and stay healthier than people who don't. For a food addict, journaling means writing your way through emotional pain rather than eating your way through it.

Researchers speculate that, for some people, writing about difficult events in a journal improves their well-being because it allows them to examine the events more closely and helps them find out and understand more about who they are. Gaining a better sense of self can, in turn, reduce certain types of stress and anxiety.

Writing in a journal helps you explore feelings and keep track of your progress toward the changes you'd like to make. Your journal is a good place to set up your goal organizer and list any habits you're trying to break. If you use it well, write in it every day, and refer to it often, your journal will keep you mindful of your intention to develop a healthier relationship with food.

A food diary is a type of journal that helps you examine your eating habits and patterns. It helps you keep track of what, when, why, and how much you actually eat so you can identify problem areas. Once you recognize patterns that are causing problems, you can take steps to change them.

Janis Jibrin, M.S., R.D., a Washington, D.C.–based dietitian and author of *The Unofficial Guide to Dieting Safely,* finds that by keeping a food diary, her clients learn about problems they weren't even aware of. For instance, she says, some of her clients have learned why, when they've been "good" all day by eating just a banana for breakfast and a salad for lunch, they wind up bingeing throughout the evening. Until they kept a written record and went over it with a dietitian, they didn't realize they were heading into the evening hours with only a few hundred calories under their belt. Many people are also able to make immediate links between stress, boredom, or other forms of unhappiness and eating once they've kept a record of when and why they eat. They can then learn to substitute coping mechanisms other than food. Without their food records, however, they couldn't have made those all-important connections.

You can also use a food diary to record your emotions and the day-to-day situations that trigger problem eating. Everyone has different triggers, and your diary will make you more aware of the specific foods, emotions, and behavior that affect you. A food diary can even help you eat less, if that's your goal, because you might think twice about overeating when you know you're keeping a written record. Later on, you can use your food diary as a tool to measure your progress.

GET PSYCHED

"You know *what* to eat, so how come you're still overeating, undereating, or falling into other destructive nutrition patterns? Your diary can point out things you never knew about how and why you eat the way you do. Once you become aware of weak areas, you can start making useful changes and setting new goals."
–*Janis Jibrin, M.S., R.D., Washington, D.C., dietitian and author,* The Unofficial Guide to Dieting Safely

To create a food diary, you can use a section of your regular journal, a calendar, a small spiral notebook, or just a few pieces of paper stapled together. Whatever you use, it should be easy to carry and have enough space for at least a week's worth of entries. Across the top of each page, write the following categories: Time, Food, Amount, Reason, Location, Partner(s), Time Spent Eating.

Every time you eat, whether it's a full meal, a planned snack, or a quick bite on the run, record the following information in your food diary:

- Under Time, write the time you started eating.

- Under Food, write the type of food you ate. Give each food its own line, and try to break down mixed foods such as spaghetti and meatballs; record their individual components so you can better judge how much you actually eat of different types of foods.

- Under Amount, fill in the quantity or weight of each food you listed in the Food column.

- Under Reason, write down your motivation for eating. A wide range of answers is possible here. If you're eating because it's lunchtime or because you feel hungry, you'll just write "lunch" or "hungry." If you're eating for emotional reasons, you'll write in something like "lonely," "bored," or "angry."

- Under Location, fill in where you were when you were eating.

- Under Partner(s), write down the names of anyone you were eating with.

- Under Time Spent Eating, fill in the total amount of time you actually spent eating.

It's a good habit to write down everything as soon as you eat so you don't forget. For that reason, it helps to use a portable diary. Try to keep an accurate record, but don't make yourself crazy. If your diary is incomplete at the end of the day, try to fill it in from memory. If you miss a day, start again the next day. Don't be afraid to keep an honest diary. You're the only one who has to see it, and there's no reason to hide any information from yourself.

Your food diary will look something like this sample:

Time	Food	Amount	Reason	Location	Partner(s)	Time Spent Eating
7 A.M.	bagel	1/2	breakfast	kitchen	Molly	10 min.
	jam	2 TB				
	0g	1 c				
10:30 A.M.	apple	1	snack break	desk	alone	5 min.
1 P.M.	veg. burger on a bun	1	lunch	coffee shop	David	45 min.
	sweet potato fries	1 c				
	iced tea	2 c				
4 P.M.	cheese	2 oz.	bored & hungry	desk	alone	10 min.
	crackers	8				
6 P.M.	lemon chicken	1 breast	dinner		Molly, Ruby, Sabrina	30 min.
	rice	2 c				
	broccoli	1 c				
8 P.M.	pumpkin pie	2 slices	de-stress	living room	alone	15 min.
	milk	1 c		couch		

What You Can Do

Changing your relationship with food takes a lot of self-reflection. Dig down deep in your heart and figure out what you need to do to make lasting lifestyle changes.

- ☐ Figure out which stage of change you're in.
- ☐ Reflect on your goals.
- ☐ Figure out what you want.
- ☐ Start setting realistic goals.
- ☐ Keep your long-term goals in mind while acting on your short-term goals.
- ☐ Use a journal to keep track of your feelings, your goals, your eating habits, and anything else related to changing your relationship with food.

Identifying Eating Triggers

It's impossible to get through the day without running into something that makes you crave food. You walk into a deli for a cup of coffee, and you smell bacon sizzling on the grill. The snack cart shows up at 10 A.M. every morning, and you can see the doughnuts from your desk. Your co-worker brings in a bag of candy. You drive by your favorite fast-food restaurant every day after work. Eating triggers are everywhere, and that makes it tough to resist overeating. In this chapter, you'll learn about different types of eating triggers and how to cope with the ones that affect you.

Many situations and emotions trigger us to eat when we're not really hungry or overeat when we've had enough. You might be encouraged to overeat at family get-togethers. You might feel you need to eat to fit in at a social occasion. You might eat in response to moods or feelings, such as when you're angry or nervous about something. You might eat because you feel bad about yourself, even if the thing that's making you feel bad is overeating! You might eat just because food or an advertisement for food is right in front of you. You might eat simply out of habit, because it's 4 in the afternoon and you always have a snack at 4 in the afternoon. All these triggers can make you feel hungry, even though, physically, you might not need food. Knowing your triggers helps you distinguish false hunger from the real thing.

Food Triggers

The mere sight or smell of real food at home, at work, in a restaurant, as you're walking through the mall—or anywhere for that matter—can make you want to eat when you're not actually hungry. A food trigger is a physical urge to eat that's very hard to avoid because it's right there, assaulting your senses. Some common food triggers that can tempt you to eat or overeat include the following:

- The smell of food cooking, whether it's your own or someone else's.

- Seeing food, such as in a bakery window, on a buffet, or in your own refrigerator.

- Vending machines filled with candy, snacks, or soft drinks in schools, offices, even hospitals.

- Your favorite comfort foods at a family gathering.

- Favorite foods such as bagels or favorite categories of food such as carbohydrates. If you overeat certain foods at home, you might want to keep them in short supply.

you're not alone

Staying on Track

"I don't think I'm an emotional eater; I just like to eat. A lot of my family members are overweight, and I didn't grow up learning very good eating habits. When I was in my early 20s I was about 20 pounds overweight. I decided I didn't want to be heavy like the rest of my family, so I joined a weight loss center and went on my first diet. I couldn't stand the food plan, but I stuck with it, and three months later, I was 18 pounds lighter. I quit the center and tried to keep off the weight on my own but that didn't work, and within a year I gained back 25 pounds.

"Next, I went on a diet I saw in a magazine and started walking long distances for exercise. Soon my walking turned into slow jogging, and I was starting to look and feel really good. I read a lot about losing weight and getting fit and instead of following the magazine diet to a 'T,' I made up my own diet plan that was similar but that included more foods I like to eat. I've been following that basic diet plan (for the most part) for four years, and I get some sort of exercise every day, even if it's just walking a mile or so. When I get bored, I look in fitness magazines for motivation and food magazines for new recipes and diet plans.

"I think the reason I've been able to keep off the weight this time is that I was really ready to make a commitment to myself. I'm almost thirty, more determined now to keep the weight off, and more interested in my own health than when I was younger. I also stay on top of it. I don't obsess about food. I pretty much eat what I want, but I don't let myself forget what it's like to be 25 pounds heavier and that helps me not overeat.

"Ever since I was a teenager, I've kept a journal. At the weight loss center, I learned about keeping a food diary and writing down weight loss goals and logging trigger situations. That helped me look at my eating patterns and see them more clearly and figure out the changes I needed to make in my life as well as in my diet. I don't keep separate diaries and logs anymore like I did while I was trying to lose weight, but I notice that my regular journal entries almost always contain something about food." *—Marianne G.*

Behavioral Triggers

Behavioral triggers are somewhat more controllable than food triggers. They are habits or activities that might have become associated with unhealthy eating in your mind—for example, snacking while you cruise the Internet or stopping at the same coffee shop for pie and ice cream. You can learn to divorce the activity from the food habit you want to stop. You can work on your computer without eating at the same time, for example. You can take a different route home after work at night so you don't pass your favorite coffee shop or fast-food restaurant on days when you're better off eating at home. Other behavioral triggers you might face include the following:

- Passive activities such as watching TV, working on the computer, or reading a magazine. When you get up for a commercial, instead of heading for the kitchen, do some stretching exercises.

- Driving in your car. Eating while driving is similar to any type of eating on the run, and it generally means you're not paying much attention to what or how much you're eating.
- Going to a party. There might be more junk food at a party than healthy food. If you're trying to eat better, contribute a tray of cut veggies and yogurt dip to the party fare, and pick from this platter for the evening.
- Eating out of habit. How often do you stand in front of an open refrigerator, mindlessly checking out the contents?
- Walking into the kitchen. This trigger is self-explanatory!
- Not sleeping. When you're tired from not sleeping the night before, you might overeat during the day to try to get more energy and keep yourself awake.
- Procrastination. Eating can be a distraction from something else you don't want to do.

Emotional Triggers

As you already know, if you attach food to your feelings, you're an emotional eater. You might use food and eating to feel better, cover up bad feelings, or cope with overwhelming feelings, even if they're positive. Emotional overeaters often report being in a "food fog" that anesthetizes their feelings while they are eating.

Everyone experiences emotional eating sometimes. But if you regularly eat in response to your emotional state rather than your physical needs, you're at risk of becoming obese or developing a full-fledged eating disorder. It is essential for an emotional eater to identify the specific feelings and circumstances that trigger overeating.

Once you identify your own personal patterns of emotional eating, you can start to separate your eating behavior from the emotions that trigger it and learn to experience your feelings without having to turn to food. This separation is an important step because it enables you to see the problem more clearly and provides an opportunity to solve emotional eating at its source. You can decide to avoid, ignore, or face the situations that trigger your eating behavior. Or you can find other ways of coping with the feelings that are healthier and make you feel better about yourself.

Boredom, guilt, disappointment, stress, job insecurity, and even happiness are all feelings that can trigger emotional eating. Try paying more attention to how you feel before you eat. The trick is to first deal with the situation that triggers the mood *before* you get to the food. Here are a few typical emotional triggers and some foodless suggestions to combat them:

- **Anger.** Some studies show that anger is the top eating trigger for women. Try taking a few deep breaths or counting to 10. Then try to articulate your feelings in a calm, clear manner to get them off your chest.

- **Family interaction.** Just being with family members is enough to make some people overeat. That could be due to traditional eating habits or anxiety from being with your family. Some people simply make it a point to spend a little less time with their families because the after-effects are just too devastating.

- **Low self-esteem.** Think back on your day and focus on what went right about it. Think about your accomplishments and any steps you took to break your food addiction.

- **Performance anxiety.** If you're nervous about taking a test or having to make a presentation or speaking to a group, you might eat in an attempt to "swallow" your anxiety. Take a deep breath, and practice, practice, practice.

- **Feeling like "I deserve this."** If you've had a particularly hard day or you've been depriving yourself of foods you enjoy, you might feel you deserve a special treat. Try rewarding yourself with something other than food (see the following "Reward Yourself!" section for some hints).

- **Depression.** Exercise is the best self-help for sadness and mild depression. Severe depression may be the result of a chemical imbalance in your brain. If you think you suffer from clinical depression, speak to your doctor.

Environmental Triggers

Like behavioral triggers, environmental triggers are external factors that affect your eating habits, and as such, they are somewhat easier to control than internal triggers that are rooted in your emotions. Some common environmental triggers include the following:

- **Cultural expectations.** It can be difficult to "break the mold" and change your eating habits when you're with family or friends who eat in traditional ways. For advice on how to handle situations with relatives and other people who expect you to eat in ways you would rather not, see Chapter 12.

- **Eating with certain people.** Some people encourage you to eat more than you would normally.

- **Seeing a television commercial featuring food.** When this happens, it's often tempting to get up and go into the kitchen for food.

- **Seeing a recipe or food advertisement.** The purpose of food photography in magazines or in ads is to make food look enticing so you'll want to buy the food or try the recipe.

- **Being out in cold weather.** Cold weather increases hunger.

- **Office co-workers bringing in goodies to share or sell.** Oh, those Girl Scout cookies!

- **Time of day.** You might eat simply because you're used to eating at particular times of the day.

- **Going out to eat.** If you're eating out for a special occasion, you want to enjoy a special meal. You probably don't want to watch what you're eating. If you eat out on a regular basis, however, you might have to modify your restaurant eating habits. For advice, see Chapter 11.

What Are Your Triggers?

One of the best things you can do to start developing a healthier relationship with food is to identify your own trigger situations and either be prepared to avoid them or take action to handle them in different ways. Ask yourself: *Are my triggers social, psychological, physiological, or situational?*

Another way to approach it is to figure out if your triggers are at home, at work, with family or certain friends, while you're doing certain activities, or because you're routinely feeling stressed or sad.

WEB TALK: For solid advice on losing weight and preventing weight gain, check out:

www.dietitian.com

Sometimes an eating trigger is a physical sign of true hunger, such as a grumbling stomach or headache. If you skipped lunch, then bought two glazed doughnuts on your afternoon break, you probably did it because you were really hungry, not just because the doughnuts were calling out to you from the snack cart. You might not have made the healthiest food choice, but you were eating for the right reason. Eat balanced meals regularly when you feel truly hungry and until you feel satisfied, and you might be able to avoid making too many unhealthy food choices.

Trigger Talk Identifying triggers is the first step to making changes. When you start making those changes, remember to think small. Your long-term goals can be big, but you reach them by taking baby steps. When you know your own eating triggers, you can focus on changes that will really make a difference because you're taking a personalized approach. For instance, you might think you should eat fewer carbohydrates because you know several people who lost weight that way, but perhaps that's not your weakness. Maybe what you really need to do is stop eating snacks of any kind while you watch TV at night.

Look for the triggers that have a big impact on the amount and type of food you eat. If you always keep bagels in the freezer and as a result, you often eat two or three toasted with butter as a late night snack, then frozen bagels are a trigger that might have to be removed from your life. If, however, frozen bagels are part of a quick, balanced breakfast you eat most mornings, then they are not a trigger food.

Expectation can be an eating trigger. You eat dessert after dinner because you expect to follow a savory meal with something sweet. It's the way your palette has been trained. You can retrain it, though. If dessert is always high in calories and fat and you always eat it even though you're full from your meal, you might want to retrain your palette to expect fresh fruit. You can, in fact, lose your taste for rich, sweet foods by replacing them with healthier foods. It just takes time.

A Trigger Log If you're keeping a food diary or a food journal of any kind, you can use that to record your trigger situations. Or you might want to keep a separate trigger log, which will not only help you identify your triggers, it will help you work out solutions. You might not come up with a better way to handle an eating trigger on the spot, but if you carry your log with you and look at it often, you'll give yourself time to come up with the best solution for each situation.

Like a food diary, a trigger log is a self-monitoring tool that will help you become more aware of the nature of your food addiction and figure out positive steps you can take to improve your relationship with food. A trigger log is a way of observing yourself and reporting your observations. It's also a way of challenging yourself and challenging a belief system that isn't working for you. This type of reporting helps you become more accountable to yourself for your eating behavior and defeatist attitudes. You increase your self-awareness and become more understanding of your own needs when you write down your triggers and your responses.

Here's what a trigger log looks like:

Time of Day	Trigger	How I Handled It	A Better Way
10 A.M.	snack cart	bought sticky bun	close office door so I don't see the cart, or bring snack from home
1 P.M.	deadline stress	glass of water	
6 P.M.	Fred invited me out after a tough day at work		suggested light meal and movie instead of usual bar food

Creating Diversions

The goal of a food addict who wants to change is to turn an adversarial relationship with food into a happy, healthy relationship. You do this by breaking old, ingrained habits and replacing them with new, healthier ones. Identifying your triggers is the first step toward breaking old eating habits. Your next step is to find alternatives to unhealthy eating when trigger situations arise.

Even if you love to eat, you've had an adversarial relationship with certain foods, and eating those foods carries negative associations for you. These associations need to be changed along with your old eating habits. To do this, try teaching yourself to associate healthful foods with positive feelings and the positive outcomes you expect from eating those foods. Focus as much as you can on those foods and those feelings until they overshadow the negative feelings you've developed about the foods that you believe may have hurt your health. Take this as another positive step toward creating new patterns of eating and thinking.

How you respond to an eating trigger depends on the trigger itself. At times, chewing gum or gargling with mouthwash might be enough to prevent you from eating until your next meal. If the urge to eat is very strong, however, you'll need to find better distractions.

Instead of Eating You can probably think of a few dozen things to do instead of eating when you're bored, upset, or feeling blue. Sometimes all you need to do is buy time with a distraction until the craving passes. Some suggestions to get you thinking about alternatives to overeating follow. Add to this list with your own ideas.

- Write in your journal.
- Call a friend.
- Send an e-mail.
- Write a letter.
- Clean your house.
- Wash your car.
- Start or add to a scrapbook or collage of your life.
- Go for a walk or do outside chores.
- Take a shower.
- Brush your teeth, use mouthwash, or chew gum.
- Go to the library.
- Drink a glass of water with lemon.
- Read a health and fitness magazine.
- Work out with an exercise video.
- Knit, sew, or work on a craft project, or take a class to learn how to do something that will keep your hands busy.
- Play with your dog, brush your cat, or clean the fish tank.
- _____
- _____

It won't hurt to keep a list of realistic diversions on your refrigerator door or carry them with you to remind yourself that there are things you can do in the moment to distract yourself from unnecessary eating.

Sometimes, however, temporary distractions aren't enough to control your moods and keep you from overeating. In that case, techniques such as meditation, mind-body exercises such as yoga, and individual or group counseling can help you address your underlying emotional issues and cope with them in healthier ways until you resolve the problem.

WEB TALK: For more alternatives to eating, go to the University of Pittsburgh Medical Center site at:

www.upmc.edu/weightloss/Attitudes/alternative_list.htm

Reward Yourself! Your best reward for getting mentally and physically fit is, of course, your own good health. Ideally, that would be enough incentive to keep you moving toward your long-term goals. But we're all human, and most humans want tangible rewards. Psychological studies consistently show that external rewards following a particular behavior increase the internal satisfaction we feel from performing that behavior. In other words, rewards work, especially when the behavior or task itself is especially difficult.

Parents know that rewarded behavior is likely to be repeated. Often the only reward necessary is a kiss, a hug, or a little bit of praise. When we're young, our rewards often come in the form of sweets—lollipops, cookies, or chocolate anything. Now we not only need self-reinforcement, we also need to come up with nonedible rewards that will give us that same pleasure.

A food addict's rewards are best reserved for changes in behavior and attitude, not changes in weight. You're learning how to break old habits and old thinking and replace them with new, healthier attitudes. That's your measure of success, not the number of pounds you lose.

If you think positive self-reinforcement will work for you, come up with a list of nonedible things you will find truly rewarding. Then, every time you meet a short-term goal or make even the smallest positive change in your thinking or eating behavior, give yourself a reward from your list. It's important to have that list of rewards handy so you can reward yourself right away.

Match the size of the reward with the size of the accomplishment so you don't run out of reinforcers. Think small at first and reward yourself often for every little accomplishment. Eating smaller portion sizes at dinner, exercising 10 minutes longer than usual, or picking up a pair of knitting needles instead of eating when you're bored are all small achievements that deserve to be rewarded. Just try not to reward yourself with food! As your small accomplishments and behavior changes turn into permanent new habits, think about bigger rewards such as books, clothes, beauty products, flowers, a massage, or jewelry. Six months or a year down the road, when you start reaching some of your really big, long-term goals, you can start thinking about a new car, vacation, or a designer dress.

GET PSYCHED

"Good health may be your best reward for getting physically and mentally fit, but that reward has always been there for you, you've known about it, and it hasn't been enough to reinforce your efforts. Give yourself more tangible rewards, whether it's simple self-praise or a shopping spree." *—Clay Tucker-Ladd, Ph.D., clinical psychologist and author of* Psychological Self-Help

When you make up your reward list, come up with some ideas that don't cost money, like giving yourself permission to sleep in on the weekend or take an extra-long bath. The idea is to fill your life with positive events—big and small, inexpensive and luxurious—that parallel the positive steps you're taking to break your food addiction. Here are a few more ideas to help get you thinking about things you can reward yourself with: a new CD or DVD, new sport or hobby equipment, a day off from work, a new wallet, a weekend escape, a new magazine subscription, a manicure/pedicure, or hiring someone to clean your house.

Rewarding yourself for small accomplishments helps you feel good about yourself and motivates you to move forward because it is positive reinforcement for a job well done. Try not to "bribe" yourself with big rewards until you've really earned them because then you'll be working for the reward, rather than for your own self-improvement. Only reward yourself when you've earned it. On the other hand, don't punish yourself in any way for lapses— that's just another way of chipping away at your self-esteem, and who needs that?

It's not okay to punish yourself, but it is okay to "correct" yourself by eating a light dinner after giving in to a junk-food snack in the afternoon, or running an extra mile on the treadmill because you chowed down after a disturbing discussion with your boss. These types of corrective behavior put a little pressure on you to pay more attention to your triggers, but at the same time, they help you reach your longer-term goals.

you're not alone

Rewards Work!

"I first got hooked on reward systems when I quit smoking cigarettes once and for all. The smoking cessation program I joined provided a list of about 100 ways you could reward yourself for not smoking. Everything was on that list, from smiling at yourself in the mirror to buying yourself a flower to using the money you save from not smoking for a vacation. At first I would give myself affordable rewards every day, sometimes more than once a day, just to stay motivated. They weren't planned; I would just look at the list for an idea, then go to a store and buy myself something. I really looked forward to those rewards, and they helped me get through the days as I cut back on smoking.

"Soon, I found I didn't need rewards as much as I needed good distractions. So instead of buying myself material things all the time, I also started rewarding myself with activities. Sometimes, I would sneak out on my lunch break and go see a movie. I took day trips on weekends. Anything that would keep me busy and keep me from getting bored. After three months, I quit smoking and left the program. I never smoked again, but luckily I held on to some of the tools they gave me, including that reward list.

continues

continued

"The 18 pounds I gained shortly after I quit smoking was the first real weight gain of my life. I was thirty-seven and had never been on a diet before, but I felt obsessive about food, and I had to do something. So there I was, counting calories and feeling miserable about it. Then I remembered my reward list. I knew that if it helped me quit smoking, it could help me stay motivated to lose weight. I went through the same routine, rewarding myself every day for eating less food, for breaking my grazing habit, for joining a gym, for *going* to the gym. I even rewarded myself for things like reading a magazine article about healthy eating, something I would have done even if I wasn't trying to get back in shape. The big reward came about three months down the road, when I not only lost those 18 pounds but could see the results of my gym routine. I was in better shape than I'd ever been in my life. I'm not sure I could have done it without all those incentives along the way."
—*Susan M.*

What You Can Do

You can't control all your eating triggers, but you can pay attention to them and develop new ways to cope with them.

- ☐ Identify your eating triggers.
- ☐ Create a trigger log you can carry with you to record your eating triggers and how you respond to them.
- ☐ Come up with new ways to respond to your eating triggers.
- ☐ If you feel a strong urge to eat when you're not hungry, try to distract yourself for fifteen minutes until the craving goes away.
- ☐ If your craving is the result of true hunger, allow yourself to eat.
- ☐ Make a list of distractions from eating and hang the list on your refrigerator or carry it in your wallet.
- ☐ Make a list of nonedible rewards you can give yourself for every accomplishment, large or small.

11

Maintaining a Healthy Relationship with Food

You know how to choose healthier foods, set goals, identify eating triggers, eat consciously, and expand your culinary horizons. Now it's time to check your attitude, find a healthy balance between your physical and emotional needs, and learn what it takes to maintain the changes you're working so hard to make.

You're not immune to the pressures and pleasures of real life, and you still have to deal with snack carts, restaurant meals, doughnut shops, grocery stores, and other day-to-day food challenges. In this chapter, I give you real-life solutions for managing these real-life situations.

How's Your Food Attitude?

Eighty-five percent of consumers surveyed in 2002 by the American Dietetic Association (ADA) about their attitudes toward health issues said they are concerned about diet and nutrition. Seventy-five percent said balanced nutrition is a factor when they select food. Fifty-eight percent said they actively seek information about nutrition and healthful eating. These results suggest that a majority of people in this country have the right food attitude.

At the same time, however, the survey found that 63 percent of respondents consider body weight an indicator of a healthful diet, 57 percent believe some foods should never be eaten, and 54 percent agreed that taking vitamin supplements is necessary to ensure good health. The popularity of these myths signals a need for better nutrition education.

WEB TALK: To maintain a positive attitude toward food, check the American Dietetic Association's (ADA) Tip of the Day at:

↑ www.eatright.org

Your attitude toward food and your willingness to make changes in your eating habits affect your ability to develop and maintain a healthier relationship with food. If you're ready to make a commitment to necessary changes in your attitude and behavior toward food, you will be successful. If you believe the benefits of making these changes outweigh any sacrifices you have to make to reach your goals, you'll be successful. And if you believe in yourself and your ability to develop new eating habits, you will be successful at maintaining a healthy relationship with your food.

You may have noticed that the more you tell yourself you can't have a particular food, the more obsessed you become with that food and the more you start to crave it. Sooner or later, you give in and, most likely, you go overboard. Then what? You end up feeling guilty, promise yourself you'll avoid that food, try to avoid it, and the cycle starts all over again. What would happen if you changed your attitude and let yourself eat whatever you like? Would you eat any more of the foods you crave than you eat when you finally give in to a desperate craving? Probably not. If you constantly tell yourself you can't have some of your favorite foods and then end up overeating them sometime later, instead of depriving and indulging, *earn* those cookies, chips, ice cream bars, and brownies.

You can do several things to earn the calories or fat you get with indulgence foods. One way is to have an advance plan. Work small portions of your favorite foods into your daily eating plan. That generally only works for people who are able to eat small amounts of favorite foods. If you get regular physical activity, it might be easier to stretch your workout an extra ten or fifteen minutes to burn off extra calories. Another good trick for anyone who can't keep certain foods in the house without bingeing is to walk to the store and buy a single serving of whatever it is you crave. And as part of the deal, you also have to walk home!

> **GET PSYCHED**
>
> "If you stick with it, you *will* improve your relationship with food. Rather than get discouraged or impatient with yourself if you're not quite where you want to be or having difficulty moving forward, celebrate every little change you make because each one brings you that much closer to success."
> *—Susan McConnaughy, C.S.W., psychotherapist, New York City*

There really are no quick fixes when it comes to losing weight and developing a healthy relationship with food. That's why it's such an achievement when someone is successful at getting and staying fit. Many small accomplishments along the way—such as learning more about healthy eating, changing the way you eat, increasing your activity, and finding ways to mentally and physically relax—all add up to the big one.

To change your behavior, there's no doubt you have to change your attitude toward food. Otherwise you are like a "dry drunk" who still has the desire and thoughts of an addicted person. If those thoughts and desires are strong enough, you'll be more susceptible to relapse. If you find you can't make the necessary inner changes on your own, individual or group counseling might help.

Finding Your Balance

What does it mean to live a balanced life? It means you feel satisfied with all or most aspects of your life. It means you devote a fair amount of time to work and a fair amount to play. If you're living a balanced life, your physical, emotional, and spiritual health are all intact.

A food addict's goal is to create a healthy balance between physical and psychological drives. Sometimes that means striking a deal with yourself between what you want to do and what you know is best for you. As you well know, too much of the wrong types of food or too little of the right types of food will throw off your body balance. Emotional eating throws off that balance. Stress throws off that balance. Not getting enough physical activity throws off that balance. You become tired. You become sick. You gain weight.

WEB TALK: For an excellent free guide to psychological self-help, visit:
➤ mentalhelp.net/psyhelp/

No specific formula exists for a balanced life; it's different for everyone. To find your balance, focus on improving the areas of your life where you don't feel happy or satisfied. Those areas need more immediate attention. That might mean devoting more time to something you're already doing to try to help yourself, but it could also mean stopping and figuring out a completely different approach. For instance, if you recognize that you overeat for emotional reasons and you're working on resolving your underlying issues on your own, you might want to devote more of your time to reading self-help books or take a completely different approach and talk to a counselor. You might need support to balance your life because the imbalance could very well have to do with the fact that you're trying to do too much on your own.

you're not alone

"I've been overweight my whole life. I grew up eating double helpings of everything, and I never knew I ate too much food because my whole family ate that way. I've been on low-fat diets, high-protein diets, high-fiber diets—you name it—and while I learned a lot about eating better, none of them actually worked for me. I never lost weight because I could never stick to a diet plan for more than a day or two. I would ride my bicycle or jog every day, as I always have, but I stayed at the same weight. One day I realized that when I eat the way I usually do, without dieting, I also stay at the same weight. So I asked myself, why do I bother to go on these diets?

"My brother suggested that I forget about dieting and just exercise more,

If one area of your life is out of whack, so are the others, because too much of one thing means too little of another. When your eating habits are out of balance, so is the rest of your life. Balancing your eating habits means eating nutritionally balanced meals, and it also means balancing your thoughts about food.

Conquering Cravings

There you are, working at your desk or walking down the street, when you suddenly feel a powerful urge to eat something sweet (or salty, or meaty, or doughy). You try to suppress the urge, but you know it's just a matter of time before you sneak off to the snack machine or duck into the doughnut shop. Sometimes you just can't say "no."

> **WEB TALK:** Get help conquering cravings from the University of Pittsburgh Medical Center at:
> www.upmc.edu/weightloss/ Attitudes/mind_games.htm

Many different theories exist about cravings. Some say cravings are related to our primal impulse to fill up on food whenever we can. Others say we crave food because food is all around us and some of it just tastes too good to resist. Still others say that when we crave certain foods, it's our body's way of telling us we need specific nutrients. Although the latter theory was once a commonly accepted belief, it's hard to believe anyone's body needs nutrients from potato chips or chocolate-chip cookies. Craving

which is what he does. I joined his gym, and for the past year, in addition to walking and jogging, I've been working out with light weights and using the treadmill to walk uphill and the stair climber just for something different. I go to the gym two or three times a week, sometimes I take exercise classes while I'm there, and on the other days, I still ride my bike or jog slowly. I don't have a strict schedule; I just make sure I exercise almost every day. In that first month of not dieting, I lost 10 pounds, and now, almost a year later, I'm down from a size 16 dress to a size 10 and holding fast. It's amazing—I feel great, I'm proud of myself, and best of all, I still eat whatever I want."
–Danielle C.

salty snacks doesn't mean you need sodium, and craving a chocolate dessert doesn't mean you're low on sugar or fat.

Nutrition experts now agree that cravings rarely have anything to do with a nutritional deficiency. Modern research links strong cravings to alterations in brain chemistry. You might also get cravings simply because you don't eat often enough. If you skip meals or wait too long between meals, your cravings might be a result of true hunger.

What We Crave When you get a craving, it's probably not for a tossed green salad drizzled with fat-free dressing. Most of the time, we don't just crave food, we crave very specific types of food. Studies show that women are more likely to crave fat-sugar combinations such as chocolate or doughnuts, while men tend to crave fat-protein foods such as hamburgers, hot dogs, or juicy steaks. When surveyed about foods that satisfy cravings, people also put salty foods, breads, and sweets at the top of the list. "Forbidden" foods—those you tell yourself you can't have for one reason or another—are a common craving.

Whatever type of food you crave, if you can satisfy the urge with small indulgences every so often, you're less likely to find yourself eating an entire tray of cookies or six pork chops in one sitting.

Why We Crave Ongoing animal studies at Rockefeller University in New York have shown that two brain chemicals are involved in food choices. Neuropeptide Y, a brain chemical found at high levels in the early morning, dictates a preference for cereals, breads, fruits, and other such foods. Another brain chemical known as galanin triggers cravings for fattier foods such as pizza and ice cream. According to Sarah Leibowitz, leading scientist of the Rockefeller University studies, the hormone insulin also plays a role in food choices because it inhibits the production of galanin and reduces the preference for fat. Thus, any change in insulin levels will affect the activity of the gene that makes galanin.

When insulin is low, such as in diabetes, the gene activity increases, more galanin is produced, and the appetite for fat increases.

In addition to encouraging a taste for fatty foods, recent studies show that eating a fat-rich diet can further stimulate the production of galanin. According to Dr. Leibowitz, eating fatty foods and experiencing cravings for them is a positive-feedback relationship, or vicious cycle. The more rich, fatty foods you eat, the more you crave them.

GET PSYCHED

"Eating a diet that's high in fat can stimulate the production of a brain chemical that, in turn, further increases your appetite for fat-rich foods." –Dr. Sarah Leibowitz, professor of behavioral neurobiology, Rockefeller University, New York

According to Drs. Judith and Richard Wurtman, a husband-and-wife team of researchers at Massachusetts Institute of Technology (MIT) who have done groundbreaking work in the area of food and brain chemistry, carbohydrate cravings are easy to explain: people who crave carbs need a certain amount of carbohydrates in their diets to keep their moods stable. In the 1970s, Richard Wurtman first showed that eating sweet or starchy carbohydrates raises brain levels of serotonin, a neurochemical that affects mood and appetite. Judith Wurtman has since shown that carbohydrate craving is associated with serotonin-related changes in mood. If a carbohydrate-craver eats a high-protein meal or snack instead high-carb, she might feel full, but her mood isn't likely to improve.

I get uncontrollable cravings for carbohydrates and chocolate for a few days before my menstrual period every month. Why does this happen, and what can I do to control it?

In general, women report getting cravings more often than men, and studies have shown that chocolate is the most craved food among American women. Premenstrual cravings are common, but no one knows for sure why they occur. Physiologically, low levels of serotonin occur at this stage of the cycle. So it is no wonder that when you experience cravings, they're for high-carb foods and chocolate, because these foods will trigger production of more serotonin. Exercise also raises serotonin levels and that might be a healthier solution if you find yourself bingeing on carbs.

Researchers say that indulging in cravings for sweet or fatty foods also triggers the release of endorphins, brain chemicals that can help us feel calm. Endorphins are also responsible for the "high" you might feel when you exercise vigorously, fall in love, or eat chocolate. That could help explain why a food addict repeatedly craves the same foods and why, sometimes, only a brownie or a thick slab of steak will satisfy the craving.

Both fat and sugar stimulate "feel-good" brain chemicals, so both are likely to be the foods we long for. Everyone has different cravings, however, and everyone responds differently to different foods, so the answer to why we get irresistible cravings is not crystal clear. Some researchers feel that what is commonly called a sweet tooth is actually a "sweetened fat tooth" because so many of the foods we eat to satisfy cravings are high in fat disguised by the stronger taste of sugar.

Although understanding of the neurochemistry is still in its early stages, most researchers do agree that food cravings have a neurological or psychological basis and rarely have anything to do with hunger or filling nutritional needs.

Resisting Cravings Caving in to cravings is only a problem if you regularly overeat. If your cravings result in binge eating or weight gain, they have to be controlled. When you're trying to resist a craving, the best thing you can do is temporarily distract yourself until the urge to eat goes away. For most people, that usually happens within fifteen minutes. You might have to get up and take a walk outside in the dead of winter, but it may be worth it to learn that you can, in fact, conquer cravings.

Like other forms of emotional eating, your cravings might be based on psychological needs. If you are an emotional eater, confronting the issues underlying your need to eat is the first step to conquering problematic cravings. If your cravings are due to real hunger, you might be able to reduce their frequency simply by eating three balanced, satisfying meals every day within three or four hours of each other and supplementing with planned snacks.

You know you're getting enough calories and keeping your blood sugar steady throughout the day. If your meals and snacks are balanced and you're getting enough carbohydrates and fat in your diet, it will be easier to avoid the abrupt chemical changes in the brain that appear to induce cravings.

Handling Snack Attacks

Do you love to snack? If so, you're in good company. Studies show that more than 75 percent of Americans snack at least once a day. If you think snacking is unhealthy, it might be because of the types of foods you associate with snacking. Products designed to be snack foods—chips, dips, pretzels, crackers, cookies, and the like—are traditionally high in fat, sugar, or salt and low in essential nutrients. More and more packaged snack foods are being made with less salt, less sugar, and healthier fats. That's a start toward healthier snacking, but it's not the whole story.

Emotional snacking is common. Do you sneak your snacks? Were snacks forbidden in your home while you were growing up? If so, you'll probably always feel some guilt if you eat between meals. Why not snack openly and enjoy it? These tips from the American Dietetic Association (ADA) can help you snack guiltlessly:

- Snack only when you're hungry.
- Make snacking a conscious activity.
- Eat snacks well ahead of mealtime.
- Eat snack-size (small) portions.

If you are snacking too often throughout the day and snacks are contributing to unwanted weight gain, you need a new snacking strategy. According to Washington endocrinologist and obesity expert Wayne Callaway, if you feed yourself six or eight times a day, pretty soon you start to feel hungry six or eight times a day. Your body comes to expect a certain amount of food at certain times every day—even if it doesn't really need it. If you continue to feed that hunger, the snacking habit can easily lead to weight gain, even if you're eating nutritious foods.

But snacking can actually be a good strategy for weight control if you snack on wholesome foods in healthier ways. Think of snacks as mini-meals, and balance them the way you would a real meal, by being sure there's some protein, some fat, and some carbohydrate on your plate. Make snacks from several different types of food, and use snacks to fill nutritional gaps in your diet. For instance, instead of grabbing a fistful of chips and then ultimately eating half the bag, arrange a small, snack-size plate with chips, cheese, and fruit. If you snack on sweets, top a scoop of ice cream with cut fruit and have a small muffin on the side. That might help prevent you from emptying the ice cream container. When you snack this way, you're filling up on an assortment of foods rather than eating too much of any one food, and you're getting a variety of nutrients at the same time. You will have no reason to feel guilty.

The secret to healthful snacking is careful planning. Be prepared for snack attacks. Have healthful, ready-to-eat snacks available at home and at work. With a little planning, snacks can …

- Help you meet your daily needs for protein, vitamins, minerals, and fiber.
- Add fun and variety to your diet.
- Help prevent afternoon "slumps."
- Supply you with energy throughout the day.
- Prevent you from becoming so hungry that you overeat at your next meal.

Although snacking is okay, there are two definite "don'ts" for people who have trouble controlling their snack intake:

- Don't snack while you're doing something else, like watching TV, working on your computer, or reading.
- Never eat food straight from its container. Portion out a reasonable serving for yourself, and put away the container.

If you make snacking a conscious activity, as you've learned to do with regular meals, you'll pay more attention to the types of food you're eating, eat your snacks more slowly, and eat only as much as you need to satisfy between-meal hunger.

The Art of Food Shopping

For a food addict, the mere thought of entering a supermarket can bring up all sorts of emotional issues. You might avoid supermarkets because you don't trust yourself to keep food in the house. Instead, you eat out, order in, or pick up just enough food to provide a single meal at home. You might only buy foods you consider "safe," such as frozen, calorie-controlled entrées or certain types of vegetables. Many binge-eaters never even step foot in a supermarket unless they're set to binge, so when they actually do go grocery shopping, it's for indulgence foods only. Standing in line with an open cart full of binge food brings up feelings of guilt and shame because you feel exposed in a public place. You might worry about being judged by other people in line. You might think other people know you're feeling out of control when they see you buying so much junk food. Some binge eaters go so far as to shop in several different stores on the same night because buying all that food in one place can feel too shameful.

Lora Sasiela, C.S.W., B.C.D., a New York City psychotherapist specializing in addictions and eating disorders, uses an anti-deprivation approach with clients who seek her help for food addictions. She helps them "legalize" all food choices so they can walk into a supermarket and pick up both the broccoli and the chocolate kisses and feel good about both choices. To do that, she says, you first have to stop thinking in terms of good foods and bad foods and allow yourself the freedom of choice.

Food addicts often have to re-learn how to shop for and prepare healthful foods, just as they have to re-learn how to eat them. When the subject turns to shopping for healthier foods, especially if weight control is an issue, two good suggestions often come up: have a plan, and don't go food shopping when you're hungry.

Both rules are designed to help you buy just enough of the foods you need until it's time to go food shopping again. Having a plan simply means knowing in advance what type of foods you want to prepare and keep on hand, as well as having an itemized list in hand when you go to the store. The real trick, then, is to only buy what's on your list. Shopping on a full stomach will help make you a pickier buyer. If your stomach is full, you won't be as tempted to fill your cart with indulgence foods.

Another common recommendation is to do most of your food shopping in the aisles on the outer perimeter of the store. In some respects, that's true, because fresh fruits, vegetables, meats, and dairy products are generally located on these outside aisles, and processed foods tend to be shelved in the center. It's an old rule, however, and these days, healthful foods can be found in the packaged, canned, bottled, and frozen food sections of most supermarkets. This aisle-by-aisle guide will help you find your best food bets in each category:

Produce The best general advice anyone can give you about buying fresh fruits and vegetables is to buy in season. Produce is more flavorful, more nutritious, and usually less expensive when it's in season. When it has all that going for it, you're more likely to want to buy and eat it. And now that so many fruits and vegetables come prewashed and precut, fresh produce is practically a convenience food. Salad bars, which are an extension of the produce department in most large supermarkets, come in handy when you want to pick up fresh, ready-made side dishes for dinner.

Meat The most deceiving meats when it comes to hidden fat and calories are cold cuts and other processed meats such as hot dogs. Traditionally, these also tend to be very high in sodium. If you do eat processed meats, it

GET PSYCHED

It might be best to stay away from grocery stores when you're in a negative emotional state. You might end up buying more food than necessary or the types of food that get you in trouble. Try to go food shopping when you're feeling good about yourself.

makes nutritional sense to choose those that have been modified to be healthier; now you can choose from many lower-fat, lower-sodium varieties of your favorite deli meats. When it comes to regular meat, the amount of fat varies from cut to cut. If you're concerned about fat in your diet from meat, choose leaner cuts such as loin, tenderloin, shoulder, leg, and foreshank.

WEB TALK: For an insider's view of marketing responses to diet and food trends, see:

www.groceryheadquarters.com

Poultry Most of the fat in a turkey or chicken is found in and under the skin, but that doesn't mean you have to buy skinless cuts. Many people prefer to cook their turkey and chicken with the skin on to preserve moisture and flavor and then remove the skin before they eat. Fat does not travel from the skin to the flesh during cooking, so when you remove the skin, the fat goes with it. If you're choosing ground turkey or ground chicken to replace higher-fat ground meats, be sure to check and compare the information on the Nutrition Facts label. There's no guarantee that a sausage or burger made with poultry is automatically low in fat.

Fish Fattier fish also contain natural oils that are thought to be good for your heart and your health. These "fatty" fish include salmon, tuna, catfish, trout, mackerel, and bluefish.

Dairy The best way to show the nutritional difference between low-fat and full-fat (whole milk) dairy products and dairy substitutes is to take a look at the labels and start comparing. This example, using 1 cup milk, shows just how big the difference is when it comes to fat and calories:

1 Cup Milk	Calories	Fat (Grams)
Whole	149	8
2 percent low fat	121	5
1 percent low fat	100	3
Skim or nonfat	90	<1

Freezer Case You can actually build a pretty nutritious meal from ingredients found in the freezer case. In some instances, thanks to technology that gets fresh food from the field to the freezer in a matter of minutes, some commercially frozen fruits and vegetables may be more nutritious than what's available fresh. Other nutritious picks from the freezer case include frozen pasta, multi-grain waffles, organic and vegetarian meals, and various ethnic foods.

Canned Foods From a nutritional standpoint, most canned fruits and vegetables can't be recommended over fresh or frozen. Canning is a high-heat process that destroys some or all of the nutritional value of most foods. But for someone who is very busy (and who isn't?), some canned foods make a lot more sense than fresh. Canned foods that retain a fair amount of good nutrition include tomatoes and tomato products such as sauces and pastes, cooked dried beans, split peas, lentils, bean and lentil soups, and canned fish.

GET PSYCHED

"When you go food shopping, allow yourself to buy indulgence foods along with more healthful foods. Once you give yourself permission to choose all types of foods, you will end up craving broccoli and chicken cutlets as often as you crave ice cream and chocolate cream pie. That's what happens when you get in touch with real hunger and stop thinking in terms of good foods and bad foods."
–Lora Sasiela, C.S.W., B.C.D., New York City psychotherapist specializing in addictions and eating disorders

Grains In Chapter 8, I give you tips on how to climb out of a rut by trying new foods. Grains are a great place to start. Supermarkets carry more interesting whole-grain products, such as quinoa and cracked wheat, than ever before. Even pasta and rice come in enough different varieties that you can eat them often and eat something different every time.

As you're shopping, always keep in mind that you're looking for healthy food, not "diet" food.

It doesn't take much to stock a kitchen for healthful cooking and eating, even in a pinch. Keep your cupboards and freezer lightly stocked with healthful foods for those times when you don't have a meal plan and you're just too tired or too disinterested to think about it. If you always have a small supply of pasta shapes, grain mixes, bottled tomato sauces, canned tuna or other fish, canned beans, and broths in your cupboard, and vegetables or other healthful options in the freezer, you've always got the makings of a quick, satisfying, and nutritious meal. In just a few minutes, you can combine some of these ingredients into a hearty soup or pasta dish.

By choosing convenience food *ingredients* rather than fully prepared entrées, you can control the nutritional value of the "fast food" you eat at home. Many frozen entrees and "TV dinner" type meals, even those that are lower in fat, are high in salt and low in fiber and essential vitamins and minerals. When you create your own quick meals, you can choose to add more healthful versions of similar ingredients and avoid saturated fats, excess sodium, and other additives.

you're not alone

Whatever Gets Me Through the Night

"I'm twenty-seven years old, and I weigh just under 200 pounds. I'm tall, and I was always a big girl, but now I'm fat. I'm fat because I overeat. I overeat because I'm tired and lonely a lot of the time so I entertain myself with food. I work late nights, so I don't have as much of a social life as most of my friends. Right now, it's 1 a.m., and I'm sitting at my computer, staring at a bag of potato chips that I bought in a health food store so I can tell myself they're healthy chips. That's the way most nights go for me.

"I like myself, but I want to like my body, too, so I'm trying to lose weight. I've gone on three diets in my life, and each time I lost 20 or 30 pounds, then gave up for one reason or another and gained the weight back. Twice I joined weight loss programs and once I followed a high-protein diet on my own. I got bored with the rules and with eating the same types of food all the time. This time I'm counting calories so I can eat whatever I want, whenever I want, throughout the day. I just have to stop eating when I get to my limit of 1,600 calories. Most days I'm able to do it because I save my calories for the end of the day (which, for me, is after midnight). And I eat plenty of healthy food and low-calorie foods as well as a little junk. I know dieting and watching calories so

continues

189

continued

closely isn't the right way to lose weight. I know I should just find other things to do when I'm bored besides eat, but right now I'm stuck. I need to do something to get myself motivated to make some big changes in my life.

"The only way I'm going to get out more and work on my social life is to find a day job. I don't think it will be hard to do, but before I change jobs, I need to lose some weight. I want to start fresh; I don't want to bring all this old fat with me to a new job. I think I'm finally ready to lose weight once and for all, and until I figure out a better way, I'll just keep counting calories. For now, it's a good, workable plan because I'm not overeating and I know it's just a temporary way of eating to lose some weight, not the final solution." *–Eileen K.*

Eating Out and About

According to the National Restaurant Association, the typical American eats out an average of four times a week. Seventy-five percent of restaurant customers modify their meals by asking for alternative preparation methods, off-the-menu orders, and substitutions, and most restaurants welcome and honor such requests.

It's not usually a good idea to "save your appetite" when you know you're going out to eat. Not eating earlier in the day only leads to overeating when you finally sit down to a meal. It's actually a better idea to have a small snack about half an hour before you go out to eat to help curb your appetite and give you more control over the amount of food you eat at the restaurant.

Different strategies work for different people. Some people choose restaurants that serve lighter cuisines; others want to forget about eating lean when they're eating out. The following tips can help you control the amount of food you eat so restaurant dining can be a healthful and still pleasurable experience:

- Avoid all-you-can-eat buffets unless you feel you can make wise choices and control the amount of food you eat. If you choose wisely and take small portions, however, you can get a very nutritious meal from a buffet, thanks to the variety of foods offered. A good trick is to take very small portions of several favorite foods, regardless of their healthfulness, and sit down to eat them. Think of them as appetizers. When you go back to the buffet, choose healthier foods for an entrée.

- Ask for a glass of water as soon as you sit down. Drink water often throughout your meal.
- Ask for the bread to be taken away until your entrée is served.
- Order a small cup of soup or a large salad to start your meal.
- If you're eating out with someone else, order an appetizer each, then split one entrée.
- If you can't split an entrée with someone and you don't feel you should eat the whole thing yourself in one sitting, ask the waiter to package half your meal in a take-home bag before you eat.
- Share a dessert or have a flavored coffee for dessert, if that will satisfy you.

For these strategies to be helpful, you have to follow them on a regular basis until they become habit. The trick to eating well, whether you're at a restaurant, a party, or on the road, is to have a plan. Planning *how* you will eat is more important than planning *what* you will eat. Focus on developing habits that will help prevent you from overeating, regardless of what you're eating.

What You Can Do

Maintain a healthy relationship with food by developing a positive attitude and basic skills that will help you make wise food choices in normal, day-to-day situations.

☐ Remember that *how* you eat is more important than *what* you eat. The amount of food you eat, how you balance your diet, your attitude toward food, and your personal eating habits generally play a larger role in your food addiction than the specific foods you choose to eat.

☐ Curb cravings by distracting yourself for several minutes to see if the craving will go away before you give in.

☐ Learn to shop wisely at the supermarket. Shop on a full stomach and when your commitment to healthier eating is strong.

☐ Give yourself permission to shop for, prepare, and eat all types of foods.

☐ Be prepared for snack attacks by planning ahead and having plenty of healthful snacks on hand at work and at home.

☐ Develop strategies for eating out at your favorite restaurants without overeating.

12

Helping Hands

I f changing your attitude about food and staying at a healthy weight were as simple as following a balanced diet and getting enough exercise, there would be no such thing as food addictions, eating disorders, or an obesity epidemic. The problem is obviously more complicated than that.

If you've been indulging in ordinary overeating or you're only moderately overweight, self-help techniques and a network of supportive friends and family might be all you need to break the bonds of your food addiction. If your problem seems insurmountable, however, and your overeating has long been associated with emotional situations and dysfunctional responses, or if your self-help strategies aren't working for you, you might need to look for additional help.

Who's in Charge?

You are the only one who knows what's right for you. The world presents you with plenty of options for normalizing your relationship with food, but you have to choose what works.

Food has been controlling your life. Now it's time to decide how you want to be different, and take responsibility for the changes that will help improve your relationship with food. In many respects, that relationship is like any other. It's not working if it's riddled with problems and causing a great deal of stress in your life. To fix it, in part you need to develop better relationship skills.

WEB TALK: Find an international resource guide for disordered and addictive eating at:

↑ open-mind.org/ED.htm

Every day, from the moment you wake up, you are presented with choices. Go for a walk, or sit on the couch? Eat an apple, or eat an apple pie? No one can make those decisions for you.

Blaming other people and situations for your food addiction is a way of giving up responsibility for yourself and your own health. It's the same as saying you don't have control over what happens to you, that other people and outside forces determine your fate and your weight. Although it might be true that your boss is a maniac, you inherited your mother's hips, and your mate insists on keeping junk food in the house, it's not true that any of these people or situations are responsible for your personal eating habits. Instead of pointing a finger at anyone (including yourself), take these steps to gain or regain control:

- Decide what you do and don't want to happen in your life from now on.
- Take responsibility for yourself.
- Learn how to deal with difficult situations.
- Be accountable to yourself.
- Restore balance to your life.
- Stay committed.

Setting Boundaries Your personal boundaries are the physical and emotional limits that set you apart from other people. When you set your boundaries, you draw invisible lines of responsibility for your own feelings and behavior and those of others. By setting these limits, you establish how you will allow other people to treat you. Setting boundaries is a way of telling yourself and the world that you deserve to be respected, that you're working hard to break the bonds of food addiction, and you're entitled to your success.

You also establish boundaries for yourself when you avoid eating triggers or learn how to cope with those you can't avoid. You establish boundaries when you set aside time, for yourself, whether it's to go to a yoga class, sit quietly, and meditate or read a book. It's up to you to stay within the boundaries you establish for yourself, and at the same time, you have to respect the boundaries established by those close to you. For instance, if your housemate fills the cupboard with junk food that you find tempting, he's not crossing your boundary. No matter how hard it is to resist eating his food, it's still his food, and he's entitled to have it in his home. If you eat his potato chips, it's not your housemate's fault.

What and how you eat is your own personal decision, and no one else's. You have the right to expect others to respect your decision. At times, you might want your family or friends to speak up and remind you of your goals. That can be helpful when you're trying to break old habits and develop new ones. At other times, however, you might want people to respect your privacy and your need to work through your changes on your own. If they don't, or if they criticize your eating habits rather than lend support, they are stepping over the line. You have to be direct and say to people, "Please don't comment on what I'm eating or how much I'm eating. It doesn't help." Once you've established clear boundaries, you know when to say "no."

you're not alone

"**E**ven when I'm at my normal body size, I'm still obsessive about how I look and whether or not I look fat. I'm still working on this. One thing other people don't seem to realize is that it is excruciating for me to hear any type of comment about my body or my weight. When someone says 'You look great!' or 'Wow, you've lost weight!' they think they're being nice, but it's too much pressure. I can't handle any attention about how I look because I'm still not comfortable with myself. I've started asking people, especially my relatives, not to comment on my looks or to say anything at all to me about food or weight until I work through this." –Allison K.

Learn to Say "No" While you're learning to say "no" to second helpings or "no" to certain foods, you also have to learn to say "no" to people and situations that can sabotage your efforts to develop and maintain a healthier relationship with food. The most well-meaning people in your life are often the ones who prevent you from reaching your goals. They can also be the hardest people to say "no" to. You have to be strong enough to say "No, thanks, Grandma. I don't want any more mashed potatoes," even if you're afraid she'll take it personally. At times, you'll have to say "No, sweetheart, I'd rather eat at home tonight," when your mate wants to go out to a restaurant. If you normally go out with friends on Friday night, you might have to decide to stay home alone. While you're learning to eat normally, you have to say "no" to people and situations that trigger emotional eating behavior. You won't always have to say "no" to everything, but for now you have to be firm when it comes to destructive situations. Only you know how easy it is to fall back into old eating habits or fool yourself into thinking "just this once."

When you're low on self-confidence, you might find it difficult to say "no" to people and situations that could sabotage your best efforts to maintain a healthy relationship with food. You might feel guilty saying "no," but sometimes you have no recourse. If you try to please someone else by doing what you don't want to do, you'll only end up feeling resentful. If an outright "no" is too difficult, there are other ways to say it: "I'm sorry, I can't"; "Not right now"; "I can't make it this time"; "I'd rather not"; "I don't like that idea"; or "No, thanks, but maybe next time" are all softer variations on a flat-out "No." You can also delay your response by saying, "I have to think about it," or "Can I get back to you on that?" "I'm not sure I can do it, but I'll let you know." Smile when you say "no" to remind yourself you're doing something positive. It might help to practice what you're going to say before a situation arises. Sometimes all you need is to have the right answer at the ready.

Family and Friends

A network of family and friends can be as important to your success as your own determination and efforts. In fact, several studies have shown that you're much more likely to stay motivated to reach your health goals if you have a solid support system in place. Family and friends can support your efforts to build a healthier lifestyle in many ways, from cheerleading to serving healthier food at get-togethers, to becoming one of your gym buddies, or perhaps baby-sitting while you go for a walk. Support can be in the form of a motivational tip, a kind word, even a recipe for preparing a favorite food in a healthier new way.

> **GET PSYCHED**
>
> Support from family, friends, and co-workers gives you more confidence to make changes. Change is almost always stressful. Getting support and letting people around you know what you're coping with can reduce some of that stress.

Don't be afraid to let people know you need their support. Whether you're trying to lose weight, develop a healthier attitude toward food, or get fit through exercise, you have to tell others what you're trying to do and ask for the support you need. For example, you might have to explain to your well-meaning grandmother or mother-in-law that even though you love her cooking, you have to pass on second helpings and would prefer she doesn't offer. Or you might need to ask friends to baby-sit so you can go to the gym or choose a different type of restaurant when you all go out to eat together. Or maybe you need to ask your spouse to refrain from eating junk food in front of you until you can trust yourself to resist.

Make it clear that you *don't* need people to tell you what to do or monitor your habits. That could be cause for rebellion! What you really need are facilitators, people who can lend an ear when you need to talk, offer encouragement, provide motivation, and share information. Help your friends and family understand that you're trying to break a lot of your bad habits and it's going to take a lot of work and a lot of positive reinforcement. Explain that when you say "no" to food or to situations that might trigger overeating, you're not trying to be antisocial or impolite. Let everyone know this isn't just another diet or stab in the dark, but that you're trying to make big changes in the way you eat and live and think so you never again feel tempted to go on a diet or abuse food. Be specific when you tell people what you need them to do and say. Let your family and friends know if their comments about your body or your weight or your eating habits are hurtful, and ask them to refrain. Let them know that it won't help to hear negative remarks or to be reminded of your past failed attempts to conquer your food addiction. They might not know what they're doing to sabotage your efforts or what they can do to be helpful.

Sometimes the people you most expect to help you will let you down. It happens. You might have friends or family members who are resistant to change, so they're unable to give you the support you need. They might simply be unavailable when you need them. It might be hard for some people to deal with the fact that you're making improvements in your health and appearance while they're not. They may be jealous or afraid that you'll change so much or so fast that they'll lose you, and they may not consciously realize that they're hurting you. You might have to point it out to them, and you might have to look elsewhere for help.

If, while you're in the process of developing a normal relationship with food, you have to miss family dinners or parties until you feel more in control, and your absence hurts family members and friends, be open and ask for their understanding and support. Or you could try to rally your family and friends to get involved in ways that result in positive lifestyle changes and healthier eating habits for everyone.

If changing your appearance means you'll be more attractive to other men and women, your mate might not be as supportive as you expect. If your best friend fears you'll soon be looking better than she does, she might not support your efforts. Everyone you know is used to the way you've always looked and behaved. They could have their own reasons for wanting you to stay the way you are, or they might not be taking you seriously. They might have problems of their own right now, and your efforts frighten them for some reason. Close friends and family might tell you that you're just fine the way you are because they are afraid that your feelings will be hurt if they agree that you need to lose weight or stop eating compulsively.

One of your goals must be to stop worrying so much about how other people feel and think. This doesn't mean you have to stop caring about the people you love, but it does mean you have to focus more on your own needs, at least where food is concerned, than on theirs. You might have to be a little selfish, at least until you get used to the new changes in your life. For help, turn to those people who seem most willing or understanding in their support—even if they aren't the people you traditionally count on. Whatever you do, don't set yourself up for disappointment by trying to get support from someone who can't give it.

Don't be afraid to approach some of the not-so-significant others in your life. If you go to a job, belong to a church or temple, or are part of any regular social group, you might be able to enlist new friends that will lend support or join you in your efforts to live a healthier lifestyle. When you're looking for people to buddy-up with or lend support, look for people who are nearby, willing to help, and, ideally, who live a similar lifestyle so they can truly be available. Look for people who can support you without indulging you at those times when you get frustrated or feel tempted to give up.

Additional Support

If you feel it's necessary, look for support outside your immediate circle of family and friends. Peer-led groups for people who overeat meet regularly in church basements, hospitals, clinics, and other community centers in just about every city and town. It is estimated that up to 25 million Americans have attended some type of specialized self-help group at some point in their lives for one type of problem or another. Groups such as Overeaters Anonymous (OA; www.oa.org), Food Addicts Anonymous (FAA; www.foodaddictsanonymous.org), and Food Addicts in Recovery Anonymous (FA; www.foodaddicts. org) specialize in overeating and food addiction.

Meetings are generally free or supported by donations and are open to anyone who is willing to abide by the rules of the group.

Successful, community-based self-help groups are sometimes affiliated with national organizations such as the American Heart Association, and often have the support of health and medical professionals. At the same time, peer-led self-help groups, such as those listed earlier, thrive without professional involvement and support themselves quite well through voluntary member contributions. These groups are based on the same *12 steps* that form the foundation of and contribute to the success of Alcoholics Anonymous and Narcotics Anonymous. These 12 steps are considered the instruments by which a personality change is accomplished.

I asked Jan H., a member of Over-eaters Anonymous for 28 years, to describe what happens the first time someone walks into an OA meeting. She explained that there are several different types of meetings. There are general meetings, step meetings (that focus specifically on one or more of the 12 steps), and promises meetings (that focus on the promises of taking action on the 12 steps). Even though newcomers are welcome at any meeting, Jan suggests looking for a beginner's meeting, because some of the lingo used at other types of meetings might be unfamiliar and confusing to a beginner.

When a general meeting opens, a chairperson or presenter speaks on a particular topic, often telling the story of his or her

PsychSpeak

The **12 steps** used as a recovery tool in 12-step fellowship programs help members identify and acknowledge the depth of their problem and admit their lives have become unmanageable and they are powerless to deal with the problem alone. Although nondenominational, 12-step programs are spiritually based.

own disorder and what it's like for them now. Then there is sharing from the floor, and you'll hear people saying things like "I can relate to that because ..." or "It's the same in my family ..." or "I'm thinking of doing something similar." What's called cross-talk, "If I were you ..." or "You really shouldn't feel that way because ..." is discouraged. At some point during the meeting, the main speaker will ask if there are any newcomers or anyone there for just the second or third time. At that point, you can introduce yourself by first name only and you will be greeted by the other members.

People in 12-step programs sometimes develop sponsorship relationships when someone feels he has already worked through all or most of the steps and is now in recovery and wants to pass his experience and guidance on, not only to be helpful but to keep himself working the program. Finding a sponsor is simply a matter of approaching someone who you believe is ready and asking.

All 12-step programs are similar in principal, but each has its own rules, expectations, and individual group dynamic, so you might have to shop around for a group that fits your needs. Overeaters Anonymous is a fellowship of compulsive overeaters with no rules about food or eating behavior, but other 12-step programs can be more regimented and might better serve people with other types of food addictions. Members of Food Addicts in Recovery Anonymous, for instance, must adapt to a disciplined way of eating that includes eliminating flour and sugar from their diet, weighing and measuring meals, no snacking, no caffeine, and no alcohol.

The benefit of any self-help group is the mutual support of people who have similar problems and similar goals. If you can't find an established group, or if the groups available to you don't suit your needs, you might want to start a small group of your own. You're probably surrounded by people who would benefit from the same type of support you're seeking and who would be willing to meet regularly.

Cross Addiction

"I have to admit that I've been a food addict since I was a little boy. I grew up in an alcoholic home and was neglected. Food was the only pleasure I had in an otherwise hostile and emotionally vacant home. I learned early that pain could be taken away by eating, and I got very good at it. In fact, I remember at five years old stealing a dollar from my mother's pocketbook and going to the corner store and buying a box of cookies because my mother wouldn't have any treats in the house.

"I have been addicted to alcohol, pot, cocaine, and nicotine, but by far, by *far*, the hardest one to manage has been food. I have been abstinent from booze, reefer, coke, and cigarettes for almost fifteen years. But food, yikes! I still struggle big time. After all, I have to eat.

"I get off the food addiction merry-go-round for a month or two, but somehow I always manage to climb back on. I consider it a true addiction. It may not be as devastating as the hangovers of alcohol, the health problems of cigarettes, or the dishonesty and bankruptcy of cocaine, but it does crush my spirit and my self-esteem, and it is the hardest addiction to break.

"For me it is always about sugar. If I have one cookie, I eat an entire sleeve. If I have a scoop of ice cream, I polish off the pint. For me, it's just like a line of coke. I cannot stop. Then, I wake up the next morning with a low-sugar headache so I get into the kids' cereal, and it's back on the merry-go-round again.

"The only thing that works for me is complete abstinence from sugary foods. Funny thing is that when I am abstinent, I feel much better physically, emotionally, and spiritually. So why do I go back? I go back because I am an addict. I have a disease that tells me I do not have a disease, and when it comes to food, I still believe what the disease tells me. My denial is such that I always come back to feeling that I can get away with eating something sweet, and the fact is that I can't. One taste, and the cravings come back, and I am absolutely powerless over the situation.

"What would really help is for me to give myself over to Overeaters Anonymous (OA), like I have with Alcoholics Anonymous (AA). The emotional support I get from the fellowship and from the higher power I found through the 12 steps are really the only things capable of filling the hole in my soul that I have been trying to fill up with food for forty-six years. I'm finding it harder to surrender to OA because I'm used to AA and the rules are different. But I know it's the only real solution so I just have to adjust. And of course, I have to be willing to give up the sweet stuff. I'm not quite there yet, but I'm on my way." —*Christopher C.*

Many legitimate, well-organized, and free discussion groups are available on the Internet; they offer invaluable support and advice to people with food addictions. Some are peer-led, and some have the benefit of professional leadership. *Caveat:* watch out for misinformation and unqualified leaders. Online groups are great for emotional support and sharing personal stories, but notoriously unreliable when it comes to facts! When you want accurate information about food, dieting, exercise, eating disorders, mental health issues, counseling, or any other topic related to food addiction, look for discussion groups that are monitored by members affiliated with professional organizations.

Individual and Group Counseling A type of psychotherapy known as *cognitive behavioral therapy* (CBT) can help food addicts change the self-destructive thoughts, feelings, and behaviors that interfere with their psychological and physical well-being. The emphasis in this type of therapy is not on reliving childhood experiences, but on a much more practical process of replacing false or self-destructive beliefs and behaviors with realistic ones. It can help you identify the underlying emotional issues that drive eating behavior such as using food for comfort, avoiding food out of fear of becoming overweight, and eating to escape from unpleasant feelings. More to the point, you can develop a plan for tackling your bad relationship with food, and figure out techniques that will make these changes more manageable and easier to cope with.

For many people, CBT is more appealing than more traditional forms of psychotherapy because it is considered a relatively quick form of treatment that focuses on giving you tools for the future rather than delving into your past. The average person undergoes treatment for about four months. Within the first few weeks, it will become obvious if CBT is going to help you,

PsychSpeak

Cognitive therapy teaches you how your own thinking patterns can give you a distorted picture of what's really going on in your life and cause symptoms of anxiety, depression, and anger. **Behavioral therapy** teaches you how to weaken the link between emotional situations and your response to them.

because that's when the most rapid progress is usually seen. The reason for this "quick fix" is that CBT is highly structured and instructive in nature. The relationship between therapist and client is like that of a teacher and a student. If you work with a CBT therapist, you might get homework that consists of reading assignments and practicing techniques you learn in your sessions. Although CBT is used to resolve all types of emotional and behavioral issues related to eating disorders and being overweight, it appears to be a particularly effective treatment for binge eating and weight loss.

A cognitive/behavioral psychotherapist who specializes in clinical and subclinical eating disorders can not only provide you with some answers, she'll also be able to ask the right questions. That's especially important if you are ever to get to the root of the self-doubt that drives your emotional eating patterns.

Many psychotherapists combine cognitive/behavioral therapy with other forms of therapy that are more centered on past experiences and emotions. Heather Ferguson, C.S.W., a psychotherapist in New York City who specializes in eating disorders and weight issues, takes an investigative approach with her clients. In the first session, she introduces the idea that she and her client will work together as anthropologists, tracing food habits back historically to try to find out how patterns developed over many years. Together, they work to understand the historical roots and emotional significance of the client's relationship with food. Most clients, she says, can remember pivotal moments, usually when family, friends, or classmates made comments about weight, when they first thought, *Aha! If I go on a diet and lose weight, I'll feel better about myself and how I look to the world.* That was the moment when they created a false sense of control over their bodies and their lives and began the destructive cycle of dieting, losing weight, gaining weight, dieting, losing weight, gaining weight—over and over again.

WEB TALK: *Psychology Today* magazine can help you find a psychologist in your area at:

therapists.psychologytoday.com

Some people benefit from group therapy. In this type of therapy, one or two therapists form a group of several patients who they feel would benefit from being a member and who also might have an effect on other members of the group. Group members share their personal struggles and feelings and practice interpersonal skills with each other. In this way, they help each other work out the dynamics of their personal relationships. According to Heather Ferguson, group therapy helps people learn that they are not alone. In group therapy, you have the opportunity to see your own qualities and difficulties mirrored in other people so you see yourself more accurately and can begin dismantling distorted thinking about your self, your body, and food.

For a young person dealing with an eating disorder such as anorexia or bulimia, a comprehensive treatment plan usually includes family therapy, which involves an assessment not only of the patient, but also of the patient's parents and siblings. A family therapist helps members identify emotionally charged topics and feelings that may have gone unexpressed, while at the same time teaching more constructive and direct ways of communicating with one another. The goal is to facilitate change within the entire family as well as to alleviate the patient's symptoms. A psychologist can guide you through the process of change, but you still will have to do most of the work. You will have to figure out how to apply what you learn in therapy to your life outside the therapist's office.

Plans and Programs Some people say you're just as likely (or unlikely) to lose weight on your own as you are by joining a commercial weight loss program, and statistics show that they're right. These programs do not have high success rates. They are based on restricted diets, and in the long run, diets don't work for most people.

But these programs *can* help certain people in certain ways. If you're overweight, need structure and attention, and want to draw from the experience of other people, you might consider one of these programs. YMCAs, YWCAs, and local community centers sometimes offer affordable weight management programs, and some of the more successful commercial programs such as Weight Watchers and Jenny Craig provide guidance and support as well. These programs also provide an educational component that can be very useful to anyone who needs to learn how to eat a portion-controlled, nutritionally balanced diet. And some people do, in fact, lose weight and keep it off with the help of these programs.

Before you sign up for any program, even one of the nationally known programs, shop around. Each program has its own approach and rules. A sound program, however, is always based on a nutritionally balanced diet combined with recommendations for regular physical activity and behavioral counseling. Your focus, and the focus of any weight control program you join, should be on eating a balanced diet that includes foods you enjoy eating, learning what it means to eat an appropriate amount of food, and becoming physically and mentally fit. The focus should *not* be on dieting. Remember that you're looking to make a lifelong commitment to a healthier lifestyle, so be sure the program also includes a transition plan that teaches you how to make better choices outside the program. Stay away from any program that promises a loss of more than a pound or two a week after the first week.

You can also check to see if your local hospital or medical center has a weight management program. Unlike most other commercial programs, medical programs usually are staffed by a team of doctors, dietitians, and sometimes psychologists and sports physiologists—the more members on the team, the better. The only drawback is that unless this type of program is covered by your health insurance, it can be very expensive.

If you're at least 20 to 30 percent above your ideal body weight or your BMI is greater than 30 and you're at risk of developing medical problems as a result of your weight, your doctor may recommend a very-low-calorie, medically supervised diet program through a local hospital or medical center. Your diet will consist of mostly or only a liquid formula that provides approximately 800 calories a day. You won't have to make any decisions about food because, for the most part, you won't be eating any. Weight loss in these programs averages about 3 to 5 pounds a week or about 44 pounds over a twelve-week period. This type of modified fast is the only near-safe way to lose this much weight this quickly. It can help a compulsive eater break bad eating habits and feel more motivated to start losing weight in a healthier way.

But very-low-calorie diets can also be hazardous to your health. That's why you can only stay on them for a short period of time and only under the supervision of a physician. It's also important to note that modified fasts don't work any better than any other diet in the long run. Once you return to normal eating, keeping the weight off is even more difficult than losing it. If you sign up for a medically supervised weight loss program, be sure it includes a maintenance plan. To be successful, that maintenance plan must include an educational component that helps you learn how to make permanent lifestyle changes such as healthier eating and more physical activity. It also must help you commit to those changes.

You might benefit from the additional support of a registered dietitian or licensed nutritionist. A dietitian picks up where a psychotherapist leaves off, focusing more on your diet and eating behavior than on the underlying causes and emotional roots of your food addiction. Choose a registered dietitian who has experience working with eating disorders and disordered eating.

You can help ensure your own success by understanding that you can't turn the responsibility for your eating habits and weight control methods completely over to someone or something else. You have to take responsibility for learning how to use and apply the tools these programs offer. In the long run, you will have to be accountable to yourself, not to any fitness program or weight loss counselor.

Treatment Centers Thousands of people with clinical and subclinical eating disorders have been treated at residential and outpatient treatment centers. According to Debra Weinberg, Program Information Manager at Renfrew Center in Philadelphia, Pennsylvania, patients come to eating disorder centers through referrals from physicians, psychologists, psychiatrists, social workers, concerned parents, and guidance counselors. Often, she says, men and women who recognize their own problems walk in on their own.

Some clinical treatment programs are hospital- or health center–based, while others are nonhospital settings. The goal of all these programs is to prevent eating disorders from progressing and, in some cases, becoming fatal. Although these programs offer similar counseling services, each has its own unique overall approach to treatment.

WEB TALK: You'll find a listing of eating disorder treatment programs at:
www.addictionresourceguide.com

Residential programs such as the Eating Disorders Program at the Menninger Clinic in Houston, Texas, and Remuda Ranch in Wickenburg, Arizona, treat anorexia, bulimia, compulsive overeating, binge eating disorder, obesity, general weight issues, and overexercising disorders, as well as the psychiatric problems that underlie these conditions. Every program is different; for example, some are faith-based, some are for women only. Rogers Memorial Hospital in Oconomowoc, Wisconsin, runs the one male-only residential center in the country, and the Eating Disorders Treatment Program at the Children's Hospital in Denver, Colorado, works with male and female patients through the age of twenty-one. The Mirasol center in Tucson, Arizona, takes an integrative approach that combines classic cognitive behavior therapy with alternative methods such as neurofeedback, clinical hypnosis, and polarity therapy. A unique program at the Avalon Hills residential eating disorders program in Petersboro, Utah, incorporates animal therapy along with more traditional art and movement therapies. According to staff psychologist Wendy Holt, horses, dogs, cats, and even reptiles have been used successfully at Avalon Hills to provide comfort and a form of connection in individual therapy sessions, to help patients think about something other than their eating disorders, and to help them develop their sense of personal power.

At the initial interview, most residential center patients are assessed to determine the level of care and length of stay required. Most residential treatment centers also offer intensive outpatient services such as individual and family counseling and day treatment programs for people in transition from the residential program or for people who don't require residential treatment. In some cases, if the "fit" isn't right between a patient and a particular center, the patient might be referred elsewhere. Most treatment centers can also help over the phone by making referrals to private psychotherapists or other local advisers.

Residential treatment programs such as Milestones in Recovery in North Miami Beach, Florida, and outpatient programs such as Diets Don't Work in Laguna Niguel, California, consider some eating disorders to be part of an addictive process. These centers are designed to address both the addictive and emotional aspects of eating disorders. Eating-disorder treatment centers that base their treatment on the addiction model often feature "dual diagnosis" programs to address cross-dependencies on alcohol or drugs. Such programs usually see a variety of people, including some who come without a secondary addiction and those who have gained a foothold on their substance abuse problem and now seek to address their food addiction. According to Dr. Marty Lerner, executive and clinical director of Milestones, many of the "dually addicted" people he sees don't initially acknowledge their other dependencies and initially are seeking to deal only with their food addiction. They then come to realize

GET PSYCHED

"When you choose a treatment center, look for one that not only helps you develop a normal relationship with food, but also helps you decide what kind of person you want to be in the world when you no longer have an eating disorder." *–Jeanne Rust, executive director and founder, Mirasol: The Arizona Center for Eating Disorders* they need to address their drug or alcohol dependencies as well. Food addiction programs generally include a mix of individual psychotherapy, family support, and group therapy. They often recommend 12-step meetings modeled on Alcoholics Anonymous and Narcotics Anonymous, if that type of group is right for the individual.

Eating disorder treatment programs, particularly the residential programs, can be very expensive, and costs are not always covered by health insurance plans. Some centers offer sliding scale fees, however, and others try to raise funds to occasionally help people in need.

> **WEB TALK:** Locate workshops, lectures, and retreats for food addicts at:
> ▲ www.foodaddiction.com

Medical Options Many physicians and other health experts believe obesity is a chronic medical condition that can and should be treated with medication, just as you would treat heart disease, diabetes, or any other chronic condition with specialized medications. Prescription weight loss medications are approved by the Food and Drug Administration (FDA) for people with a body mass index (BMI) of 30 or more, or with a BMI of 27 or more with at least one of several weight-related conditions such as diabetes and hypertension. Clinical studies have found that people who use weight loss medications lose up to 20 percent more weight than people who try diet and exercise alone. One problem with drug therapy for weight control right now is that chronic conditions require ongoing treatment, and, due to their side effects and potential for addiction, most of the prescription weight loss medications available are approved only for short-term use.

Whether or not you decide to take weight loss drugs is between you and your physician. If your weight is really high and your ability to lose weight is very low, you might be a good candidate for drug therapy. Keep in mind, however, that many people regain the weight they lose once they stop taking the medication. Also, all drugs, including prescription and over-the-counter (OTC) weight loss formulas, have side effects, and some can be serious. Your doctor can help you decide which weight loss medication might be right for you and if the health risks associated with being overweight in your particular case outweigh the risks of taking that medication.

Every drugstore and health food store stocks an array of over-the-counter diet supplements that supposedly burn fat, rev up metabolism, or put a brake on your appetite. Some will do nothing at all for you and others might help you lose a pound or two initially, although there is no evidence that any OTC weight loss supplement works in the long run. And because dietary supplements are not regulated the same way prescription medications are, taking them can be dangerous to your health. Like prescription medications, OTC drugs and supplements can have serious side effects.

In the past, several OTC weight loss supplements have been associated with dangerous side effects and even a number of deaths, and as a result, the FDA has banned many once-popular products. For instance, throughout the 1990s, the FDA received reports of circulatory problems, including high blood pressure, in people using products that contained an herbal ingredient known as ephedra or ephedrine. By late 2003, following the death of baseball player Steve Bechler, who had been using a product containing ephedra, the FDA started warning consumers not to use any product that contained ephedra. By early 2004, these products were banned from sale in this country. In another recent example, OTC diet products imported from China were found to contain an amphetamine-type drug known as fenfluramine, which was once sold by prescription only in the United States and has since been withdrawn from the market because of a link to heart valve problems.

There is evidence that antidepressants, particularly selective serotonin reuptake inhibitors (SSRIs), are helpful in treating eating disorders and weight and body image issues because undiagnosed depression often underlies the more evident symptoms.

WEB TALK: For up-to-date FDA warning and safety information on dietary supplements, check:

vm.cfsan.fda.gov/~dms/supplmnt.html

Remember, though, that if you decide to take any type of weight loss medication, you still have to change your relationship with food if you are to be successful at maintaining weight loss.

Role Models

Earlier in your life, your parents, family members, teachers, and young friends all served as your role models. Whether you realize it or not, much of what you learned from these people throughout your childhood is still with you, including your ideas about who you are and what you look like. For better or for worse, early role models tend to have a lasting effect.

Unfortunately, many of the beliefs and attitudes we carry from childhood end up directing our lives in ways that leave us feeling frustrated and unhappy. If you grew up hearing a message that you were unattractive or imperfect in any way, you might still view yourself that way. If you were raised to believe you weren't capable of making your own decisions, you might still mistrust your judgment. You may not have known why you feel this way, but once you put your finger on the source of your discomfort, you can start to fix it.

Most of your life you may have been dreaming an impossible body dream based on what you've seen in movies and magazines. If so, maybe it's time to get real about your role models. Actors, dancers, athletes, entertainers, and fashion models aren't realistic physical role models for most of us, and many of these celebrities are thin because they suffer from eating disorders. In addition, the picture you see in a magazine or onscreen has often been enhanced to appear much more perfect than the person is in real life. It's unrealistic and simply a waste of time to compare yourself to an image that was created on a computer or perfected with an airbrush, or, worse yet, to model yourself after someone who maintains weight with the help of an eating disorder.

Good role models can provide inspiration and motivation to maintain a healthier, more positive lifestyle. The best role models are people you feel you can relate to, often because they've been in a similar situation and have gotten through the tough times, dealt with setbacks, and still came out on top. You're able to see just how long it took someone else to achieve success so you won't feel as discouraged when your own goals seem unreachable.

> **GET PSYCHED**
>
> Your best role models are everyday people who live happy, healthy, hopeful lives. Find people in your life who inspire you to think in new ways and move in new directions. Look for people who have successfully transformed themselves and their lives.

The people who are most successful at changing compulsive eating behavior and other forms of food addiction are people who take responsibility for themselves. They have a great deal of determination and are committed to living healthier lives. They want to give up their preoccupation with food more than they want to continue practicing self-destructive behavior. When you go looking for role models, look for other people who have active food addictions or are recovering from food addictions and who are as determined as you are to be successful at maintaining a healthier weight and a better attitude toward food.

What You Can Do

When it comes to making difficult lifestyle changes, you have to be your own best friend and cheerleader. But you also need all the support you can get, from wherever you can get it.

- ☐ Avoid blaming other people and situations for your food addiction. Instead, take responsibility for charting this new course in your life.
- ☐ Ask family and friends for support, but don't be shocked if they can't give you what you need.
- ☐ If you don't get help and support where you expect it, look elsewhere.

☐ Compare the different types of group programs that can provide guidance, therapy, and support for people with food addictions and eating disorders.

☐ Have a complete physical check-up once a year. If you are having emotional problems, you can discuss those with your family physician, who should be able to recommend professional help.

☐ Get referrals for psychotherapists, nutritionists, and other professionals from people you know and trust.

☐ Look for role models you can relate to and who inspire you by their own experiences.

Part 4

A Personal Plan for Healthy Living

Building a healthier relationship with food requires a commitment to positive changes in the way you think about yourself and the way you treat yourself. In Part 4, you'll find exercises to strengthen your mind and your body. You'll also find motivational techniques and ways to handle the inevitable bumps you'll encounter on your road to success.

13

Affirmative Action

The more flexible you are and the more easily you accept change, the easier it is to let go of an obsession with food and move on to a happier, healthier lifestyle. As you feel your life improving, you will experience many changes in the way you see yourself and in the way you see the world around you. Even though these might be changes for the better, they can be scary simply because they are different. You'll be thinking in new ways and doing many things differently than you've done them before. Remember, fear can prevent you from letting go of self-destructive habits and truly enjoying the rest of your life. Don't let it happen!

Accept Yourself

When you free yourself from your food addiction, you will be a different person from who you are now. You will think, look, and feel different. Getting to that truth, that place of *self-acceptance,* comes from exploring yourself from the inside out. Defining who you are and what you want from life is the first step to knowing yourself and getting what you want—a happier, healthier life.

Self-knowledge—a clear vision of your own character, powers, strengths, limitations, and potential—isn't something you're born with; it's something many people struggle to learn, and it can take a lifetime. You have gathered a great deal of knowledge and experience in your life so far, which helps you understand who you are. That's not your whole story. You are also everything you have the potential to be, if you give yourself the opportunity to reach that potential.

PsychSpeak

Self-acceptance means loving yourself and approving of yourself, without judgment, in spite of your limitations.

Self-acceptance means you'll stop being your own worst enemy. You'll stop picking on yourself for things no one else even notices. You'll feel more comfortable in your own skin and have an easier time being true to yourself. You'll stop worrying so much about what other people think and have more control over the direction of your own life.

When you accept yourself, you stop comparing yourself to other people. There is such a thing as healthy competition, but as a food addict, it's generally not a good idea to compare yourself too closely to others. Inevitably, you'll compare yourself to someone who can do something much better than you can or who has already achieved success in an area in which you're still striving. If you're trying to lose weight, you'll compare yourself to someone who's skinnier. If you've just joined a gym, you'll compare yourself to someone who's been working out for ten years. In the end, you'll feel bad about yourself. And don't think you'll feel better by comparing yourself to someone who hasn't been as successful at overcoming food and weight issues. Looking down on someone else and propping up your own ego by feeling superior to another person isn't the way to go. Better to turn all that attention you give to others back around to yourself.

Remember, the people who count the most in your life—close family members and good friends—like you for who you are and for the things that make you unique. You're the only one who's comparing yourself to anyone else.

Accepting yourself also means accepting your limitations. That doesn't mean you have to give up hope or stop striving to improve. But rather than focusing on the things you can't change, rather than setting impossibly high standards for yourself and setting yourself up to fail, concentrate on what you do well and on all you've done to get yourself to this point. Stay focused on realistic goals. As you begin to accept yourself, you ...

- Grow in self-esteem.
- Stop struggling to win approval from others.
- Believe that you have value and believe that others know it, too.
- Can take more risks without worrying about the consequences.
- Become more independent.
- Live your life to please yourself, not to please others.
- Show your flaws to others and expect them to love and respect you anyway.
- Give yourself plenty of leeway when it comes to making mistakes.
- Feel a sense of freedom.
- Are less afraid of failure.
- Accept yourself and expect others to accept you for who you are, not what you look like or what you accomplish.

Self-acceptance doesn't mean giving up on yourself. You can accept who you are, what you look like, and how much you weigh right now and still be determined to change what you don't like about yourself. When you're no longer struggling against who and what you are, you'll be more effective at making changes because you'll be starting from a more positive, clear-minded place.

GET PSYCHED

"Acceptance is not approval. It means you've stopped struggling emotionally against reality. You may not like the idea of being a food addict; you may not want it in your life. Acceptance says, 'Here it is anyway. Now what am I going to do about it?'"
—*Theresa Wright, M.S., R.D., president, Renaissance Nutrition Center, Inc., Plymouth Meeting, Pennsylvania*

Express Yourself

To get through any process of change, it usually helps to talk about your feelings and concerns with the people you most trust. Expressing yourself in words helps you clarify how you feel and prevents problems from festering and growing larger than life inside your head. The people who care about you probably have a different perspective on your life, and might be able to shed new light on your problems and help resolve any fears you have. Getting help is part of taking care of yourself. Start with family, friends, teachers, school counselors, or whoever is most available to you. If you feel your food issues are serious, however, you should consider professional help. You might avoid relapses or more serious problems down the road if you ask for the right help at the right time. (See Chapter 12 for more information on finding support.)

WEB TALK: Share your feelings and experiences with food addiction at:

www.something-fishy.org/ online/bulletinboard.php

People who have been hurt in the past often have a hard time trusting and confiding in others, even the people they love, often because the people they love have been the very ones who betrayed their trust. To rebuild trust, you have to risk being open with people, expressing how you feel, and sharing your vulnerabilities. If you don't take that risk, fear will weaken your ability to change your thinking and behavior patterns by restricting your communication with other people. Working on self-acceptance is an important first step toward being able to trust others and communicate better, because when you accept yourself for who you are, you'll be able to let down your defensive guard.

For so many people, the struggle with food addiction is really a struggle with unresolved feelings. You know now that you have to find a way to express these feelings one way or another so you don't continue to suppress them with food. One tactic that may help you stop overeating in response to strong feelings is learning how to express your feelings to other people without putting them on the defensive:

- Avoid blame. By not blaming, you show that you understand your perspective is not the only one, and that you're not the only one who has suffered.
- Speak about your own feelings and actions, not the other person's. This avoids putting the other person on the defensive. For example, if, when you were young, everyone in your family was allowed to have dessert except you, rather than confront your mother with her unfair rules, tell her how you felt when you were a child and about the secret relationship you developed with food as a result.
- Be honest to yourself and to the other person.
- Make it clear that you're open to hearing the other person's side—and try hard to follow through!
- Stay focused on your feelings, rather than the problem itself. If you repeatedly say "I feel" or "I felt," you're less likely to sound confrontational.
- If the conversation provokes anger on either side, stop and take a break.
- Admit your own mistakes.
- Be willing to listen, forgive, and move on.

Openly and directly expressing your feelings in emotionally tense situations isn't always easy. Sometimes it's impossible. You can't always lay it on the line with your boss if you need your job. You probably can't tell your mother-in-law exactly what you think of her if you want to preserve your marriage. You might not be able to tell your parents exactly how you feel about having grown up in a household that destroyed your self-esteem.

In these situations, you can take the second-best step, however, which is to talk to someone else about it, preferably someone who is sympathetic and familiar with the situation and people involved. If that's not possible, you can put your words down in writing. Address an angry letter to your boss or in-law that will never be delivered but that serves to unload some of your feelings. Get your feelings out of your mind and heart and onto that piece of paper, then destroy the letter once it's written. It may seem pointless, but writing it out can help clarify your thoughts and move your hurt and angry feelings outward, letting you forget about it.

you're not alone

Asking for Help

"I've been overweight most of my life, so when I lost more than 60 pounds a few years ago, I felt like I finally had my life under control. I saw a psychotherapist once a week for two years and really learned a lot about myself and how I use food. At the same time, I joined a weight loss center and learned how to eat better. These were two very big steps for me because I have always been reluctant to ask for help when I need it. When I lost the weight, I felt like I had done an amazing thing, and I was very proud. Even though my weight fluctuates, I still feel like I did an amazing thing because I've never been that heavy since. But I still struggle with the idea of asking for help, and it can be my downfall when I'm trying to maintain my weight.

"Whenever my life gets stressful and I have too much to do, I fall off the food wagon. It happens all the time. I stop taking care of myself. I don't eat regular meals, so when I finally do eat, I eat too much. I use stress as an excuse to eat fast food. I start to feel the weight coming on pretty quickly. Then I feel ashamed of myself and guilty, and I start thinking that it's just too hard to keep weight off, and I want to give up.

"I can always tell when stress is getting to me and I'm heading for a relapse, and the problem is I don't do anything to prevent it. I end up doing just the opposite of what would be best for me. I clam up and hide away from people rather than reach out for help. There are plenty of people in my life who are happy to lend a hand, but I still don't ask. I don't want anyone to know I've let things get out of control.

"My therapist used to do role-playing exercises with me to teach me how to ask for what I need. She would pretend to be someone else in my life and I would be me, and we would act out a hypothetical situation where I would have to ask her for help with something. That way I got to practice expressing myself in situations that were very difficult for me. I don't feel like I need to go back into therapy, but I do feel like I need to somehow practice again so when my life starts to feel out of control, I'll have an easier time doing it for real." —*Teri G.*

Coping With Change

To break the bonds of your food addiction, you'll first have to come to terms with the idea of change. To be successful, you have to change something about the way you think and the way you eat. You'll need to make internal changes, like thinking about food differently and paying more attention to your body, and you'll need to learn to cope with events in your life or new situations in ways that don't involve food. And when you free yourself from a food addiction, your work isn't done. Maintaining a healthier relationship with food takes just as much patience and open-mindedness to change as it took to develop it.

Some people thrive on change; more commonly, people don't like the prospect of varying their routine. If you are afraid of or threatened by change, it will be harder for you to break old eating habits and thinking patterns and allow yourself to move forward. Eating might have been the way you coped with change in the past, but for a recovering food addict, relying on food is no longer an option.

The changes that create the most turmoil are those we feel we have no control over. It helps to understand and accept the fact that you have no control over most external events in your life. You cannot change the outside world or the people in it; you can control only the way you respond to situations and maintain your self-control. To a food addict, that means your greatest power lies in changing your response to your eating triggers.

Theresa Wright, a registered dietitian and owner of the Renaissance Nutrition Center in Plymouth Meeting, Pennsylvania, points out that when you are overweight, you have fantasies and expectations about what your life will be like when you've reached your ideal weight. When you lose weight, those ideas either come true or they don't. Either way, it's scary. If your dreams don't come true, it's disappointing and frustrating. If they do come true, it can be downright scary because it's such a big difference.

Now that I've lost a good deal of weight, I find I'm often uncomfortable walking around in this new shape and doing normal things like shopping for clothes. This is what I wanted, what I worked so hard for, so why doesn't it always feel good?

You're in the early stages of the "new you," and you're still adapting to the change. Nutritionist Theresa Wright explains that a big change like dramatic weight loss inevitably brings other changes into your life. You might be getting more attention or a different type of attention than you're used to getting. People who have known you for years might be looking at you differently, perhaps more closely. You might feel self-conscious. You might have social or professional expectations of yourself that you're not ready to fulfill, such as rekindling your love life or pursuing a new career. Others might have expectations you don't want to fulfill. You might choose to slow down your weight loss for a time to allow yourself to adjust emotionally to the change. Try to avoid other major changes until you are more comfortable with your new weight. This is a good time to re-examine how you want your life to be and to reach out for support from the people you trust most.

All change can be stressful, and the way stress affects you depends on how you react to it. If you react in negative ways, such as with anger or overeating, stress will take more of a toll on your mental and physical health. That's why it's important to develop good coping skills. Some things you can do to alleviate the stress of change include the following:

- Face your fears about change. Fear of change can mean fear of failure or fear of success. Either way, these fears stem from self-doubt, and the antidote is to work to improve your self-esteem and learn to have faith in yourself.

- Learn to adjust your plans when things don't go as you intended.

- Trust your own judgment when it comes to making decisions.

- Look at mistakes as learning opportunities.

- Try not to get discouraged.

- Pick yourself up as soon as you fall.
- Leave room in your schedule for unexpected events.

Sometimes you can change your behavior directly, but at other times, you might have to change your attitude and your approach before you can successfully change your behavior. If you need to have a difficult conversation with your parents or your mate before you can change your eating behavior, you might first have to confront your fears about expressing your feelings. If you're looking for inspiration to get more physical activity into your day by changing your exercise routine, ask yourself if it's enough to try a new machine at the gym, or do you need to boost your attitude toward exercise in general? When changes in attitude and behavior are difficult, particularly when those changes involve other people, it might help to think about what kind of physical and emotional shape you want to be in six months from now. You probably can't get there without taking a risk or pushing yourself in a different direction. When you're clear about how you feel and what you need to do, it's easier to take action.

You can make small changes in your life to help you get used to the idea of bigger change. Even some simple, everyday things such as these will help you become more flexible:

- Change what you eat for breakfast.
- Try a new food you've never eaten before.
- Change your exercise routine.
- Walk short distances instead of driving.
- Shop in a different grocery store.

What other changes can you think of to fit into your life?

GET PSYCHED

"Never give up! Most people blow it several times before they are successful at any lifestyle change. You can't let frustration or fear of failing stop you from moving forward again. If you try to change your behavior and slip up within the first month, you're still twice as likely to succeed in the next six months as someone who didn't try at all."
—*James O. Prochaska, Ph.D., author of* Changing for Good

Opening yourself to change is scary because it involves taking risks. The biggest risk you face when you decide to change your attitude and eating behavior is that you might do a lot of hard work and then fail. The outcome is uncertain, that's true. Once you take an honest look at your lifestyle and review your options for improving your health, you'll realize it's worth the risk.

The next time you have occasion to make a resolution—your birthday, an anniversary, or New Year's Eve, for instance—remember that the changes you want to make will be easier and longer-lasting if you focus on eating and exercise habits and behavior rather than on the number of pounds you want to lose, how many calories you're eating, or how you want to reshape your body. Whatever you do, don't promise yourself you'll go on a diet! Resolve to take small steps and make gradual changes in the way you eat, the way you think about food, the way you look at yourself, and the amount of exercise you get on a regular basis. Deal with one change at a time. It will be much easier to stick to your resolutions if you keep them manageable and don't over-whelm yourself with too many changes at once.

A Positive Approach

Psychological research supports the notion that an optimistic viewpoint—feeling hopeful and expecting positive results from your efforts—often results in better physical and mental health. A negative attitude, on the other hand, can be self-defeating because the way you think affects the way you act and a defeatist mind-set often results in destructive behavior. No matter how well you can do something, no matter how successful you could be at losing weight or getting fit or developing a healthier attitude toward food, you have to believe in yourself and expect success, or you won't even try.

Adopting a positive attitude has nothing to do with living in a state of denial. You can adopt a positive attitude and still accept the unpleasant realities of your food addiction. You will have to accept that certain people and situations that have triggered your destructive eating behavior in the past aren't going to change. To accept that means to give up the struggle of trying to change other people and external events so you can focus on the changes you need to make in yourself. You can see your own self-destructive habits, self-defeating thinking, and poor food choices for what they are and at the same time have an optimistic attitude about changing them.

Sometimes eating disorders combine with other psychological problems and other addictions. Research shows that the longer someone suffers from an eating disorder such as compulsive overeating, anorexia, or bulimia, the more likely it is they will also suffer from anxiety or depression. Some food addicts are cross-addicted to alcohol or drugs or find other self-destructive ways to help block out emotional pain. In these cases, it is important to get an accurate diagnosis and get the right treatment. It's difficult to begin a program of positive change when you are feeling sad, hopeless, and pessimistic about your future. If you feel this way and it's been going on for more than a couple weeks, consider seeking professional help.

> **WEB TALK:** If you think depression is preventing you from feeling optimistic, check your symptoms at:
>
> **www.nimh.nih.gov/ healthinformation/ depressionmenu.cfm**

Have Patience! Patience is valuable for coping with long lines, being put on hold, or interacting with disagreeable people. Without realizing it, however, you might be especially impatient with yourself. Real inner change takes time, and the danger of impatience is that you can end up feeling angry and frustrated with yourself when you don't see quick results.

Patience takes a great deal of inner strength. In fact, patience *is* inner strength—and you need a lot of it to stay on the slow road to recovery from a food addiction. Every breakthrough in food addiction recovery, no matter how small, should be thought of as an extraordinary achievement. All your small accomplishments along the way to recovery add up to the big one—freedom from addiction. There are no quick fixes when it comes to changing a lifetime of self-destructive thinking and bad eating habits. It's a day-by-day process that can go on for many years or decades. If you have the patience, if you can wait for yourself to get there, it can happen.

Your lack of patience might stem from false beliefs about yourself. For instance, you might think you should be able to handle everything yourself or that you'll never really be able to change. You might think that there is only one way to accomplish your goals and become impatient with yourself when that way doesn't work. If you've been dieting your whole life and it hasn't worked for you, you might feel impatient with the idea of trying a new approach to losing weight. If you're impatient, it will be difficult for you to take the baby steps often necessary to reach your goals.

Rather than get discouraged or anxious when your progress is slow, remember that change is supposed to take time. Remind yourself that you are on the path to recovery from a food addiction that's been with you for a long time. Continue to give yourself credit for everything you've accomplished so far.

GET PSYCHED

When you lack patience, you feel upset, anxious, tense, irritated, nervous, frustrated, out of control, ill-tempered, rushed, and often ignored. When you have patience, you feel calm, peaceful, tolerant, content, accepting, compassionate, and often relaxed. You choose.

Short-term goals are useful when you're feeling impatient with yourself and change is going slowly. Set a small goal for today and think about what you need to do to achieve it. This helps you feel in charge of your life again because you're making something happen while waiting to reach your long-term goals.

If you need help developing more patience, try one (or all) of these exercises:

- Focus on daily, short-term goals rather than on your long-term goals.

- Approach life a day at a time.
- Stay in the present. Don't spend too much time dwelling on the past or worrying about the future.

Patience means taking the time to gather your resources, doing your homework, and waiting until the right moment to make a big decision. You might want to lose weight and, if you're impatient, you might be tempted to go on yet another crash diet, even though the odds are against your long-term success. In all likelihood, you'll lose some weight, you'll gain it back, and you'll have to start again from scratch. In the long run, you'll have to wait longer for what you want than if you had the patience to lose weight a little more slowly and by healthier, more natural means.

Developing a Can-Do Attitude To be successful at anything, you must believe in yourself and in what you're doing. You have to be motivated by the belief that you can do whatever you set out to do, because your attitude will affect your behavior. Other people might help motivate you by cheering you on or giving you a gentle push in the right direction, but it's up to you to stay actively involved in your own life and to take the steps necessary to develop a lasting, positive relationship with food.

Having a positive, can-do attitude doesn't mean you have to jump for joy whenever you think of the emotional work that lies ahead of you. It doesn't mean you're happy all the time or that you'll always be successful. That's not realistic. It does mean you'll look for solutions rather than giving up and you'll be more likely to make more changes in your diet and exercise because you feel confident that your efforts will be rewarded.

If you let yourself think you'll never improve your relationship with food, or that the changes you have to make are just too difficult, you'll start to lose hope. If you stop believing in yourself,

WEB TALK: Read about the Women's Campaign to End Body Hatred and Dieting at:

www.overcomingovereating.com

you won't be able to help yourself. Develop and maintain a more positive attitude. Here are some suggestions:

- Surround yourself with positive-thinking, successful people.
- Keep a journal of any positive changes you experience in your thinking and behavior.
- Praise and reward yourself often, especially when you accomplish one of your goals.
- Give yourself all the time you need to develop new habits and reach your goals.
- Come up with new and satisfying ways to spend your time as you work toward change.
- Try to replay your successes in your mind; try not to replay your mistakes.

Nutritionist Theresa Wright advises her clients to take a look at their good qualities and strengths and ask themselves, "What can I do to make my positive qualities stronger?" "What strengths do I have that will help me solve this problem?" She points out that people often spend so much time and effort berating themselves for having a food problem that they have no time left to work on the solution. Whatever you focus on, she says, will grow and take up more space in your life. Focus on the positive, on your strengths, and use them to get the life you really want.

Anything you can do to incorporate more fun into your life and try to develop your sense of humor will certainly help you have a more positive attitude toward yourself, your life, and the emotional work that lies ahead of you. Do what you can to help lighten your emotional load and distract yourself from obsessing about your weight—find healthy role models, develop new hobbies and interests, get out more, take more vacations, begin to enjoy your meals, and surround yourself with fun and funny people.

What You Can Do

Some of the most important steps you need to take to improve your relationship with food have nothing to do with eating or weight control and everything to do with putting yourself in a healthy emotional state.

- ☐ Accept yourself for who you are right now so you're not struggling with the past at the same time you're struggling to improve your future.
- ☐ Define what you want for yourself. It's important to have a clear sense of who you want to be and how you want your life to proceed when you conquer your food addiction.
- ☐ Talk to someone—a friend, family member, counselor or fellow member of a reputable online support group—about your feelings.
- ☐ Take risks. What you've been doing so far to fight your food addiction hasn't been working, so it's time to try something new. That might mean ending a destructive relationship, joining a 12-step program, or simply adopting a new attitude toward yourself and your eating habits. Risk-taking is scary, but sometimes it's the only path to change.
- ☐ If you're having a hard time feeling hopeful about the changes you must make, consider professional counseling.
- ☐ Practice patience.
- ☐ Come up with new ways to make your life more fun.

Emotional Makeover

After you've decided to break the bonds of your food addiction once and for all, you will enter a new stage. Life is no longer about quick fixes or frantically trying to figure out how you're going to get in shape for a high school reunion, and it's not about eating out of boredom, unhappiness, or habit. When you made the decision to free yourself from your food addiction for good, you decided to make big changes in your emotional life. You also chose to live a healthier, more active lifestyle than the one you were living before. Maintaining a healthier relationship with food—and with yourself—means an ongoing commitment to that new lifestyle.

Motivation and Commitment

You have eating habits that are strongly ingrained: You're accustomed to eating a certain amount of food at certain times. If you need to lose a substantial amount of weight, you're probably talking about changing lifelong habits—habits you've probably had longer than you've carried your excess weight. Even if you're only trying to shake off 10 or 15 pounds, you still have to be committed to making changes in your thinking patterns, eating habits, and exercise routine. Commitment is especially important when you're trying to maintain a healthy weight because for most people, sticking to it is harder than losing the weight in the first place.

If you make a commitment to better health rather than to a change in your appearance, you'll be less likely to fall for diet gimmicks or "magic bullet" solutions that don't work. You'll realize that these false solutions only get in the way of real progress because they distract you from getting to the root of your food addiction.

GET PSYCHED

Commitment means you're not going to give up on yourself. You're going to keep at it until your new eating and exercise habits become just that, habits. You're going to stick with it until you get to the point where you're more motivated to move forward than backward.

Get motivated to stick with your plan by figuring out what matters most to you, what makes you feel happy and satisfied. Motivation comes from the rewards you get for working so hard to improve your attitude and behavior. Using the following suggestions or coming up with your own, figure out what motivates you and use that information to remind yourself why you're doing all this hard work:

- Losing weight
- Maintaining weight
- Staying healthy
- Getting healthier
- Controlling disease
- Getting in a better mood
- Feeling a sense of accomplishment
- Getting stronger
- Staying in control
- Boosting energy
- Looking more attractive
- Getting tangible rewards
- Leaving obsessive thinking behind
- Setting a good example for my children
- Overcoming self-doubt

- Feeling proud
- Living longer

Your best motivators are the things that really matter to you. If you're not concerned with your health right now, then preventing heart disease won't motivate you to take an aerobics class or cut back on saturated fat in your diet. On the other hand, if you want to lose weight and feel better about yourself, those are your best motivators for going to the gym and watching what you eat.

Approach-avoidance conflict, or a push-pull situation, is normal for people who want to change their behavior. You want to be physically healthy, but at the same time, you don't want to give up any pleasures. You have to decide whether to struggle against the problem or give in.

Under these circumstances, a good coach—whether it's a friend or professional counselor—can help keep you motivated. When you are distracted by conflicting desires or other events in your life, you might need someone to remind you to focus on your goals.

> ### PsychSpeak
>
> **Approach-avoidance conflict** occurs when your goal has both positive and negative aspects. You want something and you don't want it at the same time, usually because the prize comes at a price. You must make a choice between struggling toward your goal or staying where you are.

Make a Promise to Yourself If you've been yo-yo dieting most of your life and gaining and losing weight as a result, or promising yourself that you'll give up your obsession with food once and for all and always breaking that promise, you might be afraid to make yet another commitment to yourself. This time, make broader promises that are easier to keep. Instead of promising yourself you'll lose weight or fit into a new dress size or avoid anything that contains fat or carbohydrates, simply make a promise to start taking better care of yourself. That's the healthiest and most honest place to start.

Look over the following checklist of promises you can make to yourself to help improve your overall health and your relationship with food. They're broad enough and open-ended enough to personalize them to fit your own situation. Check off the promises you feel you need to make to yourself, or create your own list, adding other promises and putting your priorities higher on the list.

☐ Put your health first by doing something healthy for yourself every day.

☐ Never go on a calorie-restricted diet again.

☐ Find and work with a registered dietitian who specializes in weight and eating disorders.

☐ Start preplanning meals and snacks.

☐ Find ways to make healthy eating easy.

☐ Find and work with a mental health professional, such as a social worker or psychotherapist, who specializes in weight and body image issues, food addictions, and eating disorders.

GET PSYCHED

"Most of my clients know how to eat healthfully; they just can't do it on their own. It's as if they are hardwired to reach for food whenever a feeling surfaces. We habitually reach for the only coping mechanism we have perfected—eating more food." —*Rebecca Cooper, M.A., registered behavioral therapist, Diets Don't Work*

☐ Reduce stress by making more time for yourself.

☐ Reduce stress by getting enough sleep.

☐ Develop new interests that will help distract you from your obsession with food and your body.

☐ Be honest with yourself.

☐ See your doctor for a routine physical checkup.

☐ Get in the habit of reflecting on your goals and regularly renewing your commitment to healthier thinking and living.

Stick With It Make healthy eating and physical activity priorities until they become habits. That could take several weeks or even several months of constant repetition. Here are some ideas to help you stick with it:

- Have a plan. It can be flexible, but be sure to outline your goals for each day.

- Do what you can. There will be days when you can't eat perfectly at every meal or bring yourself to do any real exercise. Do the best you can, then call it a day.

- Know your limits. If you push yourself too hard, you'll exhaust yourself and give up.

- Stick with your existing eating and exercise plan until you're sure you're ready for a change.

- Work up to a maximum—don't try to give it your all at once. Always start slow and make gradual changes.

- When you make a mistake, pick yourself up right away and start moving forward by doing something productive to counter the mistake.

- Don't try to do anything you truly hate to do, or you won't be able to stick with it.

- Stay motivated by reminding yourself of where you want to be six months, a year, and five years from now.

- Instead of thinking about how difficult it is to eat a healthy meal or put in a half-hour of exercise, think about how good you're going to feel once you've done it.

- Develop a long-term relationship with someone who can help keep you motivated—a workout buddy, a nutritionist, a counselor, someone you meet at a support group—anyone you feel you can work with right now and whom you can check in with from time to time, even after you've achieved your goals.

WEB TALK: Find a guide to behavior change from the National Institutes of Health at:

www.nhlbi.nih.gov/health/public/heart/ obesity/lose_wt/behavior.htm

you're not alone

Why Me?

"I found out I was fat in fourth grade when my neighbor's uncle told me I had legs like a man. That was also the year everyone was wearing leotard sets—tight-fitting shorts, pants, and tops that came in horizontal stripes or solids. They were comfortable and good for climbing trees and playing kickball and riding bikes. Those were my favorite things to do in third grade. I'd throw on my clothes, not giving a thought to how I looked, just wanting to feel able to move in my clothes, and go off to play with the neighborhood kids.

"Fourth grade shouldn't have been any different, but along came Heidi and Jan, who lived around the corner from us and became my sister's and my best friends in fourth grade. We did everything together. They wore leotard sets, too. But they always had the horizontal striped sets, while my mom always bought me the solids. Heidi and Jan were skinny. I was not. I started to feel like I was all wrong, and they were clearly right. They tried to soothe me and tell me it was just baby fat and I'd grow out of it. But the clincher was that they ate massive amounts of frozen French toast, dripping with butter. They ate double-scoop ice cream cones dipped in chocolate. They had junk food in their house with no limits on when or how much they could eat. And they did eat. And eat, and eat. And they were still skinny.

"Although I was only nine and had not yet studied genetics, I was, unknowingly, getting my first introduction to being a loser in the gene game. It was also the beginning of a life-long obsession with comparing my body to every other female I would come in contact with. My compulsive eating behavior didn't start until much later. In fourth grade, I ate less than Heidi and Jan did. I started to sneak-eat in seventh grade. From there I got caught up in the dieting game—a game I could never win.

"Over the years, I have done an enormous amount of work on my food addiction. I have identified the emotional reasons behind my using food. I have replaced my unconscious eating behavior with healthier habits. I have found that my compulsive eating behaviors have subsided enormously, but although my food addiction is resolved, I am left with a thin addiction. Even though I look at other women who are big and beautiful and honestly see them as sexy and appealing, the standard I hold for myself seems to be different. I continue to compare myself to other women, and I'm still not at peace with my body type.

"When I look back at pictures of me in third and fourth grade, what I see is an athletic girl, not fat by any standards, but short and solid. I am forty-seven now, 5'1", weigh 135 pounds, and even though I'm not tremendously overweight and I am told that I have a sexy, curvy body, I still see my legs as tree stumps. But there are bright spots, the brightest being the times my seven-year-old son hugs me and says, "You have the perfect snuggling body, Mom, all soft and squishy." In that respect, I know my body is okay." —Deah S.

Mind Over Matter

In some food addiction circles, there's a lot of talk about self-love and learning to like yourself before you can develop a healthier relationship with food. It's easy to see why self-love can help you get to a healthy weight and stay there. When you love someone, you naturally want to treat that person with care and respect. You don't want to pick apart or find fault with that person. When you love yourself, it's the same thing. You don't have to shower yourself with terms of endearment or be blind to your own faults, but you do want to treat yourself better.

Never underestimate how hard it is to change addictive behavior and how much support you'll need to stay motivated and committed to changing. Most people who lose motivation do so because they've set their sights too high and have unrealistic expectations about how much weight they can lose or how much exercise they can fit into their schedules. Be realistic when you set goals, and be flexible about changing them. Even though permanent change in attitude and behavior comes slowly, you can help yourself stay motivated by paying attention to every small success.

Instead of thinking of yourself as fat, try thinking of yourself as out of balance. To some degree, you've been eating an unbalanced diet. An overzealous approach to exercise or a lack of exercise has thrown your health out of balance. At times, your emotions have been out of balance, too. Once your emotions and lifestyle become balanced, so will your body.

You won't be able to change your eating habits until you change the way you think about food. In Chapter 2, you learned how your internal dialogue, or self-talk, affects the way you feel about yourself and how negative self-talk can easily make you feel quite

GET PSYCHED

If you want outside help to stay motivated, look for people at home and on the job who will remind you, without criticizing, that you don't want to eat certain foods or that you're slipping back into an old, destructive routine such as putting yourself down or isolating yourself. These people could play a major role in your early success.

WEB TALK: Find tools for balancing your lifestyle at:

www.coping.org/balanced/
content.htm

bad about yourself. In the same vein, negative "food-talk" can turn into negative opinions about foods that could ordinarily have a place in a healthy diet. If you hear yourself saying "I shouldn't eat this" about foods you're constantly eating, then you are viewing these foods as "bad." That wouldn't be such a problem if those negative feelings prevented you from overeating, but that's rarely the case for a food addict because when you get to the root of the problem, it's not really about the food. Instead of thinking in "should's" and "shouldn'ts" or "good foods" and "bad foods," try to figure out how you can fit all the foods you like into a healthier diet so you have only positive feelings about your eating habits.

To maintain physical and emotional balance, you need to do only five things:

- Maintain a positive outlook.
- Eat nutritionally balanced meals.
- Get a reasonable amount of physical activity; not too much and not too little.
- Build up your support network.
- Don't ever give up.

These are simple rules, but you have to discover how to apply each to your own life. For a food addict, that's not always simple. If you're not eating enough, eating balanced meals means you will have to start eating more food than you're used to. If you overeat, balance means watching your portion sizes. If you eat a lot of junk food, you have to find a way to include small amounts of these foods in an otherwise balanced diet or go "cold turkey," if you think it's the only way, and eliminate these foods from your diet altogether.

What role, if any, does willpower play in managing a food addiction? Willpower is a struggle against your own desires. Exercising willpower means not letting yourself eat a piece of chocolate when you really want a piece of chocolate. To exercise willpower, you have to make an on-the-spot decision about whether or not to give in to temptation. It's a short-term solution, if it's a solution at all, that has no role in food addiction. It's just too short-lived to be useful.

WEB TALK: To learn about a natural approach to wellness and balanced living, check out:

www.drweil.com

Willpower and *self-control* are terms that are often used interchangeably, but exercising self-control is more about establishing a personal set of rules to live by. It can be a long-term solution that helps you keep destructive behavior in check by substituting new behaviors. It is the power you have over your own actions, the ability to ignore momentary impulses, no matter how powerful they are, in the interest of achieving something you really care about. It doesn't mean punishing yourself, or preventing yourself from living well. It really means keeping the big picture in mind. When you exercise self-control, you are sending a message to yourself and the world that you care enough to take responsibility for yourself. Good examples of ways food addicts can help themselves by exercising self-control include the following:

- Eating a balanced diet
- Mending personal relationships
- Forgiving mistakes
- Keeping a food diary
- Letting go of dependencies
- Reducing the amount of stress in your life
- Finding ways to stay motivated
- Stopping negative self-talk
- Setting emotional boundaries

The more you practice these acts of self-control, the sooner they'll contribute to permanent lifestyle changes.

A lack of self-control is often the result of illogical and immature thinking along the lines of *There's just too much to do so I'm not going to do any of it.* You might be so overwhelmed by the emotional work that lies ahead that you don't know where to begin. Self-discipline helps prevent loss of control. When you have identified the emotions and situations that send your eating behavior out of control, you know the areas in which you need to work harder. Whatever you do, don't confuse self-control with self-deprivation. They're not the same thing. Some food addicts might have to learn to do without certain foods for physical or psychological reasons, but most people don't have to deprive themselves completely of indulgence foods. Here are a few examples that illustrate the difference:

Self-Deprivation	Self-Control
I can never eat chocolate.	I can eat a little chocolate once in a while.
I can never eat at my favorite restaurant.	I can eat smaller portions when I eat out.
I have to stop snacking.	I have to plan my snacks more carefully.
I have to eat boring meals.	I have to eat balanced meals.
I can't have dessert.	Dessert is part of a balanced meal.

Take small steps, and just keep moving until you get there.

Nobody's Perfect

A perfectionist believes that anything short of perfection is unacceptable. In the case of a food addict, that usually means trying to live up to impossible standards of physical beauty. Researchers at the Eating Disorders Program of New York Presbyterian Hospital and the Virginia Institute for Psychiatric and Behavioral Genetics, along with eating disorder specialists across the country, have found that *perfectionism* is especially common in people with eating disorders.

You might think perfectionist traits motivate you to do your best and be your best, but there's a huge difference between perfectionism and striving for excellence. Perfectionism is driven by and focused on fear, as in a fear of being fat or a fear of being unloved. Perfectionists are afraid to fail. If you are a perfectionist, you might undereat or overexercise in an attempt to stay thin because you equate being thin with perfection. Perfectionists can be particularly hard on themselves because they don't easily forgive mistakes, in themselves or others. It tends to undermine people's progress, leaving them so afraid of failure that they get trapped in unhappy and unhealthy situations.

PsychSpeak

Perfectionism is a personality style in which a person is overly critical of his or her own performance. Perfectionists have an excess need for approval and view simple mistakes as personal failures.

Nonperfectionists, on the other hand, focus on achievements like eating a nutritionally balanced diet to stay healthy or exercising just enough to be fit and strong. Their focus is on success.

When Dr. Wendy Hoyt, staff psychologist at Avalon Hills Eating Disorder Treatment Center, Petersboro, Utah, talks to her patients about perfectionism and fear, she relates to them her own irrational fear of heights and how, when standing on top of a mountain, she develops an irrational belief that the mountain will suddenly crumble below her. Her natural inclination, therefore, is to avoid the edges of mountains. Instead, she challenges herself and climbs mountains, because if she were to give in to her irrational thoughts, she would never get to see the beautiful views that are afforded only from the top. She encourages her patients to also "look over the edge of the mountain" and prove to themselves that their irrational beliefs about never being thin enough or being "bad" for not eating perfectly are simply wrong. The next step is letting go of those beliefs.

If you're a food addict who is also a perfectionist, you are probably setting unachievable weight and fitness goals for yourself and at the same time, setting yourself up for failure. Instead, set yourself up for success. Learn to accept that your natural weight and body shape might be a little less perfect than you think it should be. If you allow yourself to be just a rung or two below perfection, you might actually reach your goal.

GET PSYCHED

"If you're a perfectionist, the fear of your perceived imperfections will have a destructive effect on your thinking and, therefore, on your behavior. Challenge your irrational beliefs by facing your fears so you can prove to yourself that your perfectionist thinking is wrong." *—Wendy Hoyt, licensed psychotherapist, Avalon Hills Eating Disorder Treatment Center*

Perfectionists are guilty of all-or-nothing thinking. Everything is viewed as black or white, right or wrong, with no allowance for gray areas. In a perfectionist's mind, "I ate bread" translates to "I failed on my diet; I'm going to get fat." But this problem lies more with attitude than with eating behavior. You can eat chocolate and still follow a healthy diet if you change your thinking to something more along the lines of "There are no good foods or bad foods, so how can I fit a little chocolate into my day?"

Here are some other suggestions to help you overcome perfectionism:

- Understand that nothing can be done perfectly all the time.
- Work on forgiving yourself and others for making mistakes.
- Accept yourself for who you are, not who you think you "should" be.
- Periodically reassess your goals to be sure they're realistic.
- When you fall off the "food wagon," jump right back on. Don't dwell on your mistake.
- Recognize yourself as a human being who does make mistakes.
- Stop second-guessing your ability to succeed.
- Choose role models who are not perfectionists.

One of the best things you can do for yourself is to try to switch your focus from the *size* of your body to the *health* of your body. Remember that you are a whole body, not just a collection of body parts. Pay attention to your entire self, not just your thighs or your chest or whatever part is making you unhappy. Ask members of your support network to point out when you're being too rigid or hard on yourself.

Not Perfect, Not Starving

"I'm a recovering anorexic, and I'll tell you what it's like. To begin with, when I was a teenager, I didn't know I had an eating disorder. I was a good gymnast, and I was striving for the physical perfection necessary to compete professionally. I was very thin, and I worked at it constantly by overexercising and counting every calorie, but I wasn't underweight enough to meet the criteria for anorexia. That's probably why no one noticed I had a problem.

"I was deathly afraid of getting fat. I really didn't think about much else. Whenever I ate more than 800 calories in a day, I felt fat. Whenever I couldn't go to the gym or ride my bike or do something physical for at least an hour or two every day, I felt fat. At five foot five, I weighed 112 pounds, and I often felt fat and disgusted with myself. This went on for four years.

"By the time I was seventeen, I realized that I was starting to feel sick, both physically and mentally. I knew my thinking was obsessive and something was wrong with exercising so compulsively and planning every meal so carefully to avoid getting too many calories. I was eating less and less. I had read a lot about eating disorders, and now I suspected I had one. My mother had me talk to my doctor, who referred me to a therapist who specializes in eating disorders and body image issues. I saw her for two years, and she helped me work on my problem with perfectionism and some problems I had at home. She helped me understand that it was okay to eat normally. I also went to see a dietitian several times to be sure I was eating a balanced diet.

"When you've gotten to the root of a food addiction, you're halfway to a resolution. The rest is about learning how to deal with your disorder by stopping the obsessive thinking and becoming a normal eater. But you can't just go "cold turkey" and stop exercising or stop thinking about food. You really have to take it one step at a time. I still planned my meals in advance, but I slowly increased my calories to about 1,800 a day. At first it was hard to eat so much food because I felt so full, but it got easier. I took up crocheting as a way of distracting myself. When I started obsessing about what those extra calories would do to my body, I started crocheting and did whatever else I could to distract myself. I went out more, and I tried to be more involved with other people.

"The hardest thing I ever did was fight the urge to focus on my weight but I did it. I stopped giving in to my obsessive thoughts. It took a long time and even now, at age twenty-eight and 135 pounds, I sometimes still think I look fat. The difference about being in recovery is that I don't act on those thoughts anymore."
—Randi E.

No Excuses!

When you decide to take responsibility for improving your health, you're taking responsibility for what you do and don't do. The excuses you give yourself for not eating well or not getting more physical activity—too tired, too busy, too stressed—could be your greatest obstacle to getting in shape and staying in shape.

Blaming someone else or some external situation for your lack of action is really just another way of making excuses to stay the way you are. It's the easy way out—for the moment. If you find yourself constantly making excuses for not doing something, you might not be ready to make the type of change you're attempting. Try working on something else for now.

You probably find time for most of the things you want to do— that is, the things you really want to do. If you're hungry, you always find time to eat, right? If you're a workaholic, you always find time to work. But when it comes to exercise or preparing healthy food or making an appointment to get help with an emotional problem, if you're procrastinating, somehow you can't seem to squeeze those things into your schedule.

One way to work toward your goals and procrastinate at the same time is to practice what I call constructive procrastination. If you can't get yourself to do the actual thing that will get the job done, do something related, or something else that will help you reach your goal. For example, if you're not ready to join a gym, start reading about different types of exercise or buy or rent a yoga video or DVD so you can do start doing something different at home. Even if you belong to a gym but don't feel motivated to go, get down on the floor and do some push-ups or stretches, or go out and take a walk. If you've been avoiding seeking professional help even though you know that's your next best step, find a self-help book written by or for someone with a food addiction.

GET PSYCHED

Procrastination keeps you in a constant state of anxiety because you're always thinking about something that needs to get done, but you're never doing anything about it. It's usually easier to just do the thing than it is to procrastinate about it. When you procrastinate, you stand still. If you want to get fit, you have to move.

Trust Yourself

If there's a single, most important message in this book, it is this: *Only you know what's best for you.* You know if what you're doing or what you're thinking is good for you or bad for you. It's up to you to point yourself in the right direction. To do that, you have to place a tremendous amount of trust in yourself. If, in the past, you've tried to develop a healthier relationship with food and failed, it might be difficult for you to trust that you will make better choices and succeed this time.

There's a saying among recovering food addicts: All you can do is the next right thing. Trusting yourself to do better is always the next right thing.

Trusting yourself often means following your intuition, or your gut feelings. Intuition is a great self-help tool because we all have it and it's with us at all times. Your intuition can tell you a lot about what you really want and don't want and what you need to do to be successful.

Unfortunately, your intuition is all too often ignored. Your gut instinct might not seem logical, desirable, or even practical, so you might disregard it and let your rational mind take over. Or you might be too distracted by emotions or external noise to pay attention to what your intuition says. But just like physical pain, your intuition is usually trying to tell you something important. Or in the past, you might have trusted diet plans to help you lose weight and when they failed, you might have attributed the failure to yourself.

By now, you have a better understanding of the physical and psychological reasons for your eating behavior, and you know diets don't work. You know there are underlying reasons why you have a food addiction, and you know you have to address those issues before you can permanently change your eating habits. That knowledge will guide you to making better decisions for yourself in the future.

WEB TALK: Read a helpful discussion on developing intuition at:

www.intuition.org/txt/vaughan2.htm

You'll find it easier to trust yourself if you believe you are in control of your own destiny, you're responsible for most of what happens to you from this point on, and you'll get what you want by working hard. If you feel your life is out of your control or you have little control over what and how you eat, you will feel anxious and less able to trust your own decisions.

What You Can Do

An emotional makeover will help you improve your relationship with food because your emotions have played such a fundamental role in your food addiction. You can do several things to start the process of change:

- ☐ Make a strong commitment to see yourself through physical and emotional change.
- ☐ List some things that will help keep you motivated to reach your goals.
- ☐ Promise yourself to take care of your physical and mental health first, before you take care of anything else.
- ☐ Plan to set short-term goals for every day.
- ☐ Self-control is not the same thing as self-deprivation.
- ☐ Take responsibility for your actions, and trust that you are making the healthiest choices and decisions for yourself under the circumstances.

Healthy Body, Healthy Mind

Whether you're overweight, underweight, or maintaining a healthy weight, a plan for healthier, happier living always includes some type of physical exercise. That certainly holds true for overeaters. For one thing, it's a great delay mechanism. You can't eat while you're working out! If you're underweight and want to "bulk up" or if you've figured out that dieting to lose weight or stay thin is a bad idea, exercise can help you maintain the weight—and the positive attitude toward your body—that you want.

Different types of exercises provide different benefits. For a food addict, exercises that help keep your mind in shape are just as important as those that keep your body in shape. The meditative qualities of mind-body exercises such as yoga and tai chi can make a difference in how you feel and how you make choices for yourself.

In this chapter, you'll find formulas for helping you figure out how close you actually are to a healthy weight, plus an overview of exercises that will help keep you mentally and physically fit.

When you do any type of exercise, it's important to know your own limits and exercise safely. If you're over the age of 40 or have any medical problems, check with your doctor before you start any new exercise program. Be sure to tell your doctor if you have chest pains, heart or lung disease, dizzy or fainting spells, diabetes, high blood pressure, breathlessness or wheezing after mild exertion, arthritis, or any type of back or leg pain.

Shaping Up

Maintaining good mental and physical health is the best reason to get in better shape, although it might not be your primary motivator. The mental health benefits of routine physical activity include positive self-esteem, reduced depression and anxiety, and increased ability to cope with stress. People who exercise on a regular basis report improved moods and more restful sleep.

The more physically fit you are, the easier it will be to walk long distances without getting tired, climb stairs without getting winded, or carry a heavy package without hurting yourself. You might also want to get back into clothes you haven't worn for a while, play a better game of basketball, keep up with your kids, eat some of your favorite foods without worrying about your weight, or simply feel good about yourself. Exercise is the one strategy that's all but guaranteed to bring you closer to these day-to-day goals, all the while improving your overall health.

WEB TALK: Find reliable fitness information on the American College of Sports Medicine (ACSM) site at:

www.acsm.org

The Many Benefits of Exercise Regular physical activity improves your mood, reduces the effects of stress, and enhances your overall outlook on life. It can also improve your sex life by improving both your physical health and mental outlook. A great thing about these benefits is that they are often immediate and help provide motivation to continue exercising. Over time, exercise can also help ease anxiety and alleviate depression.

Exercise releases "feel-good" hormones known as endorphins, morphinelike substances that are thought to induce the exercise "highs" reported by so many active people. Research is also looking into a possible relationship between exercise and the neurochemical serotonin, which is known to have a positive effect on depression, anxiety, sleep patterns, and mood shifts.

Just as exercise affects your state of mind, your state of mind affects your motivation to exercise. Research shows that people who trust their own capabilities and have faith in their own potential are more likely to stick to an exercise program than people who suffer from self-doubt. There you have it—another great reason to trust yourself and work on self-acceptance.

Research consistently shows that exercise has powerful psychological and physical benefits. It's been proven again and again that people who regularly exercise are more successful at maintaining a healthy weight than people who don't exercise. Besides helping with weight control, regular exercise will give you an immediate energy boost. In the long term, exercise will also help reduce your risk of developing any number of medical problems, including high blood pressure, diabetes, bone loss from osteoporosis, insomnia, stroke, and heart disease. Exercise strengthens every part of your body. Aerobic exercise strengthens your heart and lungs, and weight-bearing exercise helps build your bones, muscles, and joints.

you're not alone

Bulking Up

"As a little boy, I was always very skinny. I was one of those scrawny kids you see at the beach who are so sensitive their teeth chatter, their bodies shiver, and their lips turn purple the minute they come out of the water. But I was never a picky eater. That was not the problem. My grandmother always made sure I ate my three full meals and snacks. I was just extremely active every minute I was awake.

"I'm a small-framed guy, and as I grew up, I would try to compensate for my height and weight by being agile, quick, and strong for my size. I never tried to get bigger by eating more food. I concentrated on being physically strong and bulking up by exercising. In high school, weighing 127 pounds, I started wrestling in the low-weight classes. I always made it a point to challenge guys

continues

251

continued

much bigger than myself. I made sure I trained hard enough that I could beat them, and I did.

"In college I was still energetic and physically active. I played soccer and worked out in the school gym to help maintain my 135-pound weight. Then I got hooked on cross-country running. I loved it, but at the same time it caused me a lot of anxiety because I started losing weight. That's when and why I began to focus more on food and getting enough calories. I realized I couldn't afford to miss a single meal.

"I am now forty-three years old and weigh 140 pounds, trying to get to 145. Unlike most people my age, I find it more difficult to gain or even maintain weight than ever before, although I am working on it all the time. It's my obsession. I check my size in a mirror and on the scale pretty much daily. I've stopped running because I just lose too much weight when I do. Instead, I work out with weights several times a week to build muscle strength, and I do a minimum amount of aerobic exercise to be sure I get the cardio benefits. These days, with obligations to my wife, my kids, and a busy dental practice, my workouts are less about my physical appearance and more about maintaining the strength, stamina, and mental outlook I need to get through every day feeling good about it.

"I think about food all the time because if I don't, I forget to eat. I have a schedule, and I watch the clock to be sure I eat on time. I know I can't afford to miss a single meal. It's been a lifetime battle—me against my metabolism. Apparently, the war's not over yet." –Phil S.

How Much Is Enough? The fitness benefits you get from aerobic exercise depend on how much oxygen your body uses while you work out. To get the most benefit, you have to take in more oxygen than usual and your heart has to beat faster to get that oxygen into your muscles. According to the American Council on Exercise (ACE), aerobic exercise should be maintained for a minimum of twenty to thirty minutes, with your heart rate maintained at 55 to 85 percent of your maximum heart rate. To determine your maximum heart rate and the safest, most effective range within which your heart should beat during aerobic exercise, see the following Web Talk sidebar. It refers you to an ACE site that contains the formula for monitoring heart rate.

The most accurate way to determine if you're within your range is with a pulse/heart monitor. These monitors are built into many exercise machines such as treadmills and stationary bikes. If you don't have one, you can use a more low-tech method. During your workout, you can briefly stop exercising and measure your heart rate by counting the pulse beats at your wrist or neck for fifteen seconds. Multiply the number of beats by 4, and you have your beats per minute.

WEB TALK: To determine your target heart rate zone, use the formula provided at: www.acefitness.org/fitfacts_display. cfm?itemid=38

When you first start to exercise, your goal is to get your heart rate up to the low end of your training range. At first, you might not even be in your range. Keep exercising at a comfortable pace, and you'll move into your range. As you become more fit, you can set a new goal to get to the top of your range.

Experts recommend starting off with at least 30 minutes of aerobic exercise 3 times a week, with an ultimate goal of exercising at least thirty minutes most days of the week. Second best: try to get at least thirty minutes total daily exercise in five- or ten-minute intervals.

How Much Is Too Much? Everyone who exercises on a regular basis appreciates the physical and psychological benefits, especially the improved sense of well-being that immediately follows a good workout. Many people report feeling an exercise "high" from the release of endorphins in the brain that leaves them with a sense of euphoria after a good workout. Also, research consistently backs up reports that exercise lowers anxiety, improves mood, and builds confidence. Those feelings help keep many people motivated to exercise on a regular basis.

For some people, however, exercise can become another form of addiction. Just as food controls the food addict, exercise controls the life of an exercise addict. The behavior is similarly obsessive, and the end result is usually the same: overload and burnout. Exercise addicts might be overeaters or chronic dieters. Both exercise frantically to work off what they ate. They are sometimes likened to people with anorexia and bulimia except that instead of starving or purging their food, they lose calories by exercising.

Although little research has been done specifically in the area of exercise addiction, experts in the field of general addiction say that both physiological and psychological factors are most likely involved, just as they are in other addictions. Like everyone, exercise addicts experience the pleasant feelings that result from physical activity and appreciate the fact that they can eat more freely if they work out on a regular basis. Like other addicts, however, their response to these rewards is excessive behavior.

So how much is too much of a good thing? No criteria has been established for exercise addiction, but if you exercise vigorously for more than ninety minutes a day seven days a week, if you think about little else, and if you work out even when you're sick or injured, you might want to speak to a fitness professional to find out if you're exercising too much and could potentially be doing yourself more harm than good.

A Measure of Fitness

You can measure your fitness in many ways, but the best methods are those that measure your overall fitness. The two most reliable indicators of fitness in both men and women are the body mass index (BMI) and waist-to-hip ratio. Together they measure how much fat you have on your body and where your body stores fat. These measurements, in turn, indicate your risk level for developing weight-related illnesses.

Body Mass Index Although no chart, formula, or measurement can tell you everything you need to know about your weight or your health, the BMI is considered a more meaningful way of measuring yourself than standard height-weight charts. The BMI uses a height-weight ratio to determine how much body fat you have. Use this formula, and a calculator, to figure out your BMI:

BMI = ([704 × (your weight in pounds)] ÷ [your height in inches]) ÷ (your height in inches)

For example, if you are 67 inches tall and weigh 158 pounds:

704 × 158 = 111,232

111,232 ÷ 67 = 1,660.2

1,660.2 ÷ 67 = BMI of 24.8

If your weight is in a healthy range, your BMI will be between 19 and 25. A BMI below 18.5 is considered underweight; 30 and above is considered obese.

Body Type If you were a fruit, would you be an apple or a pear? One look in the mirror will tell you. If you have a pear-shape body, your body fat collects around your hips and thighs. If you have an apple-shape body, your body fat settles more around your waist. If you can't figure out what kind of body type you have, use a tape measure and the following method to determine your waist-to-hip ratio:

1. Stand up, relax, and let your stomach hang out. Measure your waist at its narrowest point. Write down that number.
2. Measure our hips around the widest part. Write down that number.
3. Divide your waist measurement by your hip measurement. The result is your waist-to-hip ratio.

Why is this important? At a healthy weight, the ratio for most women should be less than 0.8 and less than 0.95 for most men. A higher ratio means you might be at higher risk of developing weight-related medical conditions such as obesity, diabetes, high blood pressure, heart disease, and certain types of cancer. The good news is that by exercising and eating a healthy diet, you can reduce stomach fat to help reduce health risks.

Are there any exercises an "apple" can do to reshape and reduce the risk of health problems?

Dr. Rod Dishman, professor of exercise science at the University of Georgia in Athens, says you can't turn an apple into a pear with exercise. There's no evidence that exercising specific body parts will help you lose fat in those parts. Although we generally lose fat first in the areas where we gain it first, no matter where your body stores fat, the only way to lose it is to burn more calories than you consume.

When you do vigorous aerobic exercises, you burn calories at a higher rate than usual, both during the activity and also for hours after you stop exercising. Weight training isn't as directly effective for burning calories, but by strengthening your muscles and preventing muscle wasting as you get older, weights and resistance exercises help maintain your metabolic rate so you burn calories efficiently, twenty-four hours a day.

Fit, Not Fat For a food addict, switching your focus from fatness to fitness is the key to success. You might be bigger or smaller than you want to be, but if you're getting enough exercise, you're probably in pretty good shape.

GET PSYCHED

"It's clear that some people become obsessive about their exercise, and sometimes it can become a medical problem. The larger problem, however, is that most Americans don't get enough exercise. The goal should be to get enough physical activity to maintain a healthy level of fitness without going overboard." –Dr. Rod Dishman, professor of exercise science, University of Georgia

When you're fit, you look and feel the best you can. You're mentally alert and physically capable of performing a normal day's work. You have energy to spare so you're able to enjoy activities outside of work. You're healthy.

Health and fitness can't be measured by the numbers on a scale. Many studies have proven that it's quite possible to be overweight and still be physically fit. In fact, one study at the Cooper Institute for Aerobic Research in Dallas, Texas, showed that the death rate for people who are thin but not fit is twice as high as for people who are overweight and fit. The way to achieve fitness regardless of your weight is through routine exercise.

Most of us must eventually face the age-old question of what to do with the extra weight that creeps up on us as we get older. Although many health experts say it's normal and okay to gain 5 or 10 pounds as we get older, you might not be happy with the direction your body is going. As we age, we lose lean muscle tissue. Exercise is the best way to hold on to some of that muscle. If you work your muscles with weight-bearing exercises such as walking, stair climbing, jogging, lifting small hand weights, skating, or tennis, you might actually gain a little weight. But that type of weight gain is okay because it's muscle weight, not fat weight. It not only looks good, it also helps you burn calories more effectively and helps keep your body in its best possible shape as you age.

Getting Physical

The way to begin an exercise program is to assess where you are right now. Unless you're in pretty good physical shape, it's not a good idea to rush into a new physical activity or to push yourself too hard. You could get hurt, or experience burnout, and there's no motivation in that! Here's how to ease into a new fitness regime:

- **Start slowly.** A ten-minute walk is better than no walk at all because that's ten minutes you won't just be sitting on the sofa or at the kitchen table.

- **Choose an exercise location where you feel safe and comfortable.** You should feel good about the environment and the instructors or trainers.

- **Choose physical activity you actually enjoy.** If you like to be alone, you might choose to walk, jog, ride a bike, or swim. You might want to invest in home exercise equipment and/or videos. If you want to be part of a group, you could join a gym with exercise classes or take up a sport such as

GET PSYCHED

"When it comes to fitness training, intensity is important. But when it comes to overall psychological and physical well-being, frequency of exercise matters more. What's most important is to be active on a regular basis." –*James Skinner, exercise physiologist, Indiana University* golf, volleyball, racquetball, or tennis. By starting off with something fun, you're more likely to stick with it.

- **Pick a time of day that's best for you and try to stick with it.** Some people prefer to get their exercise over with first thing in the morning. Others prefer to work out on their lunch hours or use their workout to release stress at the end of the workday. Some people choose to work out during those times when they are most prone to overeating or excessive snacking. Find what time of day you're most apt to stick with the activity.

- **Develop a routine.** Start off exercising just a few days a week and build from there. Gradually, over time, increase the length and pace of your workout. If time is a problem, break your daily exercise routine into mini-workouts you can manage throughout the day.

- **While you're exercising, remember how good you're going to feel about yourself *afterward*.** Always keep sight of your goals.

- **Do just as much exercise as you can from day to day.** Whatever you do, however, don't set yourself up for failure by doing too much too soon or setting exercise goals that you can't accomplish. If you're sick, take a day off.

- **Develop motivational strategies.** If you've started and stopped exercising in the past, figure out how and why you lost motivation and come up with a plan to deal with obstacles in the future.

If you haven't been exercising, you can probably come up with countless excuses for putting it off even longer. James Messina, a psychotherapist in Tampa, Florida, suggests you practice replacing unhealthy excuses with positive thoughts and affirmations. For instance, instead of telling yourself *I don't have time to exercise,* tell yourself, *I will make the time to exercise because it's important.* If you find yourself thinking, *Exercise is too much work,* switch to, *I will find an exercise that's fun.* Instead of saying to yourself *I don't want to exercise in front of people,* promise yourself, *I will exercise on my own until I feel better about joining a gym.* And if all you can think is *I just don't like to exercise,* remind yourself that everyone needs some form of physical activity to live a longer, happier, healthier life. You deserve that as much as anyone else and to have it, you must tell yourself that somewhere out there is an exercise you will enjoy. Then, keep looking.

Warming Up to Aerobics *Aerobic* means "with oxygen," and during aerobic exercise, you're breathing a lot of oxygen into your body, and that oxygen is being delivered to your body cells. How effectively that happens is a measure of your aerobic fitness. However, don't judge your workout by the amount of sweat you produce. Sweat is just your body's way of cooling off when you start to overheat; it's not necessarily an indicator of how hard you're working.

Although most types of exercise provide psychological benefits, aerobic exercise has been shown to produce the greatest effects when it comes to lowering anxiety levels and alleviating symptoms of depression. When it comes to depression, aerobic activity has been shown to provide immediate relief. In the case of both anxiety and depression, the most benefit was seen after at least ten or fifteen weeks of exercise. Because exercise also provides so many physical health benefits, many mental health experts agree that aerobic activity is a helpful supplement to traditional psychotherapy.

Aerobic activities include the following:

- Fast walking
- Running/jogging
- Biking/spinning
- Climbing/stepping
- Rowing
- Jumping rope

- Fast dancing
- Playing handball, racquetball, or squash
- Skating
- Cross-country skiing
- Swimming

Always warm up for at least five or ten minutes before you start exercising. The best warm-up exercises for aerobics use the same muscles you'll be using when you get to the actual exercise. A warm-up simply starts you off slowly. You can warm up to a bicycle ride with a slow bike ride. You can warm up to a run with a walk and then a slow jog. It's also important to cool down for at least five or ten minutes after exercise to allow your heartbeat to slowly drop back to its normal rate. To cool down, gradually slow the pace of whatever exercise you're doing.

Strengthening Your Muscles Although aerobic exercise is most often credited for providing the most mental health benefits, all forms of physical activity have been shown to enhance self-esteem, relieve stress, and play a role in reducing the symptoms of anxiety and depression. In at least one study, strength training provided depressed people with relief similar to that offered by antidepressant medication. Similar results have been found in research on sleep improvement, comparing the benefits of strength training to that of sleep medication. Muscle strength-ening exercises help improve physical appearance, which in turn increases self-confidence and self-esteem for many people, including children and older adults.

The more healthy muscle tissue you have on your body, the more efficient you'll be at burning calories, not only while you're exercising, but throughout the day. Aerobic exercise alone won't strengthen your muscles or increase their size. The way to build more and stronger muscles is through strength training exercises such as lifting free weights, using weight machines, working with elastic resistance bands, and doing strength-building mat exercises.

Sit-ups, crunches, pull-ups, push-ups, and exercises done in body-shaping classes are all designed to increase muscle strength and endurance. Presses, curls, and extensions all work your muscles when you use free weights or work out on weight machines.

Different exercises work different muscle groups—shoulders, arms, trunk, upper back, chest, and legs and buttocks. Experts say it's important to work all muscle groups to balance your strength and prevent posture problems.

Whether you do your muscle work in a gym or at home, it pays for a beginner to hire a certified personal trainer for a few sessions to teach you proper form and safe procedures. Otherwise, you might not be getting the full benefit of your exercise and you could be hurting yourself without realizing it. Experienced exercisers can also benefit from personal training to get through a workout plateau or learn to use new equipment. Trainers are coaches, and as such they can be a good source of the motivation and positive feedback you need to begin and sustain an exercise routine.

WEB TALK: To find a certified personal trainer, visit the National Strength and Conditioning site at:

www.nsca-lift.org/trainers/locator.org

Getting Flexible Your flexibility is a measure of how well you can move your muscles and joints through their natural ranges of motion. The wider the range, the more flexible you are and the less likely you are to injure yourself while you're doing aerobic and muscle work. Stretching exercises release muscle tension, and relaxed muscles move more freely and are less likely to suffer damage. They improve your flexibility and your range of motion so you can bend and stretch your body more easily during routine daily activity.

Research indicates that stretching and toning exercises can be as beneficial to self-esteem as any other physical activity, particularly for older adults. This is especially true when it comes to lifting self-esteem and feelings of self-worth that are related to body image and strength.

The more flexible you are, the less risk you have of injuring yourself while doing other types of exercise. Stretching exercises release muscle tension, and relaxed muscles move more freely and are less likely to suffer damage.

How flexible you are depends on your age, gender, genetics, and fitness level. The more active you are, the more flexible you will be. Some people are naturally more flexible than others, but anyone can improve their flexibility with regular stretching.

The best time to do stretches is when you're cooling down from other exercises, while your muscle temperature is still elevated. In any event, you should never stretch a muscle that hasn't been warmed up. If stretching is the only exercise you're doing, you can warm up by swinging your arms in wide circles while walking around for five or ten minutes. To avoid getting hurt, always ease into a stretch; never bounce or throw yourself into it.

Walking the Walk One of the easiest, safest, and most convenient forms of exercise is one you already do every day—walking! If ease and convenience aren't enough to motivate you to walk more, think about this: studies have found that people who walk at least thirty minutes a day have a significantly lower risk of dying prematurely than people who rarely exercise. On a lighter note, if you do it often enough, long enough, and fast enough, you might just walk your way to a healthy weight.

To turn normal walking into a safe and enjoyable fitness activity, follow these tips from the American Council on Exercise:

- Wear comfortable, loose clothing. Well-made running shoes and trail shoes with good arch support and heel elevation are also good for walking.
- Always begin with a brief warm-up. Walk around the house or walk in place for a few minutes to get your blood flowing to your muscles before you stretch them.

- Before you start out, stretch your back, shoulders, and arms, in addition to your legs. This helps relieve tension and will make your walk more enjoyable and more effective.

- If you're a beginning walker, walk short distances at first. Start with a five-minute stroll, and gradually increase your distance.

- Forget about speed. Walk at a comfortable pace and focus on good posture, keeping your head lifted and your shoulders relaxed.

- Swing your arms naturally, and breathe deeply. If you can't catch your breath, slow down and avoid hills.

- Be sure you can talk while walking. If you can't talk, you're walking too fast.

- Once you've worked up to a point where you can walk a few miles with relative ease, start to vary the intensity. Walk up hills, lengthen your stride, or increase your speed.

- Lively music is a great way to energize your walking workout, but if you wear headphones, keep the volume down and watch out for traffic that you might not hear. To be on the safe side, wear reflective clothing, just as you would at night.

- Experts recommend walking at least twenty minutes a day, but you should stick to any schedule that works for you and keeps you walking. That might mean two ten-minute walks each day or one hour-long walk two to three times a week.

- Remember to cool down with a slow walk and a few minutes of stretches to help prevent sore muscles.

Moving Right Along If you're not doing some sort of formal exercise on a regular basis, you can do other things to get yourself moving, settle your mind, and burn extra calories while trying to come up with a better fitness plan.

The easiest exercise is to walk whenever you can:

- When you have a choice, take the stairs instead of an elevator or escalator. At the very least, get off the elevator one floor above or below where you need to be and take the stairs the rest of the way.

- If it's safe, park your car a good distance from your job, your school, the movie theater, the mall, or wherever else you've driven so you're forced to walk a little farther to get there and back.

- If you take public transportation to work or school, get off the train or bus a little earlier so you can walk part of the way. Better yet, if you don't really have that far to go and don't have to carry anything heavy, walk or ride a bicycle instead of driving.

- Use most of your lunch hour and work breaks to take walks.

- Whenever you find yourself heading for the kitchen when you're not hungry, go straight out the door and take a walk.

- If you can't go out, clean the bathroom or vacuum the rug. Unless you spend most of every day cleaning or repairing your home, you won't get much of an aerobic workout doing housework, but everyday activities still count as exercise. Keep moving and stay busy in active ways.

For more ideas, check out the "Instead of Eating" section in Chapter 10.

Reaching the Peak

"My recent trip to Israel shows just how far I've come since I lost weight. This was a first-of-its-kind trip for me in one very important respect: Instead of eating my way through the country, I exercised my way through. I made sure to get a hotel that had a gym instead of looking for the one with the biggest breakfast buffet. Instead of taking the cable car up Masada, I climbed that steep hill in just thirty minutes. I worked out three times at the hotel gym. And for my grand finale, I went rock climbing on cliffs in the Negev desert. If this was a few years ago, I'd most certainly be heading for the dessert, not the desert!

"Whenever I went on vacation in years past, it was all about food. Vacation meant living from meal to meal, wondering where I would eat and what I would order and what tasty tidbit (or two or three) I would try for dessert that afternoon, that night, or both! But since I broke my food addiction, eating has become much less important to me, whether I'm on vacation or just living my everyday life.

"The shift has been gradual, but life has changed radically for me, not just on vacations but every day. I've maintained an 80-pound weight loss for more than a year. Exercise has become an essential component of my everyday life, and food has become something I use to nourish—not weaken—my body. For the first time in my life, I actually enjoy buying clothing—and I look forward to looking good. I can't tell you where the self-control comes from, but I am able to stop myself from snacking when I visualize a new pair of size 8 pants (down from a 22 just two years ago!).

"When I first started losing weight, I didn't exercise much, but as I became stronger and felt better, I began to do Pilates. My personal trainer would charge me less if I bought a 10-session package, and if I didn't make it I'd get charged anyway, so I became a regular weekly exerciser. This was all the exercise I did for the longest time, but as my body got stronger, I added a second class per week. A year later, I added belly-dancing to my routine. The movement made me feel thinner as it was toning my abs, where most of my weight had been stored for so many years. Then I added on Brazilian Jiu-Jitsu, a form of hand-to-hand combat that has made me feel empowered by teaching me self-defense skills and helping tone my body even more.

"And here I am, back from a fabulous vacation where I lost weight instead of gaining it! The emotional and physical rewards of being active and fit are my best motivators. I'm already planning a trip back to Israel to beat my own mountain-climbing record. Who would have thought this was possible?" –*Judy L.*

Strengthening Your Mind

When stress plays a role in compulsive eating, mind-body exercises such as yoga and tai chi can be helpful because they promote relaxation. Just like meditation, breathing exercises, guided imagery, Pilates, and dance therapy, these exercises are also stress-reduction techniques that help develop self-awareness and promote overall wellness.

As Dr. Warren Berland, a psychotherapist in New York City, explains it, a part of every one of us knows what's best for us, and when we slow down and focus on our inner selves, we can tap into that deeper wisdom. Mind-body exercises are useful for food addicts because they help you find the deeper wisdom necessary to make the best possible choices for yourself. Rather than making food and behavior choices that are driven by your emotions, you can learn to listen to the inner voice that will guide you to healthier choices.

Until the 1990s, these ancient exercises were considered too alternative to be incorporated into most health club programs, and you could only take yoga classes at a yoga studio, if you could find one, or tai chi at a martial arts studio. Now, you'd be hard pressed to find a gym, library, church, or community center that doesn't feature yoga and martial arts classes.

GET PSYCHED

"Mind-body work does two things at once and does them well. It slows you down so you can gain access to your own deeper wisdom and at the same time, it reduces stress and physically exercises your body in ways that are very healing." –Warren Berland, Ph.D., author, Out of the Box for Life

Yoga and tai chi are two completely different types of exercises, but they are both meditative in nature and they share a common goal of improving both physical and psychological well-being. These ancient practices are not only part of a national trend of integrative exercise that teaches you how to connect your mind, body, and spirit, they are now widely recognized by medical doctors, psychologists, exercise physiologists, and other health experts for their many physical and psychological benefits.

Uniting With Yoga Yoga, which originated in India, helps you develop physical strength, endurance, balance, and flexibility. The word *yoga* means "yoke," or "unite," and that's its purpose: to unite your body, mind, and spirit. The focus of yoga is on self-awareness and mental well-being. The goal is a quiet mind in a physically healthy body.

According to the International Association of Yoga Therapists, yoga provides numerous psychological benefits. These include improved mood, increased self-acceptance, decreased anxiety and depression, and decreased feelings of hostility. Anyone who practices yoga will tell you that the practice leaves them feeling deeply relaxed and more in tune with their bodies. This deep relaxation is where some medical experts believe the mental and physical health benefits come from. Yoga is often recommended by conventional therapists in combination with other therapies to treat various depression, anxiety, and stress-related disorders.

Several types of yoga exist:

- **Ashtanga yoga,** which is sometimes called "power yoga," is aerobic in nature and focuses on constant movement.
- **Bikram yoga,** or "hot yoga," focuses on flexibility and uses very specific breathing techniques. Classes are often held in rooms with temperatures reaching 100 degrees and higher.
- **Bikram yoga** is favored by people with back problems and some forms of arthritis.
- **Iyengar yoga** focuses on skeletal alignment.
- **Kundalini yoga** focuses on higher awareness and greater flexibility.
- **Sivanada yoga** concentrates on simple, gentle postures and mental relaxation. Sivanada classes usually begin and end with chanting and prayers.

Ease into yoga just as you would any other form of exercise. While yoga ultimately helps you relax, and many people use it just for that purpose, it is also a stretching, toning, and strengthening exercise.

Relaxing With Tai Chi   Tai chi, which is also known as shadow boxing, began as a system of self-defense in China but is now used in both China and Western countries as a stress-neutralizing low-impact exercise. Tai chi is a series of slow, graceful, and precise dancelike movements that teach balance, alignment, and coordination. They also teach you to relax both body and mind.

Researchers at Johns Hopkins University School of Medicine found that practicing tai chi lowered blood pressure nearly as much as a program of brisk walking and low-impact aerobics. Other research has shown that tai chi can help improve heart and lung health, boost immunity, reduce joint pain, increase flexibility, and relieve insomnia. Because it helps improve balance, tai chi can also help reduce the risk of injury from falling—a benefit for older people, who often have balance problems.

Although physical in nature, the focus of all mind-body exercises is on the inner self. These are not exercises you do while watching the news on a TV monitor or with music pounding through your headphones. In yoga and tai chi classes, you concentrate on your breathing, posture, alignment, and developing a better sense of how energy flows through your body and how your body moves through space. Everyone in the room, regardless of level, is practicing; there is no competition.

Keep It Up!

Unfortunately, short stints of exercise don't have long-lasting effects. To continue to reap the physical and psychological benefits of exercise, you have to keep exercising. Early on when you get into an exercise routine, a lot of the motivation to continue comes from seeing yourself shape up relatively quickly. The psychological benefits of exercise are often immediate. After a while, however, you might reach a plateau where you don't see or feel any more changes in your body and you're simply maintaining a higher level of fitness. For some people, physical change doesn't happen soon enough to keep them motivated for more than a few weeks. That's when sticking to an exercise routine can be more difficult than starting one. Here are several ways to stay motivated:

- If you enjoy company, find a running partner to jog with or a gym buddy to work out with, or join a group activity such as an exercise class or a sports team.

- If you join a gym, be sure it's convenient to where you live or work so it's easy for you to get there on a regular basis.

- Keep an exercise journal or log. You can use it to plan exercise into your daily routine, and you can also use it as motivation to keep going. By keeping track of your day-to-day progress, you will have a written record of where you started and how far you've come.

- Don't let exercise get boring. Vary your routine from time to time to keep it interesting. This not only prevents you from falling into a rut, it keeps your body physically challenged in new ways.

- Keep your long-term goals in mind—both physical and psychological—and remember that exercise can help you reach them.

- Reward yourself for an especially good workout with something other than food.

- Strive for commitment and endurance, not perfection.

Whatever you do, don't let yourself burn out on exercise. If you feel yourself dreading your workouts, cut back on the amount of exercise you normally do, but keep going. Skip a workout if you must, but rather than stop altogether, try a new form of exercise. Instead of going to the gym, ride a bicycle or, if you take a class, switch instructors for a while.

What You Can Do

Regardless of your age, weight, or exercise history, you can start right now to improve your fitness level.

- ☐ Find the type of exercises you like to do and decide how you can fit them into your schedule on a regular basis.
- ☐ Calculate your target heart rate so you can monitor your aerobic activities.
- ☐ Figure out your body mass index to determine if your current weight is within a healthy range for you.
- ☐ Develop an exercise plan that includes aerobic activity plus some muscle-strengthening and flexibility exercises.
- ☐ Incorporate mind-body exercises into your fitness routine for relaxation and stress reduction.
- ☐ Use relaxation and focusing techniques learned from mind-body exercises to practice mindfulness at other times, such as when you are eating or when you are trying to get through a tough experience.
- ☐ Aim for at least thirty minutes of exercise, three days a week, with a long-term goal of exercising at least thirty minutes most days of the week.

Managing Setbacks

When you overcome a food addiction, you become stronger than the destructive thoughts, cravings, and habits that have reigned over your life for so long. As soon as you decide to take charge of your life and take responsibility for the way you respond to challenging situations, those behaviors can no longer control you.

You'll still get stressed out sometimes, and you'll still have ups and downs, but by learning to take better care of yourself, you have strengthened your resilience and your ability to deal with difficult circumstances. The struggles you've faced with your food addiction have expanded your self-knowledge and proven your ability to survive through tough times. To manage setbacks in the future, try to keep challenging situations in perspective. Trust your instincts, and try to see every situation, no matter how painful, as an opportunity for further growth and self-discovery.

Sticky Situations

No matter how committed you are to change, you might face a situation that will threaten your resolve. That's especially true if overeating is something you've always done to deal with stress and emotions. When you eat out at restaurants, travel, celebrate special occasions, visit relatives, or when you're faced with any type of emotional challenge, you will have to work to keep your goals in mind.

Theresa Wright, a registered dietitian in Plymouth Meeting, Pennsylvania, refers to eating triggers as "hot buttons," or situations that push you into self-destructive eating behavior. You have to know what your hot buttons are and be prepared to deal with them in the moment so you don't turn to food for a solution. Most trigger events are predictable. When you're in a calm, peaceful place, you can think back on what happened when you were faced with a trigger and plan out future responses to these predictable situations.

WEB TALK: Help for bouncing back from a stressful or traumatic event can be found at:

helping.apa.org/resilience

When she works with food addicts who are prone to relapse, Theresa uses the analogy of a fender-bender. Let's pretend you bought a brand-new car and drove it to your best friend's house to show it off. As you were backing out of the driveway, you smacked into the mailbox and crumpled a fender on your new car. How would you feel? Angry? Aggravated? Embarrassed? Would you then go out and crumple the other three fenders? Most likely not. You would probably move the car to a safe place, clean up any debris, and ask your insurance company to help you get the fender repaired. But from that point on, whenever you visited your friend, you would keep a careful eye on that mailbox to be sure it did not jump into the driveway and get you again!

In some ways, recovery from food addiction is similar. You will have times when you return to your inappropriate eating behaviors, even though you don't want to and did not intend to. When it happens, Wright suggests you immediately do these three things:

GET PSYCHED

"At times you will find yourself lapsing into old eating habits. Don't magnify your mistakes by eating everything in sight. If you catch yourself halfway through devouring a gallon of ice cream, stop eating and pour hot water over the remainder. Figure out how to get back on track, and move on."
—*Theresa Wright, M.S., R.D., Renaissance Nutrition Center*

- Stop eating right away and get back on track. Go back to your regular eating plan at the next meal or snack. Don't maximize the error by continuing to eat.

- Clean up whatever you can. Get rid of the inappropriate food. Move yourself to a better place or situation. Be aware that you might feel stronger cravings or urges to eat inappropriately for the next few days. Talk to someone you trust about your situation and ask for their help to get you back on track.

- Later, take a long, hard look at how the relapse happened without being overly self-critical or obsessing over the incident. How did you get into this again? Is there a hot button you can identify that will signal trouble next time? Is it your boss? Is it a worrisome financial situation? Is it stress from too much work or residual anger from a disagreement with your mate? Or have you not been taking care of yourself, not getting enough sleep or not eating enough? Think back to the hours or day before your setback. Try to find an objective, measurable signal you can use in the future to warn you trouble is ahead.

Recovery from food addiction is the process of creating a new lifestyle, a new way of living in the world, and a new way of relating to yourself and others. It takes time, and setbacks are natural. As Wright points out, setbacks and lapses mean your stress level has grown beyond your skills to cope with it. It doesn't mean you should throw in the towel and give up. Use your mistakes to learn what does not work for you. Use your creativity and the help, support, and experiences of others to create a lifestyle plan that will work consistently for you.

There are more situations that can cause distress and trigger emotional eating than there are solutions. The triggers can be as traumatic as illness, death, or divorce, or as routine as a phone call from a troubled relative. Although eating disorders are most common in young people, a Cornell University study showed that more and more women in their 40s are dealing with eating disorders as

WEB TALK: Vanderbilt University's Health Psychology site has links to nutrition, weight, and eating disorder information at:

www.vanderbilt.edu/AnS/psychology/health_psychology/healthps.HTM

they struggle with the physical and emotional issues of middle age. Some of these women have relapsed years after overcoming eating disorders when they were younger, and some are developing eating disorders for the first times in their lives. Any life event that leaves you feeling out of control could be an eating trigger. When you are faced with a difficult situation, call on past experiences to guide you. What have you done in other stressful situations that was helpful? Think back on who gave you the best advice and the most support. Also try to remember how you came to feel more hopeful about the future.

you're not alone

"The college I attended was far away from home, and I was scared and lonely that first year. Mix those feelings with an endless supply of cafeteria food, and you've got a young girl out of control and gaining a lot of weight!

"When I was home visiting one year, one of my brothers commented on how fat my legs were. I reacted to his remark by immediately going out to buy a pocket calorie counter. I circled all the foods that had the lowest calorie counts—carrots, celery, lettuce, etc.—and that's all I ate. I soon learned about fasting and using enemas and overexercising to make up for what I considered overeating. I developed a preoccupation with eating or not eating that progressed over the years to anorexia, overexercising, then compulsive overeating.

"After college, I became very ritualistic about eating and exercise. For five years, I never ate breakfast, walked 2 miles to work every morning, and went to a forty-five–minute aerobic class on my lunch hour. After class, I bought a buttered bagel, which I would cut up into tiny pieces and keep in my desk drawer. Throughout the afternoon I would do a little work, open the drawer and eat a little piece of bagel, close the drawer, and repeat this until the workday was over. Then I would walk another 2 miles home from work, change into running clothes, and run 5 to 10 miles. If I ate dinner, I ran more to make up for it.

"I began drinking alcohol and using drugs to take away the hunger. When I did eat, I would binge. I would go out on a date, and after the guy dropped me off, I would go back out to a deli or diner and buy another full meal. I never gained weight because I never stopped running. In fact, I started running as punishment for bingeing. I would binge and then starve myself and run extra miles the next day.

"After years of this, I finally admitted I was losing control of everything. I couldn't control my food, and my life was equally out of control. I hadn't had my period in fifteen years and as a result developed early osteoporosis. I had ulcers. I was dependent on enemas. My relationships were a mess. Food was still more important to me than people. I knew there was a huge psychological hole in me that wasn't getting filled no matter how much I binged. It was very scary.

"With the help of a psychotherapist, I healed the emotional issues I had from growing up with two alcoholic parents. I saw a nutritionist, who helped me develop better eating habits. I also joined Overeaters Anonymous. I learned to create boundaries, get out of co-dependent relationships, and have some self-control around food. OA was a place where I could share my deepest, darkest, most shameful secrets about food and no one would blink an eye. The common bond of being with so many people who struggle with compulsive eating behavior was the solution for me. The change that came over me from attending meetings and working the 12 Steps was nothing short of miraculous.

"I'm no longer in OA. It was a bridge back to life for me, and now I live life on life's terms, on my own, and it's okay. My food habits aren't perfect, but I eat normally. I'm generally more flexible, and I don't beat myself up for my mistakes. I am so much more at peace with myself." —*Kristine S.*

It's a Process

You say you want to be thin, so why don't you just lose weight?
Simple. It's a piece of cake.
How many times have I lost weight and just gained it back?
Maybe I don't want to be thin …
My fat's been good to me. My fat has protected me when no one else did. I feel safer when I ride the bus at night. When I work with men. I don't have to deal with them sexually. I'm just "one of the boys" and I can work, and I like it and I'm going to keep it that way!
I want …
I want …
I want out of here! I do!
I want to breathe.
I want to feel.
I want to feel sensuous and sexy and earthy.
Yes, I do. I do.

—Excerpted from *Leftovers: The Ups and Downs of a Compulsive Eater*

The internal musings of a frustrated yet eternally hopeful character, standing alone on a darkened stage in a poignant off-Broadway theater piece starring three compulsive overeaters, reflect the feelings of millions of men and women who suffer from food addictions.

If at some point in your life your eating behavior protected you in an abusive, negligent, or frustrating situation, food might have been a survival tool. Lacking a nurturing personal relationship, you cultivated a relationship with food, and throughout the years, you continued to turn to food for solace. It's been a long, intense relationship. It's going to take some time to replace destructive eating habits with healthier behaviors.

WEB TALK: Find information on less-well-known eating disorders at: www.anred.com/toc.html

Managing an addiction begins with accepting that you have an addiction or, at the very least, a fixation on food, weight, or body image that is interfering with your health and happiness. To overcome that addiction, you must truly want to change your behavior—not for someone else, not for any external reason, but for yourself.

The process of freeing yourself from a food addiction obviously involves much more than eating well or losing weight. It's about reinventing yourself and writing a new life script. Stay open-minded while you're rewriting that script. Resisting new ideas will only slow your progress. Right now you probably don't know how it's going to turn out, but you want your story to have as happy an ending as possible.

Stretch Yourself Stretching your muscles when you exercise helps you become more physically flexible; stretching your emotional muscles by letting go of old beliefs and habits helps you become more mentally flexible and open-minded to change. You want to be able to recognize new and healthier ways of thinking and eating, grab a good idea when it comes your way, and put it right to use.

Dr. James Messina, a psychologist and recovering overeater in Tampa, Florida, has outlined several examples of the type of irrational thinking that is sure to sabotage your recovery efforts:

- Habitual ways of thinking about your life that keep you locked in your compulsive behavior
- Unhealthy ways of reacting to emotional situations
- Beliefs and behaviors that are founded in reality as you think it should be, not in actual reality
- A need for instant gratification
- Believing it is easier to master compulsive behavior than it actually is
- Thinking there is some magic pill, potion, or prescription to make your behavior go away
- Reluctance to accept a program of recovery or change in lifestyle that puts the ultimate responsibility on yourself
- The belief that professionals do not have your welfare at heart

> ## GET PSYCHED
>
> "If a lifestyle change is to become permanent, it requires an overhauling of the way you act, react, and interact. This requires time management, social support, and replacement of old personal habits with new, healthier habits."
> –Dr. James J. Messina, licensed psychologist

Discouragement, disillusionment, and backsliding on your original desire and commitment to change are a few of the negative consequences of this type of irrational thinking, says Dr. Messina. If these types of thinking patterns go unchallenged, you won't be able to achieve a permanent lifestyle change and eventually, you will revert to your old problem behavior.

Stay in the Moment The more you practice living in the moment, rather than dwelling on the past or worrying about the future, the easier it will be to develop and maintain a positive attitude and stay motivated. You cannot change the mistakes you or anyone else made in the past, and anxiety about the future won't help you facilitate change.

To begin to get control of your thoughts and stay in the moment, try to relax and quiet your mind. Just as you can teach yourself *mindful* eating, you can teach yourself to be mindful in other areas of your life.

Mindfulness is an approach to life borrowed from Buddhist meditative traditions. When you live mindfully, you are able to stay in closer touch with what is going on right in front of you. When you're trying to overcome a food addiction, mindfulness enables you to be more aware of your day-to-day progress. If your life feels like it's spinning out of control, mindfulness can bring you back to a quieter reality. Pay more attention to your thinking process so you can slow it down when necessary and ask yourself *What am I doing? Where am I going?*

> **PsychSpeak**
>
> **Mindfulness** is being aware of the present and living in the moment, without judgment of yourself or others.

The simplest exercise for practicing mindfulness is to sit in a comfortable position in a quiet place, close your eyes, and breathe. Focus on your breathing. Do nothing more than pay attention to the sound and feel of your breath. After a couple minutes of this, you can start to pay attention to your thoughts in the same quiet way.

Mindfulness can help you eat more discriminately and exercise more purposefully, simply because you are paying more attention to what you are doing. When you practice mindfulness, you will ...

- Slow down your eating.
- Relax your mind and body.
- Become more aware of your eating behavior—and enjoy your food more.
- Observe your feelings so you can start to better understand their relationship to your eating behavior.
- Start to see that you react the same way (by eating) to a variety of situations.

- Be able to stop destructive eating behavior before it occurs.
- Feel fuller and more satisfied at the end of your meals, even with less food.

Head-On Solutions When you feel yourself lapsing, gather all your resources as if preparing for a fight. Go back to the journals and logs and food diaries you've kept along the way, and read through them for motivation. Your writing will serve as a reminder of where you once were in your struggle against food addiction, how far you've come, and how hard you had to work to get where you are now. Reading these notes again might give you more determination.

When you are confronted with triggers, remember these alternatives to eating:

- Deal with your emotions straight on. Express yourself in words, not in food. If it's not something you can say out loud, write it down.
- Move yourself physically away from food, and stay there for a while to see if the temptation to eat goes away.
- If you're free to leave the situation, go out for a walk, go rent a video, or buy a magazine—anything that doesn't put you in the path of food.

It's never easy to deal with painful or stressful situations, even when you're armed with helpful techniques. But you always have a choice between taking positive and negative steps to ease the pain. You know the negative choices: giving up on yourself, overeating, purging, and choosing other self-destructive behavior. Addressing a stressful situation directly—or simply removing yourself from it until you can get some perspective on it—is usually the most positive way to handle it.

Sometimes you might find that all your attempts to resolve a problem haven't worked. At that point, the most positive response might be to give up trying to manage the situation and move on.

Don't worry—giving up on a hopeless situation is not the same as giving up on yourself.

Following a regimented diet and practicing complete abstinence from junk food works for many people. That's why programs such as Food Addicts Anonymous and others with strict dietary rules continue to be successful. If you're a compulsive overeater or you've been starving and bingeing your way to a food addiction, abstinence from trigger foods is probably your best bet, especially early on. But it's not for everyone. If you feel you are in control of your emotions when you eat, "cheating" from time to time, even early on, might help you reach your goals in the long term.

WEB TALK: You'll find a comprehensive weight control and obesity resource list at: www.nal.usda.gov/fnic/pubs/bibs/topics/weight/consumer.html

Clinical dietitians often find ways to help their patients who must stick to special diets, such as people with kidney disease or diabetes, "cheat" in ways that making eating more fun without harming their health. It's just a matter of fitting those forbidden foods into an otherwise healthful diet by figuring out how much you can get away with. The secret is in the planning. Scheduling special treats gives you something to look forward to on tough days and also helps you control your cheating so it doesn't get out of hand.

Think about it. If you eat 3 meals a day, that's 21 meals a week. If 2 of those meals are less than perfect, you're only indulging 10 percent of the time. The rest of the time you're still eating healthfully. If you eat 3 relatively unhealthy meals in a week, that's still only 15 percent of your diet. Giving yourself those two or three opportunities each week to have more fun with food might be just what you need to avoid the feelings of frustration and deprivation that are inherent to any big change in diet and lifestyle and help you exercise more self-control at other times.

Overcoming a food addiction is a personal matter, and everyone has to create his or her own path to success. Along the way, you probably will have to ask for directions, and that's another situation in which it helps to be open-minded. You might find help in unexpected places. For instance, if you want to learn about healthy cooking and there are no cooking schools in your area, check with your local hospital. Cooking and nutrition classes designed for people with heart disease and diabetes are well suited for anyone who is trying to get to or stay at a healthier weight. In addition to creating tasty meals, the lessons they teach include calorie and portion control, as well as balanced meal planning.

Don't Kick Yourself!

If you slip up and overeat or skip a day of exercise, the last thing you need is to give yourself a hard time. If the voice in your head is getting too critical, it might help to review Chapter 2 to remind yourself of the effects of emotional self-talk.

Avoid using the words *should* and *shouldn't,* as in, "I should know better," "I should have gone to the gym," or "I shouldn't have eaten that marshmallow." Saying *should* or *shouldn't* implies you did something wrong or, at the least, that you could have done better. Instead, think toward the future, and resolve to do something healthy as soon as you can.

Move on quickly from lapses. There's nothing to be gained from kicking yourself for making a mistake. Here are several ways you can avoid feeling bad about yourself:

- Be accountable to yourself. Take responsibility for your thoughts and actions, good or bad. Don't blame or credit anyone else for your behavior.
- Live up to your own expectations, not the expectations of others.
- Be sure your expectations are realistic.
- Be flexible. There are exceptions to every rule.
- Push yourself to do better, but don't kick yourself when you can't.
- Expect to be successful.

Some people use affirmations, or uplifting personal thoughts, to counter negative self-talk and put themselves in brighter or more hopeful moods. Like meditation, yoga, and other relaxing techniques, affirmations can help lift some of your emotional weight. See if any of these affirmations are helpful to you, and try to come up with some of your own:

- My mind is getting stronger.
- This binge was just a temporary lapse.
- My life is improving.
- My diet is becoming more balanced.
- This problem is an opportunity for growth.
- I'm excited about losing some of this weight.
- I will get what I want.
- I'm in control of my eating habits.
- My opinions matter just as much as anyone else's.
- I like being healthier.

you're not alone

"During my pregnancy I gained almost 65 pounds, and that brought my weight up to 225. I lost 30 pounds within a couple months after delivery, but I wasn't able to lose the rest. I suffered from postpartum depression, and because food had always been one of my coping mechanisms, I just kept overeating. My husband wasn't very supportive, and that was a big disappointment. I think he was disgusted by my weight. Even though I've always been big and I didn't always eat right, I was always fit. I was involved in sports when I was younger and exercised right up until a few weeks before I had the baby. Everything about my life seemed to change once I had the baby, and she was really the only bright spot.

"Finally, my ob-gyn suggested short-term psychotherapy and antidepressant medication, so I did both. That helped pretty

The Road to Success

If you've read this book from beginning to end, you have all the information you need to start improving your physical and emotional health. You probably came to this book with a great deal of knowledge, even if you haven't always put it into practice. Now is as good a time as any to begin a program for overcoming your food addiction once and for all. Use the following key points from each chapter as a guide to begin creating your own plan for overcoming food addiction:

- Look at your history of eating behavior, and consider your thought processes to help you decide where you fall on the eating behaviors continuum (Chapter 1).

- Understand that you have an emotional as well as physical relationship with food. Learn to recognize the difference between emotional hunger and true physical hunger (Chapter 2).

- Develop mindful eating habits (Chapter 3).

- Promise yourself you'll never go on a low-calorie diet again (Chapter 4).

quickly with my depression, but after several months, I was still overeating and still overweight. I started talking about my weight concerns and eating habits in therapy, and I finally figured out that I had to make some serious lifestyle changes, or I would never lose the weight and get back in shape. I joined a weight loss center because I felt I needed a plan and some supervision. I also bought a jogging stroller and started running in the mornings. It took another eight months, but I gradually lost not only the rest of my 'baby weight' but another 25 pounds—60 pounds total. I was fit again from my morning runs and feeling great about myself. I guess the lesson I learned is that anything can happen, and when it does, I have to be prepared to pick myself up, stay out of the kitchen, and just keep running." –*Linda O.*

- If you suspect you have a true eating disorder, get professional help right away (Chapter 4).
- Pay attention to outside influences such as advertising and media reports that might affect your choices when you shop for food or eat at a restaurant (Chapter 5).
- Think about how your family, ethnicity, culture, and personal choices have affected your eating habits over time (Chapter 6).
- Instead of focusing on losing weight, focus on being healthier, eating better food, and being fit (Chapter 6).
- Learn about healthy eating from a reliable source that teaches from a perspective of balance, variety, and moderation (Chapter 7).
- Get over your fear of foods, and climb out of your food rut by trying new foods, new ways of preparing foods, and checking out new restaurants (Chapter 8).
- Set goals and begin to keep a journal (Chapter 9).

GET PSYCHED

"Recovery is usually not a straight path to the finish line, but more of a commitment to a process that requires consistent action in spite of the inconsistencies of everyday living. Recovery involves learning the skills and discipline to simply do the next right thing despite how we may be feeling at the time."
—Marty Lerner, Ph.D., executive director, Milestones in Recovery

- Identify your emotional, behavioral, food, and environmental triggers (Chapter 10).
- Develop strategies for dealing with the eating triggers you've identified (Chapter 10).
- Remember that *how* you eat is more important than *what* you eat (Chapter 11).
- Develop a solid support network of family, friends, and professional helpers (Chapter 12).
- Accept yourself, once and for all, as someone who has a food addiction. Work forward from that place of acceptance (Chapter 13).

- Take responsibility for yourself, and make a commitment to see yourself through changes and tough times. Trust yourself to make better choices from now on (Chapter 14).

- Develop a physical exercise routine that includes mind-body work such as yoga (Chapter 15).

WEB TALK: Check out the politics of eating disorders as a public health priority at:

www.eatingdisorderscoalition.org

- Finally, be prepared for inevitable setbacks. Learn to pick yourself up and get right back on track (Chapter 16).

Always be on the lookout for new resources to help you maintain a healthier lifestyle. Keep setting new goals for your life and your health. Buy self-help books, try new foods, keep up with the latest ideas in exercise and fitness, and stay actively involved in your physical and mental health. Think of it as continuing education. Think of your life as a work in progress, and keep updating yourself, expanding your interests, and setting new goals so that even as you are learning to live in the moment, you are setting groundwork for the future.

What You Can Do

To manage setbacks and maintain a healthy relationship with food, you might have to redo some of the things you learned while you were developing that relationship in the first place.

- ☐ One way or another, deal with trigger situations head-on as they arise.
- ☐ Be open to new ideas.
- ☐ Practice techniques that will help you maintain a positive attitude, and avoid self-defeating thoughts and behavior.
- ☐ Stay abreast of the latest information related to all aspects of food addiction.
- ☐ Use all your resources, and when you've used them up, find new ones.

☐ Reassess your goals from time to time, and set new ones if necessary.

☐ Practice mindfulness in all areas of your life. Try to live in the moment and spend less time buried in the past or worrying about the future.

☐ Remember this mantra: Food is not the problem and it's not the solution.

☐ Don't be too harsh with yourself if you backslide. Setbacks are a normal part of recovering from a food addiction.

Glossary

addiction   A state of physiological or psychological dependence. More broadly, a destructive relationship with a substance or behavior that involves craving for more, tolerance for increased amounts, and physical or psychological withdrawal symptoms when the activity stops.

anorexia nervosa   An eating disorder marked by extreme fear of being overweight. Anorexics diet excessively, to the point of serious ill health and sometimes death.

anxiety   A state of extreme apprehension or fear of real or imagined danger. The physical symptoms of anxiety can include increased heart rate, trembling, sweating, weakness, and stomach discomfort. Anxiety often underlies the behavior of a food addict.

appetite   A strong desire or craving. Your appetite is a psychological need not to be confused with true physical hunger.

approach-avoidance conflict   A situation wherein you are both attracted to and repelled by the same goal or behavior. For example, you want to eat a certain food because you like the taste, but at the same time you don't want to eat it because you know it will start you off on a binge.

behavior modification   Substituting new behavior and habits for less desirable behavior.

behavioral therapy   A psychological treatment that helps a patient replace destructive habits with new, healthier habits.

binge eating disorder   An eating disorder that is characterized by recurring episodes of eating large amounts of food in one sitting.

body mass index (BMI)   A tool that is mathematically designed to measure body weight as a health risk by measuring body fatness.

bulimia nervosa   An eating disorder in which overeating is followed by purging through vomiting or overuse of laxatives.

calorie   A unit of measurement of the amount of energy supplied by food. Calories are useful for comparing the energy value of one type of food to another. For instance, a sweet pepper supplies 20 calories, and a baked potato supplies 220. A balanced diet consists of a variety of foods both high and low in calories.

carbohydrate   A nutrient that is an important source of energy for both the body and the brain. Foods that are high in *complex* carbohydrates—grains, legumes, vegetables, and fruit—supply essential nutrients and fiber; foods that are high in *simple* carbohydrates—baked goods and desserts made with refined flours and sugar—generally make less of a contribution to a healthful diet.

carcinogen   A substance with the potential to cause cancer.

central nervous system   The brain and spinal cord; controls and coordinates most functions of the body and the mind.

cholecystokinin   A hormone that plays a role in digestion and acts as a neurotransmitter, sending "stop eating" messages to the brain.

cognitive behavioral therapy   A form of short-term, future-oriented psychotherapy that can help food addicts and others change destructive thinking and behavior patterns.

cognitive therapy   A form of short-term psychotherapy that teaches you how your own thinking might be giving you a distorted picture of what's going on in your life, and also gives you tools for changing destructive thinking patterns.

compulsion   A ritualistic, repetitive, irresistible, and often irrational behavior or impulse that provides temporary relief from anxiety.

depression   A psychiatric disorder that manifests in persistent feelings of sadness, hopelessness, poor concentration, and often sleep disturbances.

***Diagnostic and Statistical Manual of Mental Disorders* (DSM)** A guide published by the American Psychiatric Association to help mental health professionals diagnose and treat patients. It is also used to help insurance companies understand patients' needs. The *DSM* defines and describes eating disorders.

diet   The food a person eats. Diet is often used to describe a controlled or restricted intake of food and/or drink for weight, health, religious, or medical reasons.

disordered eating   An eating behavior that is not necessarily a symptom of an eating disorder but that, to some degree, is similar to the behavior of someone with a diagnosed eating disorder.

dopamine   A brain chemical that is thought to help induce feelings of contentment after eating and other pleasurable activities. Studies show that when dopamine activity is disrupted, the level of pleasure from these activities is reduced. More and more of the activity is required to reproduce those positive feelings.

dysfunctional   Abnormal, incomplete, or impaired, usually used to describe a negative relationship.

eating disorder   A psychological condition such as anorexia, bulimia, or binge-eating disorder, that meets very specific criteria as established in the *DSM-MD*.

eating trigger   A food, emotion, person, or situation that might make you feel hungry even when your body does not necessarily need nourishment.

emotional eating   Eating to ease intense feelings rather than to satisfy true hunger.

endorphins   Brain chemicals that are released in response to pain or stress that work like natural painkillers.

enzymes   Proteins produced in body cells that are responsible for chemical actions and reactions in the body. Many enzymes are involved in the process of digestion.

food biotechnology   The use of genetic engineering or cross-breeding techniques to modify foods and create new foods.

galanin   A brain chemical that triggers cravings for fatty foods.

genes   Basic units of heredity.

ghrelin   An appetite-stimulating hormone produced in the stomach that sends "I'm hungry" signals to the brain.

hormones   Chemical "messengers" secreted by glands in the body in response to changes in the body or in the environment. Hormones travel to specific sites in the body to help restore normal conditions.

hypertension   High blood pressure.

hypothalamus   Part of the brain that controls many body functions, including hunger and thirst.

ideal body weight   A body weight that falls within the range of weights for heights suggested by health experts. Ideal body weight is not necessarily an indicator of healthfulness, however, because a person might still carry too much of that weight as fat.

insulin   A hormone produced by the pancreas to carry sugar from the blood into muscle and fat cells. By doing so, insulin helps regulate hunger and fullness.

junk food   Food that supplies calories but little or nothing in the way of essential nutrients.

leptin   A hormone produced by fat cells that helps control how much we eat.

macronutrients   The three nutrients—carbohydrates, protein, and fat—the body can use to produce energy.

metabolism   All the chemical reactions that go on in body cells, including burning calories for energy production.

mind-body exercises   Structured physical activities such as yoga, tai chi, or Pilates that enhance awareness and reduce stress while improving both physical and mental strength and flexibility.

mindfulness   An awareness of what's going on in your life at the present time, without regard to past or future events.

neurological   Pertaining to the brain and central nervous system.

neuropeptide Y   A neurotransmitter thought to be involved in the regulation of food intake, certain aspects of metabolism, and the preference for foods high in carbohydrates.

neurotransmitter   A brain or spinal cord chemical that controls nerve cell signaling by affecting the transmission of an impulse between nerves or between a nerve and a muscle.

night-eating syndrome (NES)   A disordered eating condition that leads someone to begin eating later in the day and to eat most of his or her food after dinner but before breakfast. NES requires professional attention if it occurs for more than two months. It is thought to be stress-induced, produces feelings of guilt and shame, and is often accompanied by depression.

obesity   A diagnosis of being extremely overweight in men with more than 25 percent body fat and women with more than 30 percent body fat.

obsession   An abnormal preoccupation or thought that can't be stopped.

olfactory center   A group of nerve cells in the brain concerned with interpretation of odors.

omega-3 fatty acids   A family of fats most noted for their roles in brain, eye, and heart health.

opiates   Drugs such as morphine, heroin, and codeine that act as central nervous system depressants to relieve pain.

opioids   Brain chemicals that produce pleasurable feelings similar to those produced by chemical opiates.

orthorexia   A pathological obsession with healthy eating and an avoidance of foods viewed as unhealthy.

perfectionism   Maintaining unreasonably high standards for oneself. People who suffer from extreme body dissatisfaction are often perfectionists. In the fight against food addiction, perfectionism can lead to frustration and bingeing in response to minor setbacks.

protein   An essential nutrient made up of chains of amino acids. Protein is found in all foods and is especially high in meat, poultry, seafood, dairy products, and legumes. In the body, proteins are essential for the production of hormones and enzymes.

psychotherapist   A certified social worker, Ph.D., or otherwise expert counselor who treats psychological disorders.

relapse   To show signs of disease or disorder after apparent recovery.

satiety   A feeling of fullness from having enough, or sometimes too much, to eat.

self-acceptance   Acceptance of your complete self, good and bad, without judgment.

self-awareness   Having an honest, well-balanced view of yourself.

self-esteem   Your opinion of your own value; high self-esteem means you have confidence in your own worth.

serotonin   A chemical distributed throughout the body, and especially in the brain, where it acts as a neurotransmitter and regulates mood, appetite, and other basic psychological functions.

supersizing   Producing and serving oversize portions of food and drinks in restaurants and grocery stores. Supersizing is often used as a form of competition—more than or the same amount of food you would get from a competitor for the same or less money.

tai chi   A Chinese martial arts exercise characterized by a series of slow, deliberate movements.

tryptophan   An amino acid necessary for growth and normal metabolism.

weight cycling (or **yo-yo dieting**)   Repeatedly losing and gaining weight by dieting. Health experts now believe weight cycling might be more dangerous to your health than maintaining a higher weight.

Further Reading

Many books have been written about the nature and healing of food addictions. Some are more reliable and accurate than others. Many of the expert contributors to this book have written successful books of their own on related subjects. These and others are listed here to help you choose the most dependable sources of information when you want to delve more deeply into any of the topics covered in this book and learn more about your food addiction.

Bauer, Joy. *The Complete Idiot's Guide to Total Nutrition*. Alpha Books, 2002.

Berland, Warren. *Out of the Box for Life: Being Free Is Just a Choice*. Dimensions, 2000.

Bliss, Kelly. *Don't Weight: Eat Healthy and Get Moving Now!* Infinity Publishing, 2002.

Brownell, Kelly. *Food Fight: The Inside Story of the Food Industry, America's Obesity Crisis, and What We Can Do About It*. McGraw-Hill, 2003.

Danowski, Debbie, and Pedro Lazaro, M.D. *Why Can't I Stop Eating?* Hazelden Information Education, 2000.

Fairburn, Dr. Christopher. *Overcoming Binge Eating*. Guilford Press, 1995.

Fletcher, Anne. *Thin for Life: 10 Keys to Success from People Who Have Lost Weight and Kept It Off*. Houghton Mifflin, 2003.

Kuffel, Frances. *Passing for Thin.* Broadway Books, 2004.

Mellin, Laurel, R.D. *The Solution, First Harper Edition.* Regan Books, 1998.

Roth, Geneen. *Why Weight?* Plume, 1993.

Ruden, Ron, M.D. *The Craving Brain, Second Edition.* Perennial, 2000.

Shapiro, Howard M., M.D., *Picture Perfect Weight Loss.* Rodale, 2000.

Tribole, Evelyn, M.S., R.D., and Elyse Resch, M.S., R.D., F.A.D.A. *Intuitive Eating.* St. Martin's Griffin, 2003.

Willet, Walter. *Eat, Drink, and Be Healthy: The Harvard Medical School Guide to Healthy Eating.* Free Press, 2002.

For a catalog of books on eating disorders, contact:

Gurze Books
Box 2238
Carlsbad, CA 92018
1-800-756-7533

Resources

I n addition to the many books you can read on subjects related to food addiction, there are organizations, websites, and treatment centers that can provide reliable information and help. Some of the most well-recognized groups are listed here.

Organizations to Contact for Information and Support

American Council on Exercise
5820 Oberlin Drive, Suite 102
San Diego, CA 92121
1-800-529-8227
www.acefitness.org

American Dietetic Association
National Center for Nutrition and Dietetics
216 West Jackson Boulevard
Chicago, IL 60606
1-800-366-1655
www.eatright.org

The National Center for Overcoming Overeating
PO Box 1257, Old Chelsea Station
New York, NY 10113
212-875-0442
www.overcomingovereating.com/centers.html

National Eating Disorders Association
603 Stewart Avenue, Suite 803
Seattle, WA 98101
206-382-3587
www.nationaleatingdisorders.org

Relevant Websites

America on the Move
A national effort to live a healthier lifestyle
www.americaonthemove.org

American Psychological Association
Includes therapist referral list
helping.apa.org

Association for Advancement of Behavior Therapy
Includes therapist referral list
www.aabt.org

The National Women's Health Information Center
www.4woman.gov/faq/eatingdi.htm#4

Overcoming Overeating
Includes therapist referral list
www.overcomingovereating.com

Partnership for Healthy Weight Management
www.consumer.gov/weightloss

Shape Up America
www.shapeup.org

Something Fishy
www.something-fishy.org

Taking Off Pounds Sensibly (TOPS)
www.tops.org

Twelve-Step Programs

Compulsive Eaters Anonymous
5500 East Atherton Street, Suite 227-B
Long Beach, CA 90815-4017
562-342-9344
www.ceahow.org

Food Addicts Anonymous
4623 Forest Hill Boulevard, Suite #109-4
West Palm Beach, FL 33415
561-967-3871
www.foodaddictsanonymous.org

Food Addicts in Recovery Anonymous
6 Pleasant Street, #402
Malden, MA 02148
781-321-9118
www.foodaddicts.org

Overeaters Anonymous
World Service Office
6075 Zenith Court NE
Rio Rancho, NM 87124
505-891-2664
www.overeatersanonymous.org

Eating Disorder and Food Addiction Treatment Centers

Avalon
346 Harris Hill Road
Williamsville, NY 14221
716-839-0999
www.avalon-eatingdisorders.com

A Weigh Out
A division of WellCentered Eating Disorder Treatment Program
3414 Edwards Road
Cincinnati, OH 45208
513-321-7202
www.aweighout.com

Canopy Cove at the Health Management Institute
2300 Killearn Center Boulevard
Tallahassee, FL 32309
1-800-236-7524
www.canopycove.com

Del Amo Hospital
23700 Camino Del Sol
Torrance, CA 90505
1-800-533-5266
www.delamohospital.com

The Menninger Clinic
Affiliated with Baylor College of Medicine
and Methodist Hospital
2801 Gessner
PO Box 809045
Houston, TX 77280
713-275-5000 or 1-800-351-9058
www.menninger.edu

Milestones in Recovery
1928 N.E. 154 Street
North Miami Beach, FL 33162
1-800-347-2364
www.milestonesinrecovery.com

Mirasol
7650 E. Broadway, Suite 303
Tucson, AZ 85710
1-888-520-1700
www.mirasol.net

Renaissance at Pine Grove Recovery Center
2807 Arlington Loop
Hattiesburg, MS 39401
866-614-3382
www.renaissance-treatment.com

The Renfrew Center
11 East 36th Street
New York, NY 10016
(Plus six other east coast locations)
1-800-RENFREW (1-800-736-3739)
www.renfrewcenter.com

Rogers Memorial Hospital
34700 Valley Road
Oconomowoc, WI 53066
1-800-767-4411
www.rogershospital.org

St. Joseph Medical Center
7601 Osler Drive
Towson, MD 21204
410-337-1212
www.eating-disorders.com

Index

Q-R

T

X-Y-Z